THE INEXTINGUISHABLE BLAZE

In The Same Series:

THE SPREADING FLAME

*The Rise and Progress of Christianity
by Professor F. F. Bruce, M.A., D.D.*

THE INEXTINGUISHABLE BLAZE

Spiritual Renewal and Advance in the Eighteenth Century

by

A. SKEVINGTON WOOD

B.A., Ph.D., F.R.Hist.S.

There let it for Thy glory burn
With inextinguishable blaze;
And trembling to its source return,
In humble prayer and fervent praise.
Charles Wesley

Wm. B. Eerdmans Publishing Company
Grand Rapids 3, Michigan

*This American Edition
is published by special arrangement with
The Paternoster Press, London*

MANUFACTURED IN U. S. A.

CONTENTS

INTRODUCTION

THE ENIGMATIC CENTURY

PROBABLY NO SINGLE ERA IN THE WHOLE RANGE OF ENGLISH history has been more extensively scrutinized than the eighteenth century. There is an abundance of literature on the subject, and only very recently has historical interest begun to veer towards the following century. It is still, however, extraordinarily difficult to obtain a clear and unprejudiced picture of the period. The very profusion of bibliography proves an embarrassment. So many apparently contradictory accounts have appeared that the novice despairs of ever acquiring a firm grasp of this enigmatic century. Adjectives tumble over one another when historians seek to describe it. John Stuart Mill called it "innovative, infidel, abstract, metaphysical, and prosaic,"[1] and a similar spate of epithets flows from other and more recent pens than his. The eighteenth century has been variously denominated as the age of reason, enlightenment, serenity, benevolence, tolerance, common sense, respectability, artistry, classicism, formalism, deism, materialism, doubt, decadence, scandal, to select only a few. It is quite evident that no epoch can be reduced satisfactorily to a single compendious formula. The eighteenth century certainly cannot be thus epitomized. It is so spacious, so complex and so fluid that any one of the descriptions quoted above is, in a measure, accurate in relation to some aspect of the period, yet none of them is comprehensive enough to characterize the whole. Any attempt, then, at a facile simplification must be firmly forsworn.

W. H. Fitchett dubbed this "the Cinderella of the centuries."[2] He complained that nobody had a good word to say for it. That was largely true when he wrote in 1906. And even since that date too many studies in black-and-white have appeared. But the trend of the best historical scholarship in recent years has been to present

---

[1] Cf. B. Willey, *The Eighteenth Century Background*, pp. 209, 212.
[2] W. H. Fitchett, *Wesley and His Century*, p. 2.

a broader and more balanced view of the century. The extremes of eulogy and disparagement have been avoided, and a saner and more impartial picture is emerging. The sweeping generalizations of the past have been subjected to factual tests and, more often than not, have been proved to be misleading, if not actually erroneous. It has also been rightly emphasized that the eighteenth century is too often set in a false perspective. We tend to compare it with the present instead of with the past. It is quite unjust, however, to judge the eighteenth century by modern standards. It must be assessed as the eighteenth century and not as the twentieth. Only the experts have any real right to pass sentence on this era. A merely superficial acquaintance does not bestow the right to a categorical judgment. The recommendation of Professor A. S. Turberville should be weighed and acted upon: "Just as it is an impertinence to criticize a foreign country where one possesses as yet only a tourist's knowledge of it, before one has learned to know its people, to speak their language, or to become at home in their surroundings; so, we must in imagination become the friends and neighbours of our forefathers before we are entitled to dogmatize about them."[1]

Holding this admonition in view, we shall beware of committing ourselves to any pontifical pronouncement. It will be possible in this Introduction only to touch and glance upon the condition of England in this enigmatic century before proceeding in the Prelude to consider the state of the Church and the antecedents of the Revival. But these factors need nevertheless to be borne in mind throughout our survey.

If the eighteenth century had hardly opened "with *all* the promise of a summer dawn"[2] that Canon Elliott-Binns suggests, both for Church and people, at least it enjoyed a generous share. In 1702 Queen Anne ascended the throne to commence what, particularly to the conservative mind in both politics and religion, appeared to be one of the most auspicious reigns in the annals of England. In her first speech to Parliament she declared her "heart to be entirely English,"[3] and throughout her sovereignty she earnestly sought the allegiance of her subjects. The strongest motive in her policy was devotion to the Church. She displayed a genuine, if partisan, interest in ecclesiastical affairs and determined to exercise her personal prerogatives in the appointment of dig-

[1] *Johnson's England*, ed. A. S. Turberville, Vol. I, p. vi.
[2] L. E. Elliott-Binns, *The Evangelical Movement in the English Church*, p. 3.
[3] Earl Stanhope, *A History of England comprising the Reign of Queen Anne*, p. 39; cf. N. Sykes, *Church and State in England in the Eighteenth Century*, pp. 37-9.

nitaries. Yet even before her death in 1714 this Tory and High Church paradise had begun to lose its lustre. The inauguration of the Hanoverian dynasty in the accession of George I heralded a significant change of royal attitude. After the expediential alliance between Edmund Gibson, Bishop of London (the virtual Primate), and Sir Robert Walpole (the actual Prime Minister) had been consummated, the King permitted the care of the Church to pass out of his hands. Henceforward, Walpole's principle of *quieta non movere* was to dominate both Church and State. Peace at any price was the motto of this leader of the Whig oligarchy; and peace, indeed, was secured, accompanied by a considerable outward prosperity. As so often before in history, this increasing national obesity had serious repercussions in the realm of morals.

A plague of insidious materialism swept over the country. It would be easy to exaggerate its extent, for no disease, whether physical or spiritual, is so deadly as to infect an entire population. There must have been many "sweet Auburns" untouched by this blight: many scenes of domestic contentment such as those depicted by Francis Wheatley; many a pure and upright character, unsullied by the spirit of the age. But that moral degeneracy found its victims in every stratum of society and that an uninhibited hedonism was the prevailing philosophy of the times can hardly be denied. Walpole himself led the way by his openly immoral life. Houghton, his country seat, was the scene of scandalous debauchery. Virtue was the constant butt of his mordant wit. Court life under the first two Georges was as replete with vices as in the days of Charles II, without the accompanying virtues of sparkling repartee and nonchalance. It is not surprising that this degrading example in high places influenced the nation as a whole in the direction of moral laxity. Not only was the sanctity of marriage widely ignored: other symptoms of decadence began to appear. Drunkenness held the nation in its grip, from the gentry to the poorest of the poor. Gambling had swelled into an obsession of such proportions that it may fairly be questioned whether the craze ever wielded such absolute sway in any country of the world. Amusements were often cruel and brutal. Cock-fighting, bull-baiting and bear-baiting were amongst the most popular contemporary sports, if such they may properly be called. Happily, other and more manly pastimes were beginning to gain the ascendancy. According to Lecky, the English stage was far inferior to that of France in decorum, modesty and morality, and, despite the commendable efforts of Garrick, continued to be so even to the

closing decades of the century.[1] Crime was rampant, and the unequal criminal law, with its barbarous punishments, only made
criminals more desperate. Such consequences were inevitable in
an age which professed indifference to moral sanctions. When
Lady Mary Wortley Montagu could cynically suggest that the
"not" should be removed from the Commandments and inserted
in the Creed, it is remarkable that virtue survived at all.

Meanwhile, the beginnings of social upheaval were bringing
additional responsibilities in their train. The population was increasing: it rose from about five-and-a-half millions in 1702 to
nine millions in 1801. Houses, wages and food had to be provided for this growing community. The agricultural revolution,
which preceded its industrial counterpart, created problems as
well as solved them. The Enclosure Movement, whereby the
common field farming, which had prevailed since the beginning
of the Saxon occupation, was converted into the modern holding
system, undoubtedly paved the way for future agricultural prosperity, just as the industrial revolution laid the firm foundations
of commercial and economic expansion. But, like the industrial
revolution, this agricultural reform involved social disruption and
some of its immediate effects were less beneficial. To quote
Professor G. M. Trevelyan: "The social price paid for economic
gain was a decline in the number of independent cultivators and a
rise in the number of landless labourers. To a large extent this was
a necessary evil, and there would have been less harm in it if the
increased dividend of the agricultural world had been fairly distributed. But while the landlord's rent, the parson's tithe, and the
profits of farmer and middleman all rose apace, the field-labourer,
deprived of his little rights in land and his family's by-employ-
ments in industry, received no proper compensation in high
wages, and in the Southern Counties too often sank into a position
of dependence and pauperism."[2] As C. S. Orwin observes, it is
impossible to assign a precise date to the beginning of the Enclosure Movement, but the tendency which first became pro-
nounced in the sixteenth century was by the early eighteenth
century starting to produce some of the effects mentioned above.[3]

This was the major social problem confronting the nation at the
birth of the Evangelical Revival. The consequences of the industrial revolution were not felt until a much later date. It is particu-

---

[1] W. E. H. Lecky, *A History of England in the Eighteenth Century*, Vol I, p. 540.
[2] G. M. Trevelyan, *English Social History*, p. 379.
[3] *Johnson's England*, Vol. I, p. 267.

larly difficult to assess the real condition of the poor in this period. We cannot overlook the increasing Government expenditure on poor relief, which inspired de Tocqueville's remark that in France it was the nobles, in England the poor who escaped the great burden of taxation. Nor must it be forgotten that in 1722 an important Poor Law Act had been passed.[1] On the other hand, it cannot be denied that there were grave defects in a system which placed the onus of responsibility upon ill-equipped local authorities, and of these the treatment of parish children was perhaps the most glaring instance. Thus, though the picture was probably not as sombre as some have thought to paint it, the social condition of England in the age of Walpole was sufficiently serious to have touched all tender, philanthropic, and still more, religious consciences. The sad fact was, however, that the prevalent creed of materialism had largely sealed the springs of human sympathy. The rich man in his castle was too engrossed in his variegated pleasures to observe the poor man at his gate. No doubt a virile Church would have aroused the slumbering conscience of the indifferent, but the tragedy was that when its quickening influence was most required, Christianity was suffering a decline. Of this we must next speak.

[1] Ibid., pp. 302-3. The Charity Schools must not be overlooked, either; *vide* M. G. Jones, *The Charity School Movement: A Study of Eighteenth Centur Puritanism in Action.*

PRELUDE

CHAPTER I

THE CONDITION OF THE CHURCH

IN WHAT SORT OF SHAPE WAS THE CHURCH IN ENGLAND AS THIS enigmatic century opened? The answer is a saddening one. At the very time when its instructive and reviving ministry was most sorely needed, religion in our land was under a cloud. Christianity had for the most part ceased to be a vital force. The spiritual life of the people had largely been smothered by the dense atmosphere of materialism. Not that religion was altogether dead: such a claim is unjustified, but a moral paralysis had crept over the nation which prevented the gospel from displaying its real power.

On the eve of the Revival three prominent ecclesiastics recorded their fears for the future. In 1736 Joseph Butler, then Prebendary of Rochester, made this melancholy complaint in the preface to his *Analogy of Religion*:

> It is come, I know not how, to be taken for granted, by many persons, that Christianity is not so much a subject of inquiry; but that it is, now at length, discovered to be fictitious. And accordingly they treat it as if, in the present age, this were an agreed point among all people of discernment; and nothing remained, but to set it up as a principal subject of mirth and ridicule, as it were by way of reprisals, for its having so long interrupted the pleasures of the world.[1]

In 1738 George Berkeley, Bishop of Cloyne, in his *Discourses Addressed to Magistrates and Men in Authority*, declared that morality and religion in Britain had collapsed "to a degree that has never been known in any Christian country." "Our prospect," he continued, "is very terrible and the symptoms grow worse from day to day." The accumulating torrent of evil "which threatens a general inundation and destruction of these realms" Berkeley attributed chiefly to "the irreligion and bad example of those . . . styled the better sort."[2] In the same year Thomas Secker, then Bishop of Oxford, in an episcopal charge, averred:

[1] *The Works of Joseph Butler*, ed. S. Hallifax, Vol. II, pp. lxxv-lxxvi.
[2] Cf. J. W. Bready, *England: Before and After Wesley*, p. 19.

In this we cannot be mistaken, that an open and professed disregard of religion is become, through a variety of unhappy causes, the distinguishing character of the age. Such are the dissoluteness and contempt of principle in the highest part of the world, and the profligacy, intemperance, and fearlessness of committing crimes in the lower part, as must, if the torrent of impiety stop not, become absolutely fatal. Christianity is ridiculed and railed at with very little reserve; and the teachers of it without any at all.[1]

This telling contemporary evidence has been substantially confirmed by later historians, representing widely divergent schools of thought.

To what extent is the Church to be held responsible for this ominous decline in religion? The student of ecclesiastical history is aware that there have been seasons of moral and spiritual degeneration which the Church of Christ, preserving its integrity and exerting its utmost energy, has been unable to check. Is this one of those periods? Did the torrents of evil and impiety, of which both Berkeley and Secker speak, burst through all the zealous restraints of a thoroughly faithful and dedicated Church? Or were there weaknesses in the breakwater itself? The latter was unhappily the case. The Church of England in the early eighteenth century was not stout enough to stem the rising tide of irreligion. It would be a mistake to condemn it out of hand as uniformly corrupt and culpably inept. In less trying times its virtues might have found room to flourish. But it was inadequately equipped to face a crisis.

In attempting to depict the condition of the Established Church immediately prior to the Revival we must beware of unbalanced and partisan distortions. There is a real danger that the enthusiastic champion of Evangelicalism should succumb to the temptation of either deliberately or unconsciously deepening the darkness behis cherished dawn. Such a subtle manifestation of *pietas* may fore result in an inequitable assessment of the Hanoverian Church. Nor are Evangelicals the only offenders. The disciples of the Oxford Movement are equally prone to this error, to which they invariably add that of depreciating the Evangelical Revival, so that they are led, as Archbishop Brilioth pungently observes, "under the influence of inferior spirits" to the production of "a vulgate in High Anglican writing of history as regards the representation of the time before 1833."[2] Since too many ecclesiastical historians have a polemical axe to grind, a truly impartial treatment of this period is something of a rarity. The invaluable work of Charles J.

[1] *The Works of Thomas Secker*, ed. B. Porteus and G. Stinton, Vol. V, p. 292.
[2] Y. Brilioth, *The Anglican Revival*, pp. 5-6.

Abbey and Canon John H. Overton stands out from the rest in this respect: it is not without significance that their chapter on Church abuses is prefaced by this passage:

> Look at the Church of the eighteenth century in prospect, and a bright scene of uninterrupted triumph might be anticipated. Look at it in retrospect, as it is pictured by many writers of every school of thought, and a dark scene of melancholy failure presents itself. Not that this latter view is altogether a correct one. Many as were the shortcomings of the English Church of this period, her condition was not so bad as has been represented.[1]

Since Abbey and Overton wrote, however, new and important sources of information, both printed and in manuscript, have been made available, many of which confirm the view that the Church of the Georges was not so utterly decayed as some would have us believe. Amongst more recent scholars who have sought to redress the balance in the interest of strict accuracy and justice, Dr. Norman Sykes must be named as the chief. His Birkbeck Lectures on *Church and State in England in the Eighteenth Century*—the scope of which, as the title suggests, was wider than that of the usual ecclesiastical history—set a new standard in thoroughness and impartiality and have already amply fulfilled the author's hope that "the volume may contribute somewhat to a juster and more equitable verdict upon the English Church and state in the eighteenth century, and may provide a foundation upon which other and wiser heads may build a comprehensive survey of all aspects of the history of that epoch."[2]

With the foregoing cautions fully in mind, and relying primarily upon the two authorities already mentioned, we may attempt a brief review of the Hanoverian Church. The major clue to a proper understanding of the Church in this period lies in the fact that it was both reformed and unreformed. The English Reformation, which had reshaped its doctrine and liturgy, had effected comparatively few changes in its internal administration. This anomalous situation is best illustrated in the episcopate. The punctilious attendance of Hanoverian Bishops at Court and in the House of Lords is often made the target of unsympathetic criticism, and, sometimes unfairly, a contrast is drawn between this assiduity and their tepid zeal for diocesan work. But it must be remembered that traditionally the English Bishop was a royal

---

[1] C. J. Abbey and J. H. Overton, *The English Church in the Eighteenth Century*, p. 279.
[2] Sykes, *op. cit.*, p. xi. For this more sympathetic view of the Hanoverian Church, cf. also W. K. Lowther Clarke, *Eighteenth Century Piety*, S. C. Carpenter, *Eighteenth Century Church and People*, and the admirable summary in A. T. P. Williams, *The Anglican Tradition in the Life of England*, pp. 53-70.

counsellor in matters of state no less than a prelate of the Church. This association can be traced back to the very origins of the English Church, when the Roman missionaries who sought the conversion of Anglo-Saxon England received their first establishment as royal Chaplains of the several ruling princes. It was not unknown, even in the eighteenth century, for a prelate to hold an important office of state. In 1711 John Robinson, Bishop of Bristol, was appointed Lord Privy Seal and was later accredited as plenipotentiary, with the Earl of Stafford, at the Peace of Utrecht. The elevation of a divine to secular office was no doubt exceptional at this late date, but, as Dean Sykes remarks, "the political influence of prelates had suffered a change of form rather than of principle since the Reformation."[1]

This had its repercussions in the method of recruitment, which has provoked much adverse comment then and since. Samuel Johnson's complaint has often been quoted: "No man, for instance, can now be made a Bishop for his learning and piety; his only chance of promotion is his being connected with somebody who has parliamentary interest."[2] It would be wrong, however, to assume that learning and piety were therefore altogether unrepresented on the episcopal bench. This was plainly not so. But the growth of parliamentary influence following upon the settlement of 1688, together with the rise of the two-party system, had important consequences for the episcopate. The establishment of party Administrations resulted in the virtual appropriation of ecclesiastical patronage by the political leaders. It was only natural that the Administration in office, whether Whig or Tory, should appoint to the episcopal bench men of their own allegiance. Thus, in this period, the Bishops became less the counsellors of the ruling prince than the allies of the party in power. The twenty-six episcopal votes were of inestimable value to any Administration in the small House of Lords before Pitt's additions to the peerage. This was precisely the state of affairs during the Whig ascendancy under Walpole, and reached its climax in 1737 when, in two vital divisions in the Upper House on 24th May and 1st June, a Government defeat was averted by the fact that out of the twenty-six Bishops, twenty-five were present or voted by proxy, of whom twenty-four were for the Court. Party political bias was thus undoubtedly responsible for some of the criticism directed against the Church of this period.

[1] *Johnson's England*, Vol. I, p. 16.
[2] J. Boswell, *The Life of Samuel Johnson*, ed. G. B. Hill, Vol. V, p. 298.

This alliance between the Bishops and the ministers of state was further cemented by the marked inequalities in wealth between the sees. Canterbury was worth seven thousand pounds a year, Durham six thousand, Winchester five thousand, whilst at the other end of the scale Bristol was worth only four hundred and fifty and Oxford and Llandaff five hundred each. Two consequences followed upon this disparity in revenue. The poorer Bishops sought to ingratiate themselves still further with their patrons so that they might gain preferment to more lucrative sees: they also contrived to augment their income by holding prebendaries and deaneries *in commendam*. Regrettable as may have been some of the results of this political involvement of the episcopate, the only apparent solution of the problem, namely, to deprive the Bishops of their seats in Parliament, appeared so drastic that even such a rabid critic as Johnson repudiated it.

But, apart from his parliamentary commitments, with their accompanying problems, how did the eighteenth-century Bishop fulfil his ecclesiastical functions? Dean Sykes devotes a lengthy chapter in his book to this very question and supplies a needed corrective to the more extreme indictments issued by previous writers on this particular score. He points out the peculiar circumstances which governed the life of a Hanoverian prelate. The Bishop was compelled to reside in London for the greater part of the year if he was to discharge his parliamentary duties and maintain an interest in public affairs. Travel was so slow and roads so bad that frequent journeys between capital and diocese were impracticable. It was the custom for Bishops to visit their sees only during the summer recess of Parliament, except in cases of emergency. Even the most zealous reformers did not quarrel with this division of labour. Again, it must be remembered that since the Reformation only five new dioceses had been established and the statute of 26 Henry VIII cap. 14 for the consecration of suffragan Bishops had never been consistently acted upon. In face of these difficulties, concludes Sykes, "it is perhaps a matter of surprise and gratification that the prelates of Georgian England achieved so considerable an approximation to the ideal of the office and work of a Bishop."[1] He then proceeds to supply valuable evidence that in each of the three essential branches of the episcopal office—ordination, visitation of the clergy and confirmation of the laity—the Bishops of the early eighteenth century, despite the adverse conditions under which they laboured, proved more faithful and

[1] Sykes, *op. cit.*, p. 96.

efficient than they have usually been given credit for. It is not
denied that, as in all ages of the Church, there were varying standards of fidelity, and no doubt some Bishops were, as we shall
see, unduly lax in the administration of their diocesan affairs and
unscrupulous in their antagonisms. But others have suffered from
misrepresentation, as Sykes demonstrates in the cases, for example,
of White Kennett and Zachary Pearce. Nor were the Bishops
themselves blind to the shortcomings of the system to which they
were fettered. They were often painfully aware of the inadequacy
of the Church to meet the situation, even if suspicious of reform
movements not emanating from official sources, but this candour
is not always counted unto them for righteousness. Dean Sykes
concludes:

> In their endeavours to grapple with the many obstacles to pastoral
> oversight and to discharge the spiritual administration of their office,
> the eighteenth century episcopate merit a juster measure of appreci-
> ation than has been their lot at the hands of subsequent historians.
> The Georgian bench indeed has been pilloried as a byword of sloth,
> inefficiency, and neglect. . . . For the appreciation of its achievement
> regard must be had to the difficulties of its situation, and comparison
> be made with previous centuries without regard to differences of
> high and low Church. In face of the many obstacles of unwieldy
> dioceses, limited means of travel, pressure of other avocations, and
> the infirmities of body incident to mortal flesh, the Bishops of
> Hanoverian England and Wales strove with diligence and not with-
> out due measure of success to discharge the spiritual administration
> attached to their office.[1]

We have noticed that the financial inequality between the
episcopal sees compelled the less fortunate Bishops to supplement
their inadequate incomes by *commendams*. This factor has its place
in the vicious circle which produced the notorious pluralism of
the eighteenth century. Since the Bishops themselves were impli-
cated in the scandal, they were prevented from taking a really firm
stand against it. The legal position, moreover, was far from clear
cut. The statute of 21 Henry VIII cap. 13, entitled "Spiritual
Persons abridged from having Pluralities of Livings," was still
in force. The Act laid down the general rule that no incumbent
with a benefice *cum cura animarum* of the value of eight pounds or
above should be permitted to hold any other benefice with cure.
But it then proceeded to list a long catalogue of exceptions, including Chaplains to the peerage, cathedral dignitaries, and the
like. Furthermore, plurality was no new problem. It was an in-

[1] Ibid., pp. 144-5.

heritance from the Middle Ages and had been prevalent even in the much-lauded Caroline Church. It must be freely admitted, however, that pluralism, with its accompanying evil of non-residence, was the most serious hindrance to spiritual progress in the Church of the Georges. Of the widespread nature of this practice there can be no manner of doubt, and even though in the main they set an improved example, Evangelicals were not immaculate in this respect. The visitation returns of Archbishop Herring of York in 1743 reveal that out of the eight hundred and thirty-six parishes which made reply, three hundred and ninety-three had no resident incumbents. Of the seven hundred and eleven clergy, no less than three hundred and thirty-five were pluralists. This state of affairs may be taken as fairly representative.

One of the collateral evils of pluralism was clerical poverty. In respect of emolument the gap between the different classes of the clergy was unjustifiably wide. Addison divided the clergy into generals, field officers and subalterns. Whilst the first two categories enjoyed an abundant emolument, in the main, and took their rank with the higher orders of society, the innumerable army of subalterns considered themselves passing rich with forty pounds a year and hardly rose above the standing of a small farmer. Widespread non-residence greatly increased the number of curates, many of whom had little hope of preferment. And, indeed, so many benefices were so poorly endowed that the transition from the status of unbeneficed to that of beneficed cleric brought scant financial advantage. A further consequence of pluralism was neglect of parish duty. The Church of England depends for its basic welfare upon the diligent and orderly working of the parochial system. Non-residence played havoc with that sheet-anchor of Anglicanism. A vicar holding two livings inadequately endowed to enable him to maintain a curate, or a curate striving to serve the parishes of an absentee incumbent, could not in the nature of things meet the needs of each of his cures. In such cases, divine service was conducted only once a Sunday in each church. In the churches represented in Herring's returns, only three hundred and eighty-three held two services all the year round. Celebrations of Holy Communion were correspondingly infrequent. The York returns indicate that only seventy-two parishes in the diocese had monthly celebrations. One hundred and ninety-three varied between four and six a year, three hundred and sixty-three had quarterly sacraments, whilst two hundred and eight had less than that. This infrequency of

celebration must not be taken to indicate a paucity of communicants. One of the outstanding features revealed by contemporary
statistics is the remarkably large proportion of adult parishioners
who communicated at Easter. And in London conditions were
very different from the provinces.

It was not only worship, however, that suffered from the effects
of non-residence: catechetical instruction and pastoral visitation
were also hindered. We shall encounter evidence which will, in
the main, substantiate this general impression of neglect. But it
must not be supposed that every parish was in similar case. The
diaries of Thomas Brockbank, William Cole and James Wood-
forde combine to testify that throughout the eighteenth century
there did exist parishes—outside Evangelicalism—where duty
was faithfully discharged and souls were shepherded with loving
care. Canon S. L. Ollard passed this verdict upon the York
Visitation returns:

> On the whole the strong impression left by the returns is that of a
> body of conscientious and dutiful men, trying to do their work
> according to the standard of their day. Over the grave of one of them,
> the Rector of Bainton, William Territt, was written when he died in
> 1783, this tribute . . . "a very learned and sound divine, cheerful and
> peacable, constantly resident and attentive to the duties of a
> minister." With the possible exception of the words "very learned"
> . . . close examination of these returns suggests that a like descrip-
> tion would apply to many others of those who made them.[1]

This is all the more remarkable when it is remembered that the
Church had lost some of its most devout families, from which a
future generation of saintly priests might have sprung, in the anti-
Puritan purge of 1661 to 1665 and the expulsion of the Non-
Jurors in 1689 and 1690. The blame for the decay of religion in the
eighteenth century cannot too lightly be placed upon the clergy of
the day. Admittedly they might have done more than they did to
stem the torrent of iniquity. They were not sufficiently militant to
meet the demands of the age. But, as Canon Overton remarked, it
is doubtful whether, even if they had been more energetic and
spiritually-minded, they could have effected a reformation.[2]
Bishop Butler, in his charge to the clergy of Durham in 1751 complained with some justice:

> It is cruel usage we often meet with, in being censured for not
> doing what we cannot do, without, what we cannot have, the con-
> currence of our censurers. Doubtless very much reproach which

[1] Ibid., p. 274.   [2] Abbey and Overton, *op. cit.*, p. 306.

now lights upon the clergy would be bound to fall elsewhere if due allowance were made for things of this kind.[1]

We turn from the life of the Hanoverian Church to its doctrine. Here the problem is a different one. As Dean Sykes observes, the survival of obsolete medieval constitutional machinery may explain many of the anomalies which hampered the efficient discharge of episcopal and parochial duty, but in order to account for the dominant belief we must have recourse to the intellectual temper of the age. The Church of the early eighteenth century was Latitudinarian in its theological orientation. An understandable reaction from the doctrinal disputes of the seventeenth century had bred an aversion to controversial topics. A dread of extremism was the hall-mark of this period. The Hanoverian Church sought to steer a safe and central course between the Scylla of High Churchism and the Charybdis of Puritanism. The Deistic controversy only served to strengthen the case for Latitudinarianism. Although the Christian apologists had emerged triumphant from the conflict, there was little exuberance in the victory celebrations. The Church was tired of intellectual sword-play and was determined at all costs to keep out of further trouble. Walpole's political maxim, "Let sleeping dogs lie," was heartily adopted in ecclesiastical affairs, and particularly in relation to theological differences.

The new scientific movement, with its recognition of law in the visible universe, which had fostered Deism, also affected the apologetics of the Church. It is noticeable that the weapons with which Berkeley and Butler and Warburton fought and defeated their Deist opponents were rational rather than revelational. Creeds and confessions were set aside as things indifferent and the case for Christianity was built up on the arguments of natural religion, fortified by the testimony of the prophecies and the miracles of Christ. "The main effort of orthodox apologetic was therefore directed towards demonstrating that Revelation was a necessary adjunct to natural religion, or, at the lowest, not inconsistent with it," comments Professor Basil Willey.[2] The effect of this outlook upon the contemporary pulpit may be measured by a scrutiny of the sermons of Archbishop Tillotson, the most popular preacher of the day. Throughout his works he constantly appealed to the tribunal of reason. He strove to prove that Christianity was "the best and the holiest, the wisest and the most reasonable religion in the world," and that "all the precepts of it

[1] Ibid., n.   [2] Willey, op. cit., p. 76.

are reasonable and wise, requiring such duties of us as are suitable
to the light of nature, and do approve themselves to the best
reason of mankind."[1] He invited men to test their faith by reason
at all points. He discouraged the appetite for the mysterious and
taught that in the pure light of reason all darkness would speedily
disappear. This gospel of reasonableness was the theme of the
Latitudinarian preacher. The spirit of Tillotson lingered in the
English pulpit long after his body had found an honoured resting-
place in Westminster Abbey. The men of latitude boasted that
they "let alone the mysterious points of religion, and preached to
the people only good, plain, practical morality."[2] The consequence
was that all the charm and vitality was taken from the Christian
faith, and cold, unattractive reason was left in its stead. It was
these considerations which prompted G. R. Balleine to stigmatize
this as the glacial epoch in English Church history![3]

Our attention has of necessity been focused upon the Establishment, but it should be noted that Dissent was as inadequately
equipped to meet the challenge of the hour as Anglicanism. This
was a period of spiritual declension amongst what are now known
as the Free Churches. Indulgence had sapped their stamina more
effectively than persecution. The worship of the Dissenters was,
for the most part, formal and lifeless. The Arian blight had fallen
upon much of their preaching. The spirit of compromise, so
prevalent in the State and the State Church, had begun to undermine their moral integrity. On the other hand, the pamphlets of
Isaac Watts and others like him who were alive to the decay of
Dissent, and the rejoinders they provoked, indicate that the
indifference to vital religion in the independent churches was by
no means universal. Nevertheless the fact remains that the
Dissenters were unprepared to lead a revival and when it came
were slow to realize its significance and to lend it their support.

There can be no serious uncertainty concerning the need for
revival. The more balanced estimate of eighteenth-century conditions, particularly within the Church, does not in any way
suggest that the Evangelical Awakening was unnecessary. The
shadows on the canvas may at times have been unduly underlined,
but of the moral decadence of Hanoverian England and the im-
potence of the organized Church to meet the crisis there can be no
possible doubt. Materialism had eaten deep into national life: new

---

[1] J. Tillotson, *Works*, ed. T. Birch, Vol. I, pp. 99, 112.
[2] T. Bisse, Visitation Sermon, 1716, cf. G. R. Balleine, *A History of the Evangelica
Party in the Church of England*, p. 17.
[3] Balleine, *op. cit.*, p. 16.

and pressing social problems were being thrown up by the Enclosure Movement, soon to be followed by those of the Industrial Revolution. The Church, fettered by its medieval constitution and deprived of warmth and vitality by Latitudinarian indoctrination, was unequal to its task. Dissent was in no better case. Nothing less than a revival could effectively deal with the situation.

CHAPTER II

THE ANTECEDENTS OF THE REVIVAL

REVIVAL IS A RECURRING FACTOR IN CHRISTIAN HISTORY. Throughout the centuries since God was made manifest in the flesh there have been successive demonstrations of the Spirit's power. The first and greatest, of course, was at Pentecost itself. In one sense the events of that initial outpouring were unique and unrepeatable. There can never again be an original gift of the Holy Ghost to the Church of Christ. But it must not therefore be supposed that the experience of Pentecost may not be renewed in succeeding generations. Indeed the course of sacred history quite clearly indicates that from time to time God has graciously visited His people with refreshment and quickening. As D. L. Moody used to insist, Pentecost was but a specimen day. As such it is capable of repetition and it should therefore occasion no surprise when the phenomenon of revival is found to recur.

It would be unwise, however, to reduce these providential irruptions to any rigidly defined pattern. Some have claimed to trace a regular rhythm of renewal throughout the Christian era, a measured ebb and flow of the spiritual tide. But these outbreaks of blessing cannot be neatly confined within any prescribed limits. They are to be credited to the mysterious operation of the Holy Spirit, blowing where He listeth. "It looks as though there were seasons in the course of history," wrote Rufus M. Jones, "which are like vernal equinoxes of the Spirit when fresh initiations into more life occur, when new installations of life seem to break in and enlarge the empire of man's divine estate."[1]

It was just such a revitalizing re-enactment of the processes of Pentecost which stirred the eighteenth-century Church from its almost fatal lethargy and led to a remarkable expansion of influence and power. Its inception and growth were alike marked by a notable spontaneity and independence of man's contrivance. "It came without organisation," says Dr. Elliott-Binns, "and almost without expectation."[2] The impotent Church was suddenly

[1] Cf. A. W. Harrison, *The Evangelical Revival and Christian Reunion*, p. 13.
[2] L. E. Elliott-Binns, *Evangelical Movement*, p. 3.

invaded by a fresh access of spiritual enablement which stemmed the drift towards rationalistic materialism and brought Britain back to God. Both in respect of its source and success the movement is altogether inexplicable in naturalistic terms. It displays its heavenly origin by strong, commanding evidence.

This is not to suggest, however, that the Evangelical Awakening in eighteenth-century Britain was altogether unrelated to the past or represents an isolated occurrence. Whilst recognizing the divine provenance of the Revival it is nevertheless possible and accurate to refer to its antecedents, both immediate and more remote. There is a distinct and discernible link between previous movements of the Spirit and this further manifestation and it is equally evident that the spiritual renascence of the eighteenth century was not confined to the United Kingdom. It is therefore to a consideration of such factors that we must now turn.

As Professor K. S. Latourette points out, the eighteenth-century Revival regarded in its broadest aspect was essentially a Protestant concern.[1] Neither the Roman nor Eastern churches saw any exceptional advance until the close of the period. The Awakening was not restricted to any one section of Protestantism. It began with the Pietist movement in Germany in the seventeenth century and was thus first associated with the Lutheran stream of the Reformation heritage. In America its principal channels were the churches of the Calvinist tradition. In Britain it was most prominent in the Church of England, but was also operative in the Presbyterian Church of Scotland and in groups which eventually dissented from both. At a later date it extended to the Reformed Churches on the continent of Europe. It may well be claimed that the eighteenth-century Revival finds its furthest antecedents in the Protestant Reformation. That, indeed, is the affirmation of W. H. Fitchett who sees it as "the translation into English life, and into happier terms, of Luther's Reformation in Germany."[2] Professor George Croft Cell regards it as "the necessary bridge between the Old Protestantism of the sixteenth and seventeenth centuries and the New Protestantism of the eighteenth and nineteenth centuries."[3] Dr. Franz Hildebrandt speaks of it unambiguously as "the revival of the Reformation."[4]

It was especially through the Pietist strand of the Reformation tradition that the Revival was related to the major awakening of

[1] K. S. Latourette, *A History of Christianity*, p. 1018.
[2] Fitchett, *op. cit.*, p. 5.
[3] G. C. Cell, *The Rediscovery of John Wesley*, p. 1.
[4] F. Hildebrandt, *From Luther to Wesley*, p. 110.

the sixteenth century. This movement in the Lutheran Church in
the seventeenth century, of which Philip Spener was the first
leader, sought to revitalize the moribund Protestantism of
Germany. It began with religious meetings in Spener's house. He
started prayer circles, Bible readings and discussion groups. These
gatherings were known as *collegia pietatis*—hence the name of the
movement. The witness was continued by Spener's disciple,
A. H. Francke, a Professor at the University of Leipzig. He established a centre at Halle and it was here that Pietism flowered. But
it could not be contained. It proved contagious. It soon extended
its influence beyond the confines of Germany and affected the
Lutheran churches of Scandinavia as well as the duchy of Württem-
berg, where J. A. Bengel was the pioneer.[1] Through Spener's
godson, Count Zinzendorf, the Pietist impulse reached and revived the Moravian *Unitas Fratrum*. It was largely by this means
that Pietism eventually touched the eighteenth-century Revival in
Britain in a more direct manner. There are many parallels between
the Pietist movement and the Evangelical Awakening, for,
although scholars are of divided opinion concerning the ultimate
contribution of Pietism to the life of the Church, there can be no
gainsaying its contemporary effectiveness. Like the later phenomenon in England, Pietism arose out of the recognition that all
was not well with institutional Christianity. It sought to renew the original spirit of the gospel by an emphasis upon personal experience rather than formal adherence. It stimulated warm
evangelical preaching in pulpits where a dull and lifeless orthodoxy had prevailed. It expressed itself in the formation of societies
for the cultivation of spiritual health. It introduced a new note of
realism and fervour into the hymnody of the Church. It led to
educational and missionary enterprise. In these and other ways it
will be seen how closely the Pietist renewal anticipated the eighteenth-century Revival. It takes its rightful place in the sequence of
Pentecostal rebirths. "Quite apart from its rejuvenation of the
dried-up Protestant Church," says Emil Brunner, "what Pietism
accomplished in the sphere of social amelioration and foreign
missions is at the least the token of that Spirit which is promised
in the Bible to those who truly believe, and is among the most
splendid records of achievement to be found in Church history."[2]

Both the Anglican Evangelicals and the Wesleys would have
claimed that the Church of England itself stood in the lineage of

[1] John Wesley's *Notes on the New Testament* are based on Bengel's *Gnomon*.
[2] E. Brunner, *The Divine-Human Encounter*, p. 23.

the Reformation and that its Articles, Liturgy and Homilies reflected the spirit and doctrine of Protestantism. But in addition to this direct tradition they would have recognized, to a greater or lesser degree, the influence of Puritanism. There are, of course, equally obvious differences, and recent writers have tended to magnify them, but the link between the Puritan revolution and the Evangelical Revival must not be overlooked. Certainly the enemies of the eighteenth-century Awakening recognized this rootage. William Warburton spoke of "the old Puritan fanaticism revived under the new name of Methodism,"[1] and Horace Walpole revealed his misgivings when he observed: "This nonsensical New Light is extremely in fashion and I shall not be surprised if we see a revival of all the folly and cant of the last age."[2] In its protest against worldliness, its evangelistic concern, its inward piety, its Scriptural doctrines, its strictness of discipline, the Puritan way of life strongly resembled those qualities which were to mark the eighteenth-century movement. Indeed, Simon went so far as to say that "if the spiritual party in the Church of England had triumphed in the seventeenth century, the revival of religion in the eighteenth century would have been anticipated."[3] The Anglican Evangelicals in particular valued their Puritan heritage and James Hervey was expressing a typical attitude when he wrote, "Be not ashamed of the name Puritan. The Puritans were the soundest preachers, and, I believe, the truest followers of Christ in their day."[4] But John Wesley was also appreciative and said of Thomas Cartwright, "I look upon him, and the body of Puritans in that age (to whom the German Anabaptists bore small resemblance) to have been both the most learned and the most pious men that were then in the English nation. Nor did they separate from the Church, but were driven out, whether they would or no."[5] In considering the antecedents of the eighteenth-century Revival we dare not by-pass the Puritans. Indeed, Canon Elliott-Binns has asserted that one of the greatest services performed by the Evangelical movement was to revive the spirit of Puritanism.[6]

Even at the close of the seventeenth century "we hear the faint sounds of the beneficent storm which vitalized the heavy atmo-

---

[1] W. Warburton, *The Doctrine of Grace*, p. 326.
[2] *Horace Walpole's Correspondence*, ed. G. S. Lewis, Vol. IX, p. 73.
[3] J. S. Simon, *The Religious Revival in England in the Eighteenth Century*, p. 116.
[4] Cf. L. E. Elliott-Binns, *The Early Evangelicals*, p. 215.
[5] *The Letters of John Wesley*, ed. J. Telford, Vol. II, p. 94.
[6] Elliott-Binns, *Early Evangelicals*, p. 98.

sphere," to borrow the language of Simon.[1] As far back as the year 1678, societies were being formed for the enrichment of spiritual life—and this in the unpropitious Restoration period. It all began with the "awakening sermons" of Dr. Antony Horneck at the Savoy Chapel.[2] Born at Bacharach on the Rhine, he had graduated from Oxford and entered the Church of England. Horneck was "the friend, or rather the father of these societies from their first rise."[3] He was assisted by Smythies of St. Michael's, Cornhill, to organize groups of young men for weekly prayer, Bible reading and religious conference. In his *Account of the Rise and Progress of the Religious Societies in London*, Woodward informs us that these were mainly from "the middle station of life" and belonged to the Church of England: being "touched with a very affecting sense of their sins" they "began to apply themselves, in a very serious manner, to religious thoughts and purposes."[4] They consulted their ministers for spiritual advice and succour and in this way were drawn together in fellowship. The clergymen thus applied to made the following suggestion, "that since their troubles arose from the same spiritual cause, and that their inclinations and resolutions centred in the same purpose of a holy life; they should meet together once a week, and apply themselves to good discourse, and things wherein they might edify one another. And for the better regulation of their meetings, several rules and orders were prescribed them, being such as seemed most proper to effect the end proposed."[5] A specimen of such resolutions was appended, copied from the society at Poplar where Woodward himself was minister. The first four run as follows:

(I). That the sole design of this society being to promote real holiness of heart and life: It is absolutely necessary that the persons who enter into it, do seriously resolve, by the grace of God, to apply themselves to all means proper to accomplish these blessed ends. Trusting in the divine power and gracious conduct of the Holy Spirit, through our Lord Jesus Christ, to excite, advance, and perfect all good in us.

(II). That in order to their being of one heart and one mind in this design, every member of this society shall own and manifest himself to be of the Church of England, and frequent the Liturgy, and other public exercises of the same. And that they be careful withal to

---

[1] Simon, *op. cit.*, p. 125.
[2] J. Woodward, *An Account of the Rise and Progress of the Religious Societies in the City of London*, p. 34.
[3] W. G. Addison, *The Renewed Church of the United Brethren*, p. 79.
[4] Woodward, *op. cit.*, p. 31.
[5] Ibid., p. 34.

express due Christian charity, candour, and moderation to all such Dissenters as are of good conversation.

(III). That the members of this society shall meet together one evening in the week at a convenient place, in order to encourage each other unto practical holiness, by discoursing on such subjects as tend thereunto; observing the Holy Scriptures as their rule; and praying to God for His grace and blessing.

(IV). That at such meetings they decline all disputes about controversial points, and all unnecessary discourse about State affairs, or the concerns of trade and worldly things: and that the whole bent of the discourse be to glorify God, and edify one another in love.[1]

Lest it should be supposed, however, that the society withdrew itself in unconcern from the corrupt milieu in which it was set, it is salutary to read on through those regulations which dealt with the establishment of a charitable fund for relieving the sick and needy and "especially for putting poor children to school," and the determination to oppose the social evils of gambling, intemperance, and degrading entertainment.[2]

The spirit which pervaded and controlled these societies can best be measured by the following extract. We are told that the members

. . . laboured to approve themselves to the All-seeing God, by the exercise of the following ornamental duties, which are in the sight of God of great price, viz.: (i) Christian poverty of spirit, in the sense of their own impurity and imperfection; (ii) A disinterested mind, wholly renouncing all carnal ends; (iii) Habitual prayer to God, with a courageous and unwearied pursuit of such things as are agreeable to His will and subservient to His glory; (iv) Unfeigned charity towards all men; especially to their souls and spiritual welfare; (v) Quiet resignation to the providence of God in all events.[3]

Despite the dissoluteness of the times, these societies grew and gathered strength. In the reign of James II there were, it is true, some who lapsed from their former fidelity, but the remainder made their influence felt in no uncertain manner. When they saw the Mass celebrated daily in the Chapel Royal and elsewhere they arranged at their own expense for prayers at eight each evening at St. Clement Dane's and also inaugurated a monthly lecture in the same church. Large numbers attended and the protest against papistry was thereby reinforced. Amongst those who supported the Religious Societies were William Beveridge, Vicar of St. Peter's, Cornhill, later Bishop of St. Asaph, and Thomas Tenison,

---

[1] Ibid., pp. 111-12. [2] Ibid., pp. 113-14. [3] Ibid., p. 65.

Vicar of St. Martin's-in-the-Fields, later Archbishop of Canterbury.

The reign of William and Mary brought a further change in the fortunes of the societies. A rule was added that each member should strive to bring at least one other into the fellowship and as a result there was a remarkable increase in numbers. By 1698 there were thirty-two groups in London itself and they had reached as far afield as Dublin. This rapid development aroused opposition and misunderstanding and the members of the metropolitan societies had occasion to address an apology to their diocesan, explaining their intentions. Henry Compton, "the Protestant Bishop" as he was dubbed, dismissed them with the comment, "God forbid that I should be against such excellent designs."[1] From 1691 onwards the same earnest men formed the nucleus of the Societies for the Reformation of Manners, which sought to elevate public morals by ensuring the enforcement of the penal statutes against vice and immorality.

In the reign of Queen Anne many of the Religious Societies were drawn up into the High Church reaction. Their increase continued and the S.P.C.K. fostered their formation in all districts where it had correspondents. There is a direct link with the eighteenth-century Revival, for as Portus has pointed out, "possibly the most famous of all the English Religious Societies was that organised by Samuel Wesley in his parish at Epworth in 1701,"[2] and it was to the London Societies that Whitefield addressed himself in 1737. Moreover, the Fetter Lane Society, from which both Methodism and English Moravianism evolved, stood in lineal relationship with the Religious Societies instituted in the latter half of the seventeenth century. As there is also evidence that the English Societies were not uninfluenced by the Pietist "colleges" it would appear that all of these agencies were coordinated in the plan of God. Certainly the significance of what Horneck launched by his "awakening sermons" cannot be ignored. Father Piette, in fact, sees in it the only force in Britain making for constructive and vital Christianity. "If the part played by John Wesley in the religious regeneration of England can be compared with the influence of the sun in the awakening of nature in springtime, let it not be forgotten that a dawn full of promise had preceded the sunrise, however beautiful it may have been. The dawn which announced and began this moral renewal

---

[1] Ibid., p. 47: cf. G. E. Carpenter, *The Protestant Bishop.*

[2] *A Dictionary of English Church History*, ed. S. L. Ollard, G. Crosse and M. F. Bond, p. 581.

was due to the Religious Societies which came into being at the end of 1678."[1]

In passing, it should be noted that although the triumph of the orthodox divines over the Deistic threat in the early part of the eighteenth century was gained purely in the intellectual realm, it was not therefore without spiritual significance. Indeed, it cleared the path for the Evangelical Revival. The message of salvation, proclaimed on the sole authority of the inspired Scriptures, reached a generation for which the issue of divine revelation was already thought through and settled in favour of the traditional view. The claim of the gospel to be received as authentic tidings from heaven had been vindicated at the scholarly level. It now only remained that it should in fact be announced as such and that with compelling persuasiveness. "It was unfortunate that there should ever have been any antagonism between men who were really workers in the same great cause," remarked Canon Overton. "Neither could have done the other's part of the work. Warburton could have no more moved the hearts of living masses to their inmost depths, as Whitefield did, than Whitefield could have written the *Divine Legation*. Butler could no more have carried on the great crusade against sin and Satan which Wesley did, than Wesley could have written the *Analogy*. But without such work as Wesley and Whitefield did, Butler's and Warburton's would have been comparatively inefficacious; and without such work as Butler and Warburton did, Wesley's and Whitefield's work would have been, humanly speaking, impossible."[2]

It is thus plain that, if the Christian apologists who countered the sallies of rationalistic Deism prepared the way for the preachers of the Revival, the Revival itself completed the work of the evidence writers by engaging the popular front and winning the multitudes of the people by an appeal to the heart as well as to the head. If we are to give the theologians their due share of credit for laying the foundations of a right presentation of the quickening Word, we must also recognize that the Revival leaders pressed the protest against Deism to its final conclusion. "It is often asserted that in the controversy of the eighteenth century in England the victory was won by the orthodox apologists over both the deists and sceptics," wrote A. C. McGiffert. "Nothing could be further from the truth," he added. "That religious faith and devotion still survived and flourished was due, not to the

---

[1] M. Piette, *John Wesley in the Evolution of Protestantism*, p. 270.
[2] Abbey and Overton, *op. cit.*, p. 313.

apologists, but to altogether different influences, of which the great evangelical revival was the most important."[1]

The man who formed the bridge between these two great forces of the eighteenth century was William Law. He was essentially a spiritual writer, conspicuous neither in theological debate nor in evangelistic enterprise, yet he was responsible, more than any other single figure, for the transference of the conflict from the one sphere to the other. Although he himself stood aloof, Law was destined to exercise a profound influence upon almost all the pioneers of the Awakening. There is scarcely one of them who does not express his indebtedness. Dr. Eric W. Baker rightly describes Law as "a herald of the Evangelical Revival."[2] He was recognized as such at the time. Charles Wesley used in old age to refer to Law as "our John the Baptist,"[3] whilst John Wesley agreed that there was truth in Trapp's description of Law as the parent of the Methodists.[4] The latter was no more sympathetic to the Revival than Warburton, who declared that "William Law was its father, and Count Zinzendorf rocked the cradle."[5] In one of the first biographies of Wesley, we are told concerning Law that "this considerable writer was the great forerunner of the revival which followed, and did more to promote it than any other individual whatsoever; yea, more perhaps than the rest of the nation collectively taken."[6] More recently G. A. Wauer, the historian of the Moravians, has called Law "the father of the English revival of the eighteenth century, and the grandfather of Methodism."[7]

The significance of William Law, however, lay not so much in his personal influence upon the pioneers of the Revival (though this was considerable) as in his reaction to the defence against Deism. He felt that only a Pyrrhic victory had been gained and he was concerned because the champions of orthodoxy, whilst guarding the strongholds assailed by immoderate reason, nevertheless allowed reason an unjustifiable latitude in matters of faith. It was his conviction that to treat Christianity as a problem of evidence was to play the Deist's own game. He himself had dabbled in controversy but he eventually came to the conclusion that to rely on reason is gross idolatry. To be formally orthodox

[1] A. C. McGiffert, *Protestant Thought before Kant*, p. 243.
[2] E. W. Baker, *A Herald of the Evangelical Revival*. The quotations which follow are found in the Introduction, p. vii.
[3] H. Moore, *The Life of Charles Wesley*, Vol I, p. 107.
[4] *The Works of John Wesley*, ed. T. Jackson, Vol. VII, p. 203.
[5] *The Works of William Warburton*, ed. R. Hurd, Vol. IV, p. 623.
[6] T. Coke and H. Moore, *The Life of John Wesley*, p. 6.
[7] Cf. H. Bett, *The Spirit of Methodism*, p. 41n.

by a merely external subscription to the tenets of the faith, without the inward assurance of the Spirit as a consequence of the new birth, is altogether futile. We are not Christians, Law said, unless our life "is a common course of humility, self-denial, renunciation of the world, poverty of the spirit, and heavenly affection."[1] "This is the sole end of Christianity," according to the *Treatise upon Christian Perfection*, "to lead us from all thoughts of rest and repose here, to separate us from the world and worldly tempers, to deliver us from the folly of our passions, the slavery of our natures, the power of evil spirits, and unite us to God, the true Founder of all real good. This is the mighty change which Christianity aims at, to put us in a new state, reform our whole nature, purify our souls, and make them the inhabitants of heavenly and immortal bodies."[2] And, although Law has sometimes been charged with a defective grasp of evangelical doctrine, he leaves no doubt as to the means whereby such a transformation takes place. "The manner by which it changes this whole state of things, and raises us to an union with God, is equally great and wonderful. 'I am the way, the truth and the life,' saith our blessed Saviour, 'no man cometh unto the Father but by Me.' As all things were at first created by the Son of God, and without Him was 'not anything made that was made,' so are all things again restored and redeemed by the same Divine Person. . . . All the precepts and doctrines of the Gospel are founded on these two great truths, the deplorable corruption of human nature, and its new birth in Christ Jesus."[2] No doubt it was such passages as these which convinced John Wesley, as he himself records, "of the absolute impossibility of being half a Christian."[4]

Wesley himself was to part company from Law almost immediately after his conversion—the first of his pilots to be dropped—but in 1744 he could still say, "I love Calvin a little, Luther more; the Moravians, Mr. Law, and Mr. Whitefield far more than either," though he was careful to correct any misapprehension by adding, "but I love truth more than all."[5] Despite the differences which arose between them—and the open letter of 1756 indicates how wide they were—Law's influence on Wesley still persisted, as it did upon the Revival as a whole. It ensured that the ethical emphasis of the gospel would never be forgotten, but most im-

---

[1] *The Works of William Law*, ed. G. B. Morgan, Vol. IV, p. 12.
[2] Ibid., Vol. III, pp. 12-13.
[3] Ibid., p. 13.
[4] Wesley, *Works*, Vol XI, p. 367.
[5] Wesley, *Letters*, Vol. II, p. 25.

portantly it supplied the experiential stimulus which enabled the advocates of the faith to press home their message beyond the point where reason fails with all her powers. It was just here that the Evangelical Awakening realized the assets and crowned the conquest of the anti-Deistic divines, and the part played by Law in blazing this vital trail is not to be disregarded. Incidentally, it must be noted that, on the accession of George I, Law refused the oath of allegiance and became a Nonjuror. Wesley's family drew on the same tradition. Stromberg is justified in remarking that, "when purged of intolerance and political prejudice, the High Church tradition contained a core of real Christian piety unique in this age. Out of it issued the religious revival."[1]

By these manifold means the plot was prepared in which the seed of spiritual life could germinate. God worked in a mysterious way to create the conditions under which another Pentecost could occur. Yet it would not have been possible to predict precisely when the fire would fall. These manifestations of the Spirit's energy are not controlled by any human schedule. They have their ultimate origin in the inscrutable will of God. When all the antecedents of revival had disclosed themselves, there was yet no inevitability about the outcome. God's hour would strike in God's time.

[1] R. L. Stromberg, *Religious Liberalism in Eighteenth Century England*, p. 93.

THE YEARS OF VISITATION

1711—1742

CHAPTER III

THE DAWN IN WALES

ALTHOUGH THE NAMES OF WESLEY AND WHITEFIELD DOMINATE
the records of the eighteenth-century Revival, it must not
therefore be supposed that they were either the only or indeed the earliest promoters of new life within the Church of this
period. Nor is England to be thought of as the sole breeding
ground. The principality of Wales was, in fact, the scene of
initial quickening. When God began to move once again amongst
His people it was in that remote and spiritually barren region that
He chose to work.

So far as evangelical witness was concerned, Wales seems to
have been a neglected area for half a century, following upon the
Stuart Restoration. During the Commonwealth protectorate
special attention had been paid to the principality. In 1649 an act
had been passed to ensure the more effective propagation of the
Gospel in Wales and commissioners were appointed to carry out
the project. Within the space of three short years no less than one
hundred and fifty ministers were settled in the thirteen Welsh
counties and in every market town at least one schoolmaster was
placed. Thirty itinerant preachers were also appointed together
with a number of lay exhorters. To this period belong the labours
of Walter Cradock and his two converts Morgan Llwyd and
Vavasor Powell.

All this commendable enterprise was halted by the restoration
of Charles II and Wales was left to lapse into its former state. In
the latter years of the seventeenth century the lack of sound doctrine with the consequent moral decline and a widespread resort
to the practice of magical arts and divination evoked the passionate complaint of the Vicar of Clun that the whole country "lay
under a veil of darkness."[1] Nevertheless, even in this saddening
period men were raised up to maintain at least a semblance of
evangelical religion. One of these was Hugh Owen. He had been
preparing himself for holy orders, but when the Act of Uniformity
was passed in 1662 he felt unable to comply with its requirements

[1] *Evangelical Library Bulletin*, No. 22, p. 2.

39

and withdrew his offer. He settled on his Merionethshire estate and gave himself to lay preaching. He received a ready hearing from a gospel-starved people and soon extended his mission into the neighbouring counties of Montgomery and Caernarvon. He arranged his stations in a circuit and usually completed his round in three months. Large crowds attended his meetings and many found salvation in Christ. He toiled unceasingly and impaired his health by riding, often through the night and in cold, stormy weather, over the bleak Welsh mountains. "He was a primitive and apostolical Christian," says one of his biographers, "eminently meek and humble; and would often style himself less than the least of all the ministers of Jesus Christ."[1]

Another burning and shining light in this cheerless era was Thomas Gauge. For fourteen years he was Vicar of St. Sepulchre's, Holborn, only to be deprived of his living in 1662. Although he was by no means a young man, he determined to continue his ministry and was providentially directed to Wales. Here he began to itinerate as a gospel preacher and, despite considerable opposition, succeeded in leading many to the truth. He was also deeply concerned with education and was instrumental in establishing free schools in many of the towns he visited. According to an account appearing in 1675, he had by that date founded fifty-one schools with upwards of a thousand children in them. He furthermore superintended the printing of eight thousand copies of the Welsh Bible and was responsible for publishing the catechism and useful devotional books. In all these ventures he was substantially helped by the generosity of friends in London.

Thus God had not left Himself without witness in the latter years of the seventeenth century. But as the eighteenth century dawned He had prepared a prophet soul to herald the great Awakening. Griffith Jones has been aptly described as the morning star of the Revival and it is to a review of his contribution that we must now turn. More than twenty years before the conversion of either Wesley or Whitefield this man of God was proclaiming the everlasting Gospel in his parish of Llandowror in Carmarthenshire and reaping the first fruits of the harvest. He was born in 1683 of a "religious and respectable family," according to the sketch of his life in the *Gentleman's Magazine* of 1762, and was baptized in Cilrhedyn Parish Church.[2] He seems to have been a

---

[1] M. G. L. Duncan, *History of Revivals of Religion*, p. 92.
[2] He was cradled within the Church, for there are no sufficient grounds for the statement of Thomas Levi in *D.N.B.* that his parents were Dissenters.

lively and rather headstrong youth and was variously employed
as a wood-turner and as a shepherd. It was whilst he pursued the
latter avocation that the call of God was conveyed unmistakably
to his heart. As he slept beside a hedge an angel of the Lord lifted
him up in a dream to show him all the joys of heaven and the
torments of hell. Then, as in the experience of Ezekiel, he was set
down again. "But not without first acquainting him by the way"
—so one record runs—"that it was one of the everlasting decrees
of the Almighty, whereby He had disposed everything from the
foundation of the world, that Mr. Griffith Jones was to be a
chosen vessel to bear His name, a peculiar instrument for rescuing
many souls, that were now far gone on their way to that place of
torment; and to fetch them back to that bliss and joy, which no
eye but Mr. Jones' had seen since St. Paul's."[1] Beneath the cheap
and unworthy sneers of John Evans's unsympathetic version of
Griffith Jones's commissioning we can nevertheless detect the
authentic notes of a divine vocation. Although doubts have been
cast upon the historicity of this incident, Professor W. G.
Grufydd has maintained its cruciality in Jones's career.[2]

In obedience to the heavenly vision, he began to prepare him-
self for holy orders. At a late age he entered the Elizabethan
Grammar School at Carmarthen and was then trained for the
Church either there or at Haverfordwest. On the recommendation
of Evan Evans of Clydan he was ordained by the erudite George
Bull, Bishop of St. David's. In 1710 he became curate to Thomas
Philipps at Laugharne and was thus introduced to the Vale of Taf
where the remainder of his ministry was to be exercised. Evan
Evans had originally sponsored him as a missionary candidate and
he actually entered into negotiations with the Society for Promoting Christian Knowledge with a view to sailing for Tranquebar.
But the spiritual need of his native Wales weighed heavily upon
his heart. As he discharged his parochial duties he realized how
great was the opportunity at home and consequently interpreted
his vision as a command to evangelize his own rather than a
distant land. So he began to preach not only within the bounds of
his appointed parish but throughout the surrounding neighbourhood. Once he was ordained, complains the critical John Evans, he
"took dog's leave to exercise his talents in the mountains of
Cilrhedyn."[3] A contemporary description of his preaching has

---

[1] J. Evans, *An Account of Some of the Welsh Charity Schools*, pp. 14-15.
[2] *Y Lenor*, Vol. II, p. 3.
[3] Evans, *op. cit.*, p. 17.

been left to us and conveys something of its passion and power:

> When he came to the application, he entered upon it with a solemn pause. He seemed to summon up all his remaining force; he gave way to a superior burst of religious vehemence and, like a flaming meteor, did bear down all before him. His voice broke silence, and proceeded with a sort of dignified pomp. Every word was like a fresh attack, and carried with it a sort of triumphant accent. No wonder that he was so successful in the conversion of sinners, when it was the Divine Spirit that made the Word effectual. By his preaching the drunkards became sober, the sabbath-breakers were reformed; the prayerless cried for mercy and forgiveness; and the ignorant were solicitously concerned for an interest in the Divine Redeemer.[1]

Further evidence is furnished in a letter from John Dalton of Clogyfran to the S.P.C.K. as early as 1713:

> When Mr. Jones is invited to preach anywhere, and also when he preaches in his own church, in which there does not belong (as parishioners) save ten or twelve small families, it is to be admired what a numerous congregation he has to administer to, having generally above five or six hundred auditors, nay, sometimes a thousand, a number not to be met with in Wales besides, on the like occasion. It mostly consists of such as seem very desirous of being instructed in the plain and familiar dialect of their native language. It is certain that Mr. Jones is one of the greatest masters of the Welsh tongue that ever Wales was blessed with, both in respect of fluency of speech and eminently in Scriptural and Christian knowledge.[2]

In the light of these tributes, John Evans's gibe that "Hums and Ha's make half his sermon" is unconvincing.[3]

Griffith Jones not only anticipated the later leaders of the Revival in his evangelical message but also in the opposition he encountered from the ecclesiastical authorities. It appears that in the year 1714, when Adam Ottley conducted the first of his three episcopal visitations, Jones was summoned to appear before him at St. Peter's, Carmarthen, to undergo what Sir John Philipps describes as "a sort of trial."[4] Several of the clergy appeared against him to complain that he neglected his own cure and intruded himself into the parishes of other incumbents without their leave. According to Philipps, the contrary "was manifestly proved, viz. that he never preached in any other place without being invited either by the incumbent, curate or some of the best inhabitants of

---

[1] *Sketch of Jones*, p. 6.
[2] *Journal Calvinistic Methodist Historical Society*, Vol. XXV, p. 3.
[3] Evans, *op. cit.*, p. 17.
[4] Letter to S.P.C.K., 9 October 1714.

the parish: that he indeed preached twice or thrice without the walls of the church, the reason of which was because the church was not large enough to contain the hearers, which sometimes amounted to three or four thousand people: that his defence was so clear and satisfying that the Bishop declared he was willing Mr. Jones should preach anywhere, having an invitation from the ministers of the place."[1] The matter, however, was not allowed to rest, and in the following year the Chancellor of the Diocese was still considering what should be done "in the case of Mr. Griffith Jones, which is a nice affair, and of consequence."[2] Eventually, in July 1715 Jones wrote a lengthy letter to the Bishop in his own defence. He held to his former denial that he had ever preached in any parish without consent. He painted a saddening picture of the spiritual starvation suffered by the people and the inadequacy of the careless clergy to meet their hunger. "Oh! miserable people, hoodwinked with stupidity and wallowing with greediness in the filth of sin, what pity is it that so many in the sacred function should be immersed in this inundation of wickedness." He gently suggested that the Bishop would be better employed "in stirring up those that preach not than silencing those that do." He concluded by indicating his readiness to resign if the Bishop so desired, "nor need there any further trouble to stop my preaching abroad . . . than your Lordship to use your prerogative to supersede it by the better performance of others."[3] The Chancellor was apparently still unsatisfied and proposed to draw up a libel *ex officio* against Jones, but, though the document was endorsed by the Diocesan Registrar, we hear no more about it.

In 1716 Griffith Jones was presented to the rectory of Llandowror at a stipend of £25 *per annum* plus a house. This was to be his sphere until his death in 1761. Here the Revival message was faithfully preached. Here the signs following were plainly visible. Here the converts were gathered and counselled. Here the work of grace proceeded. It was his custom to summon his household daily for morning and evening prayers and on Sunday evening to catechize them all. Nor were his ministrations exclusively spiritual. He possessed a social conscience. We are told that he was careful to deal his bread to the hungry. He fed, clothed and doctored many of his needy parishioners. Indeed his charity to the poor led John Evans to declare unkindly that he was "as great a quack in

[1] Ibid.
[2] *Transactions Carmarthen Antiquarian Society*, Vol. XXIV, p. 81.
[3] *Op. cit.*, 88-9.

physic as in divinity."[1] That this latter insinuation is as groundless as the former is evidenced by the encomium published after his death in the *Gospel Magazine* where we are informed that "he was well versed in the writings of the most eminent English and foreign divines."[2]

The outstanding contribution of Griffith Jones lay, of course, in the realm of education. His name is written into the history of the Charity School movement. Already the S.P.C.K. had established a number of centres, but Jones supplemented these with an organization eventually known as the Circulating Welsh Charity Schools. It developed from the catechetical class he held in his rectory each Sunday evening. The ignorance he discovered led him to devise a means to provide his parishioners with regular and more general instruction. He first trained teachers and then sent them on circuit from parish to parish, remaining only for a few months in each and then moving on to the next centre. In this way a much wider area was covered than would otherwise have been possible. The schools were by no means confined to children but were attended by adults as well, even up to sixty and seventy years of age. Beginning from the winter of 1731-2 the movement expanded with astonishing rapidity until at his death almost four thousand such schools had been opened and one hundred and fifty-eight thousand scholars were enrolled. He received considerable encouragement and financial support from Bridget Bevan, one of his converts, and wife of a local Member of Parliament. It was she who continued the work after Jones's death. This enterprise—according to Lecky "one of the few important steps in religious education that were taken in the empire during the early Hanoverian period"[3]—was the fruit of revival. As Kelly points out, "Griffith Jones' parish work gradually forced him to the conclusion that for an ignorant populace preaching alone was insufficient as a means of salvation. It must be accompanied by positive teaching, and such teaching, in turn, was impossible unless people were first taught to read. From about 1730 onwards, therefore, we find him turning his attention more and more to educational work as the necessary foundation of all religious endeavour."[4] His literacy campaign both stemmed from and led to evangelism.

But we are primarily concerned in this chapter with the more

[1] Evans, *op. cit.*, p. 94.
[2] *Gospel Magazine*, 1777, p. 291.
[3] Lecky, *op. cit.*, Vol. III, p. 105.
[4] T. Kelly, *Griffith Jones Llandowror: Pioneer in Adult Education*, p. 25.

direct relationship of Jones to the Evangelical Revival as a whole.
He well merits his title of morning star. He proclaimed the new
birth and saw its gracious fruits long before the onset of the
Awakening proper. He was a pioneer of field preaching. He anticipated the circuit system which was to become a leading feature of
the Methodist section of the movement. He tasted the lash of
persecution. Later he had contacts with the recognized leaders of
the Revival. He heard John Wesley speak in the open air at Bath,
standing on some steps at the end of a house in Gracious Street.
At the close of the meeting the two men met and spent about an
hour together, being refreshed with each other's company. It was
in Bath, too, that Jones met George Whitefield and gave him
some account of the many obstructions he had encountered in his
ministry and convinced the rising evangelist that he "was but a
young soldier just entering the field."[1] Whitefield in turn recognized Jones as one of the shining lights of Wales. From 1748 onwards Griffith Jones was associated with Lady Huntingdon and
supplied some of her chapels. His attitude towards those of other
denominations is reflected in the following extract from an
obituary notice:

> Though as a minister of the Church of England he had a steady
> attachment to her communion, yet to persons of a scrupulous and
> tender conscience, dissenting from the Church, he left the rights of
> private judgment. Therefore he hesitated not to give the right hand
> of fellowship to all upright and pious men of every denomination
> being fully sensible that all godly men are in Christ.[2]

The influence and importance of Griffith Jones, however, is
nowhere more apparent than in the fact that the three most significant leaders of the developing movement in Wales looked to him
as their spiritual father: namely, Rowland, Harris and Davies. To
these we must now turn.

Daniel Rowland found himself in holy orders as an unconverted
man. He was curate to his brother John at Llangeitho in Cardigan-
shire. He had been ordained at an exceptionally early age, in consideration, it is said, of his superior scholarship, although he
lacked a University education. He was a keen athlete, far more
interested in sport than in Christianity. Even Sunday afternoon
was spent with the young men of the parish in the popular games
of the time. His clerical duties were something to be got through
as best he might. He had no deep convictions about the faith he

---

[1] L. Tyerman, *The Life of George Whitefield*, Vol. I, p. 184.
[2] *Sketch*, p. 22.

preached. Like so many of the contemporary clergy, he regarded his high vocation simply as a convenient means of earning a livelihood, and no more. Nevertheless he was restless and dissatisfied. In his heart of hearts he realized that he was called of God to something more than this. The Lord was troubling the waters of his soul. There was then in the county an Independent preacher named Philip Pugh who was attracting large congregations, far more than Daniel Rowland could draw. So Rowland went to hear him, hoping to learn the secret of his success. He came to the conclusion that Pugh made such an impression because he "thundered" at his congregation and warned them of judgment to come. Without at all believing in the doctrines he declared, but merely to discover whether he could fill his empty church in some way, Rowland began to model himself closely on Philip Pugh. He magnified his voice to twice its normal proportions. He bellowed from the pulpit until the pillars shivered and shook. He searched out the most terrible texts of Scripture. He launched into unaccustomed delineations of the sinner's miserable plight and everlasting punishment to come. To his amazement, the experiment worked. The people flocked to hear him and many, like Peter's audience at Pentecost, were pricked in their hearts and enquired, "What shall we do?" It is calculated that more than a hundred members of Rowland's congregation were brought under conviction of sin before he himself had begun to be touched at all. "What shall we do?" Rowland could not tell them. He was an unregenerate man himself. He had been speaking beyond his own experience. He had awakened in his hearers a sense of sin, but he knew no Saviour to whom he could point them. Their last state was likely to be worse than the first.

Soon the crisis in Rowland's life was reached. There came to preach at the nearby village of Llandewi Brefi—the second of three places under his charge—none other than Griffith Jones himself. When he entered the pulpit to deliver his sermon he could not fail to notice the sceptical look on the young curate's face. Jones paused to pray. Even in the split second between announcing his text and embarking on his discourse he was able to dart a plea to heaven for the conversion of the supercilious hearer. But Jones not only claimed Rowland's salvation. He was even more ambitious. He requested that being saved he might become the instrument of turning many to righteousness. What a tremendous prayer to sandwich between a text and a sermon! It was abundantly answered. In that very service Rowland was convicted and converted and returned to Llangeitho a new creature in Christ Jesus. Little did Jones suspect at the time that Rowland stood at the crossroads of his ministry.

Daniel Rowland now had the remedy to meet the cry that rose from his congregation: "What shall we do?" He was able to direct them to Jesus. His preaching gained unusual power. Multitudes, we are told, trembled in his presence and the church sometimes rang with the shouts and shrieks of those with whom the Holy Spirit was deeply dealing. His fame spread throughout Wales and he travelled far and wide as a messenger of the gospel. Many were of the opinion that he even exceeded Whitefield as a sacred orator, and in his *Eminent Welshmen* William Williams hailed him as "the greatest and most wonderful preacher ever heard in Wales,"[1] whilst Howell Harris described him as "a second St. Paul in his own pulpit."[2]

Soon Llangeitho began to gather hearers like moths to a lighted candle. Distance was no hindrance. On one occasion forty-five people set out from Caernarvon, sailed as far as Aberystwyth and then walked the rest of the way. They had planned to return by the same route, but a gale prevented the ship from putting out, so they made the whole journey on foot. Rowland's preaching soon took on a new and tenderer note as he proclaimed the comforts of the gospel as well as the terrors of the law. In this change of evangelistic tactics we may discern the influence of his friend and counsellor, Philip Pugh, who advised him to press upon his congregation the need to trust in Christ alone for salvation. "Preach the gospel to the people, dear sir," he said, "and apply the balm of Gilead, the blood of Christ to their spiritual wounds, and show the necessity of faith in a crucified Saviour." "I am afraid," replied Rowland, "that I have not that faith myself in its vigour and full exercise." "Preach on it," urged Pugh, "till you feel it, in that way no doubt it will come. If you go on preaching the law after this fashion, you will kill half the people in the country, for you thunder out the curses of the law and preach it in such a terrible manner that no one can stand before you." "From this time," writes William Williams, "there was a great and happy change in the tone of Rowland's ministry; now it was as full of the gospel as it had been before of law. It became as remarkable for its sweetness as it had been for its terrors, and as effective to comfort as it had been to alarm. When he proclaimed free forgiveness through the

<hr>

[1] *Evangelical Library Bulletin*, No. 22, p. 3.
[2] Ibid., p. 6.

sufferings and death of the Saviour of the world, sinners ready to perish felt that there was hope even for them. In realising that hope, they rejoiced with joy unspeakable and full of glory, and great numbers expressed their ecstatic joy in shouts of praise."[1]

Rowland was not given to lengthy sermons, but once at morning worship he was so led on by the Spirit that he continued to preach, with the congregation hanging upon every word, until a ray of light stole through the west window to announce that it was near sunset. Such preaching and such hearing does revival bring.

Griffith Jones and Daniel Rowland were ordained clergymen of the Established Church. Neither of them found favour with the authorities, though no charge could be upheld against them. It has been stated that Rowland's licence was revoked in 1763 and that he was thus deprived of his cure. The Diocesan Register contained no record of such a revocation. It is more probable that when his brother John died in 1760 his license expired and was not renewed. In any event, he was no longer permitted to exercise his ministry in Llangeitho and for the remainder of his life he preached in a large meeting house built for him by his supporters. The next leader who engages our attention, however, was a layman and depended entirely upon an itinerant programme. His conversion heralded the great Revival in Wales. It was on Whit Sunday in the year 1735 that Howell Harris was brought into the experience of salvation and assurance. He was the village schoolmaster at Talgarth in the county of Brecon, but he had little interest in his vocation. He was more concerned with dice playing, drinking, gossiping and love-making than with caring for the scholars in his charge. Nevertheless some early stirrings of prevenient grace were to be observed. In his diary he admitted that his conscience was not finally hardened and that he often felt yearnings for a better life. "I used to commune, meditate and pray to God," he tells us, "and at the same time behave like a hypocrite." He began "to be anxious and to grieve somewhat for sin" and grew "conscious of the worldliness of such a sinful life."[2] God was preparing him for the transformation which was to take place in the spring of 1735.

On Palm Sunday he attended morning worship at Talgarth Parish Church when the Vicar, Pryce Davies, read the exhortation which the rubric of the Prayer Book requires to be employed when the minister "shall see the people negligent to come to the

[1] W. Williams, *Welsh Calvinistic Methodism*, p. 32.
[2] G. T. Roberts, *Howell Harris*, p. 14.

Holy Communion." In that solemn address some of the excuses commonly advanced for such negligence are rehearsed. When he had finished reading the prescribed words the earnest incumbent added further pleas of his own. "You plead your unfitness to come to the Holy Communion. Let me tell you, that if you are not fit to come to the Lord's Supper, you are not fit to come to church, you are not fit to live; you are not fit to die." Those words struck right home to Harris's heart. He resolved to prepare himself to receive the sacrament on Easter Day and spent the intervening week in such an exemplary manner that he was fully satisfied with his own righteousness when he presented himself. But as he repeated the confession in which the communicants declare that the remembrance of their sins is grievous to them and that the burden is intolerable, he realized that he was dissembling before God. He had no such sense of the exceeding sinfulness of his sin. He was tempted to rise and leave the church, but he recalled his resolve to mend his ways and so, still trusting in himself, he partook of the holy sacrament for the first time in his life. During the weeks that followed he was subject to much doubt and fear. He earnestly endeavoured to keep his heart and thoughts fixed on God, but it was all in vain, as might have been expected, for he was trying to make the fruit good when the tree was corrupt. He was greatly helped by a book by Bryan Duppa on the Ten Commandments: through it he was constrained to abandon any reliance upon himself, his own amended life and good works, and to seek salvation solely from Christ. In another devotional manual, *The Practice of Piety*, he read: "If we would go to the sacrament simply believing in the Lord Jesus Christ, we should receive forgiveness of all our sins."[1] Howell Harris determined to put these words to the test and so it was with genuine repentance and firm faith that he approached the Lord's Table on the morning of Whit Sunday. Then, to use his own language, "at the sacrament, by viewing my God on the Cross, I was delivered from these temptations" and he obtained an assurance that his sins were indeed forgiven. His chains fell off, his heart was free. "I was convinced by the Holy Ghost that Christ died for me, and that all my sins were laid on Him. I was now acquitted at the bar of justice, and in my conscience. This evidenced itself to be true faith by the peace, joy, watchfulness, hatred to sin, and fear of offending God that followed it."[2] This blessed experience was ratified later as he

[1] Cf. Simon, *op. cit.*, p. 140.
[2] *Brief Account of the Life of Howell Harris*, pp. 13-14.

was engaged in private prayer in Llangasty Church. "I felt suddenly my heart melting within me, like wax before the fire, with love to God my Saviour; and also felt, not only love and peace but a longing to be dissolved and be with Christ. There was a cry in my soul which I was totally unacquainted with before—'Abba Father!' I could not help calling God my Father. I *knew* that I was His child and that He loved and heard me. My soul, being satiated, cried, 'It is enough. I am satisfied. Give me strength and I will follow Thee through fire and water!' I could say I was happy indeed."[1]

This experience made Harris an evangelist. His heart was filled with "the fire of the love of God."[2] Though his temperament inclined him to reticence, he was moved by an irresistible inward compulsion to communicate his secret to others. He could not remain indifferent to the spiritual deadness of the neighbourhood. On the Lord's day no sooner was worship concluded than sport and revelry began. The practice of family prayer was almost wholly abandoned. "A universal deluge of swearing, lying, reviling, drunkenness, fighting and gaming had overspread the country," he informs us.[3] No man seemed to care for their souls. Harris appealed in vain to the clergy to raise their voices. At length he could hold his peace no longer. He started by reading to some of his neighbours in his mother's house. Then he extended his ministrations to the sick. He began to visit his former companions and urge them to forsake their evil ways. Finally he went from house to house not only in his own parish but also in those adjacent. Great concourses gathered to hear him. A notable change took place in the district. Family worship was reinstated in many homes, the church services were crowded and the number of communicants much increased. Such success evoked the hostility of the clergy and magistrates, but Harris pursued his onward course in the fixed conviction that he was commissioned by God.

In 1736 he was introduced to Griffith Jones and in the same year, when episcopal ordination had been refused him, he resumed the work of a teacher until he was removed from his school at Trevecka. From this point he devoted himself to the task of itinerant evangelism. He travelled from town to town and fearlessly faced the violence of the mob in order to declare the unsearchable riches of Christ. He had exceptional power as a

[1] Roberts, *op. cit.*, p. 18.
[2] Simon, *op. cit.*, p. 142.
[3] Ibid.

preacher. His presence was commanding and his voice, though often hoarse through over-use, was of such strength that he had no difficulty in making himself heard. He thundered against sin and one man said he used to speak of hell as if he had been there himself. But he could also depict the attractions of righteousness in such a way as to make men desire it above rubies. His language was homely yet compelling and he had the knack of adorning truth with an effective tale. George Whitefield's tribute to him is worth transcribing:

A burning and shining light has been in those parts; a barrier against profaneness and immorality, and an indefatigable promoter of the true Gospel of Jesus Christ. . . . He is of a most catholic spirit, loves all that love our Lord Jesus Christ, and, therefore, he is slighted by bigots and dissenters. He is contemned by all that are lovers of pleasure rather than lovers of God: but God has greatly blessed his pious endeavours. Many call and own him as their spiritual father; and, I believe, would lay down their lives for his sake. He discourses generally in a field, from a wall, a table, or anything else, but at other times in a house. He has established near thirty societies in South Wales, and still his sphere of action is enlarged daily. He is full of faith and the Holy Ghost. . . . Blessed be God, there seems to be a noble spirit gone out into Wales; and I believe ere long there will be more visible fruits of it.[1]

Dr. Thomas Rees calls Harris "the most successful preacher that ever ascended a pulpit or platform in Wales" and adds that "he was an extraordinary instrument raised by providence, at an extraordinary time, to accomplish an extraordinary work."[2]

It was in the autumn of 1736 that Harris's first societies were established, on the advice of Griffith Jones, and thus was laid the foundation of Welsh Calvinistic Methodism. But we are not here concerned with these developments, nor with the later ministry of Harris which linked him so closely with so many of the evangelical leaders. We simply pause to salute him as one of the pioneers of revival.

Amongst Harris's converts was Howell Davies and with him our account of the dawn in Wales must terminate. Davies was a pupil at Griffith Jones's school at Llandowror and felt the call to the Christian ministry. He was eventually ordained to the curacy of Llysfra in Pembrokeshire. His preaching made a marked impression. Crowds flocked to hear him and many received a spiritual blessing. But opposition was aroused and Davies was removed.

[1] *Brief Account*, pp. 31-2.
[2] T. Rees, *History of Protestant Nonconformity in Wales*, pp. 364-5.

He thereupon undertook a wider commission and was the agent of conversion to thousands. Remarkable scenes were witnessed when he administered the Lord's Supper in the tiny churches of Pembrokeshire. Sometimes the building had to be filled two or three times to accommodate the communicants. Davies was much admired by the Countess of Huntingdon who invited him to preach at her London tabernacle. But he is best and deservedly known as the apostle of Pembrokeshire. In later years he ministered at Haverfordwest where a chapel was erected for him.

Referring to Rowland, Harris and their associates, John Owen has observed: "The revival of religion in the Church was their avowed object from the first and their professed object through life."[1] We may thank God that their aim was achieved and that under their faithful ministry the dawn light broke on Wales.

---

[1] J. Owen, *A Memoir of Daniel Rowland*, p. 27.

CHAPTER IV

THE AMERICAN AWAKENING

A S WE HAVE SEEN IN THE PREVIOUS CHAPTER, THE REVIVAL proper cannot be said to have been inaugurated in Wales until the year 1735. It is true that there were gracious anticipations in the ministry of Griffith Jones from as early as 1711, but the unbroken chain of fire was not touched off until after the conversion of Rowland and Harris. This means that although intermittent kindlings appeared in Wales, the first outbreak of sustained revival occurred not in Great Britain but in America. The earliest name in the immediate succession is not Wesley or Whitefield but Jonathan Edwards. We must cross the Atlantic to trace the source of this Pentecostal overflow. The eighteenth-century Revival was, historically speaking, part of American aid to Britain. Even if the relationship between the American Awakening and that in the homeland was not so obvious as in the following century, the links were nevertheless strong and real. What happened in the new world and in the old may be regarded as part of a single movement of the Spirit.

Before recounting the stirring story of the Northampton revival, we must indicate the condition of the Church in the American colonies at the turn of the century and consider some of the earlier manifestations of blessing. The Thirteen Colonies had fallen far from the religious fervour of the Puritan immigrants who had sailed in the *Mayflower*. The crusading spirit which characterized the pioneers had largely died out. The profound moral earnestness and spiritual passion of the first generation of colonists had waned. Although the declension was neither so evident nor so disastrous as on the continent of Europe, yet, nevertheless, the church life of America was suffering from a creeping paralysis. The concern of the enlightened few is reflected in the observations of some of the leaders. Here, for example, is an extract from a sermon preached in Boston in 1698, probably by Cotton Mather:

> What changes have we seen in point of religion! Certainly the power of godliness is now grievously decayed among us. As the

prophet of old exclaimed in Joel 1 : 2: "Hear this, ye old men, and give ear, ye inhabitants! Hath this been in your days?" Thus may I say: "Hear this, ye old men, that are of the inhabitants of the town: can't you remember that in your days a prayerful, watchful, fruitful Christian, and a well-governed family, was a more common sight, than it is now in our days? Can't you remember that in your days these abominable things did not show their heads that are bare faced among us? Here then is a petition to be made unto our God": Lord, help us to remember whence we are fallen, and to repent, and to do the first works.[1]

Here is Increase Mather writing in 1702 in his book *The Glory Departing from New England*:

We are the posterity of the good old Puritan Nonconformists in England, who were a strict and holy people. Such were our fathers who followed the Lord into this wilderness. Oh, New England, New England, look to it that the glory be not removed from thee, for it begins to go! Oh, tremble, for it is gradually departing. You that are aged persons and can remember what New England was fifty years ago, that saw these churches in their first glory: is there not a sad decay and diminution of that glory? How is the gold become dim.[2]

And again in 1721 he wrote:

I am now in my eighty-third year, and having been for sixty-five years a preacher of the Gospel, I cannot but be in the disposition of those ancient men who had seen the foundation of the first house, and wept with a loud voice to see what a change the temple had upon it. The children of New England are, or once were, the children of godly men. What did our fathers come into this wilderness for? Not to gain estates as men do now, but for religion, and that they might leave their children in a hopeful way of being truly religious. Oh, degenerate New England, what art thou come to at this day? How are those sins become common in thee that once were not so much as heard of in this land![3]

Nor was the situation any more reassuring in the remainder of the colonies. Jonathan Dickenson reported that in New Jersey religion was in a decline, with most church members moribund and the body of the people careless and carnal. In Pennsylvania Samuel Blair bemoaned the fact that true religion was dying and ready to expire its last breath of life. In Virginia and Maryland the bankruptcy of the Establishment was patent. From Connecticut, Samuel Whitman complained in 1714 "that religion is on the

---

[1] *Select Works of Jonathan Edwards*, ed. I. Murray, Vol. I, p. 24.
[2] J. Gillies, *Historical Collections*, Vol. II, p. 18.
[3] Ibid., pp. 18-19.

wane among us. 'Tis languishing in all parts of the land. . . . Is not religion degenerated into an empty form? We are risen up a generation that have in great measure forgot the errand of our fathers."[1]

The causes for such apostasy are not far to seek. The clear convictions and glowing zeal of the original crusaders did not appear in their children. The Church life of the day was dank and unattractive, not at all conducive to vitality and progress. Services were long and drab: they bore little relation to life and reflected the prevailing theological petrifaction of the day. The element of feeling was absent and thus no corresponding reaction was evoked from the hearers. Leslie Stephen remarked that a critical vocabulary of dull, duller, dullest was sufficient to describe the English homilies of this period and the situation was no more satisfactory across the Atlantic. Such a lack of fervour in the pulpit had its inevitable repercussions in the pew and the spiritual temperature of the churches dropped to zero. "As religion became institutional and less personal," observes E. S. Gaustad, "more a product of instruction than of experience, and more an affair of the intellect than of the emotions, piety waned. Brattle Street Church, founded in Boston in 1699, eliminated the testimony of personal religious experience as a concession to the modesty of potential members: it was more a recognition that there was little such experience to relate. Religion was losing its dramatic, experiential quality."[2]

Much of this decline is attributed to the notorious "Half Way Covenant." It had been the insistence of the earliest New England divines that "visible saints are the only true and meet matter, whereof a visible Church should be gathered."[3] But midway through the seventeenth century a concession had been made to parents who were not actually members of the Church in order that their children might nevertheless be presented for baptism. This involved a basic alteration of principle and in the eyes of many was responsible for opening the door to a further incursion of worldliness into the Church. At the Reforming Synod of 1679, held in Boston, an attempt was made to check the drift and in 1705 a set of proposals was presented to ensure greater control over local congregations. But these measures had little effect and the condition of New England when Jonathan Edwards came to

[1] Cf. G. L. Walker, *Some Aspects of the Religious Life of New England*, p. 73.
[2] E. S. Gaustad, *The Great Awakening in New England*, p. 14.
[3] T. Hooker, *A Survey of the Summe of Church-Discipline*, preface: cf. Gaustad, *op. cit.*, p. 9.

Northampton as depicted in a letter contained in Gillies's *Historical Collections* may be taken as typical.

> A very lamentable ignorance of the main essentials of true practical religion, and the doctrines nextly relating thereunto, very generally prevailed. The nature and necessity of a conviction of sin and misery, by the Holy Spirit opening and applying the law to the conscience, in order to a saving closure with Christ, was hardly known at all to the most. It was thought that if there was any need of a heart-distressing sight of the soul's danger, and fear of divine wrath, it was only needful for the grosser sort of sinners. . . . The common names for such soul concern were, melancholy, trouble of mind, or despair, and trouble of mind was looked upon as a great evil, which all persons that made any sober profession and practice of religion, ought carefully to avoid. According to these principles, and this ignorance of the most soul-concerning truths of the gospel, people were very generally through the land careless at heart, and stupidly indifferent about the great concerns of eternity; and indeed the wise, for the most part, were in a great degree asleep with the foolish. It was sad to see with what a careless behaviour the public ordinances were attended, and how people were given to unsuitable worldy discourse on the Lord's day. In public companies, a vain and frothy lightness was apparent in the deportment of many professors.[1]

Such was the condition of the American colonies prior to the Great Awakening. If ever revival was needed it was then.

The initial stirrings were discernible in the work of Solomon Stoddart, Edwards's predecessor at Northampton, Massachusetts, and his own maternal grandfather. Perry Miller rightly describes him as the first great revivalist in New England.[2] For almost sixty years he laboured faithfully and saw much fruit. He reaped five harvests, as he called them, in 1679, 1683, 1696, 1712 and 1718. "Some of these times were much more remarkable than others," according to his grandson, "and the ingathering of souls more plentiful. Those about fifty-three and forty and twenty-four years ago [Edwards wrote in 1736] were much greater than either the first or the last: but in each of them, I have heard my grandfather say, the greater part of the young people in the town seemed to be mainly concerned for their eternal salvation."[3] But in the remainder of Stoddart's ministry there was "nothing of any general awakening" and when he died in 1729 "the greater part seemed to be at that time very insensible to the things of religion, and engaged in other cares and pursuits."[4] Although proclaiming the absolute

---

[1] Gillies, *op. cit.*, p. 35.
[2] *Harvard Theological Review*, Vol. XXXIV, p. 316.
[3] Edwards, *Works*, Vol. I, p. 72.
[4] Ibid.

sovereignty of God, Stoddart preached a covenant theology which offered hope to all. His evangelistic approach was broader and more tolerant than that of his contemporaries and some of his pamphlets were reprinted during the Great Awakening. Like the Wesleys after him, he regarded the Holy Communion as a converting ordinance and laid down no condition of acceptance at the Lord's Table save repentance and faith.

We hear of an outbreak of revival in 1705 at Taunton under the pastorate of Samuel Danforth. It is interesting that this began when, having read some account of the Religious Societies in England, Danforth called together a group of his more zealous parishioners to join him in prayer and consultation for the reformation of manners in the town. The observance of family worship was reinstated and young people were gathered in societies after the manner of those under Horneck and Smythies. More than three hundred renewed their covenant with God and a real work of the Spirit was inaugurated. "Religion flourishes to amazement and astonishment," reported Danforth in a letter, "that so we should be at once touched with soul-affliction, and this in all corners of the place; and that our late conversions should be attended with more than usual degrees of horror, and Satan permitted to wrestle with them by extraordinary temptations and assaults, and hours of darkness. But, I hope, the deeper the wound, the more sound may be the cure; and I have little time to think of worldly matters; scarce time to study sermons, as I used to do; but find God can bless mean preparations, whenever He pleases: that such shall be most cried up and commended, which I have scarce had time to methodize. I think sometimes that the time of the pouring out of the Spirit upon all flesh may be at the door."[1]

The year 1720 marks the beginning of spiritual renascence in New Jersey. As early as 1685 the Gospel had been preached there by Walter Ker, but there had been a pitiful declension by the time Theodore Freylinghuysen of the Dutch Reformed Church began his mission to the settlements in the Raritan Valley. His earnest, faithful, impassioned preaching, produced many conversions and considerable opposition. By 1726 the revival was spreading to the Presbyterian churches of the district.

Meanwhile in 1721 we hear of "a remarkable concern" among the people of Windham, Connecticut, under Samuel Whiting, as a result of which eighty new members were added to the church

[1] Gillies, *op. cit.*, p. 23.

within the space of six months. Other manifestations of revival appeared so that "the town was full of love, joy, thanksgiving and praise."[1] Considering the fact that the population of the place was only about two hundred families this accession to the church was quite unprecedented. "It is surprising to see what an happy alteration there is made when God is pleased to bless the dispensation of the Gospel, and the institutions of His house, and confirm His Word in the mouths of His servants," runs a contemporary account.

> Now, the eyes of the blind are opened, the ears of the deaf unstopped, the dumb are taught to speak, and they that were spiritually dead raised unto life. To behold obstinate sinners that went on frowardly in the ways of their own heart, yielding themselves unto God, such as were careless and unconcerned about their own souls, now brought to the last distress and concern about what they shall do to escape from the wrath that is to come, and such as were fond of their several vicious courses now quitting them with shame and indignation, that they may endeavour for the future to lead their lives, not "according to the lusts of men, but the will of God." "Shall it not from this time be said, What hath God wrought?" Surely it is the work of Him that at first "commanded the light to shine out of darkness" and "called the things that were not as though they were".[2]

Finally, there was a considerable revival from 1730 to 1732 at Freehold, New Jersey, under John Tennent and his brother William, who succeeded him. Previously a third brother, Gilbert Tennent, had been the principal instrument of awakening amongst the Presbyterians of the province. Placed at New Brunswick in 1726, he had worked closely with Freylinghuysen and had seen encouraging fruits amongst his Scots-Irish congregation. John Tennent was appointed to Freehold in 1730 and in the brief eighteen months before his death a most remarkable quickening was witnessed, despite the fact that the congregation was in a most distracted condition when he arrived. He preached with exceptional unction and effectiveness. "During this short time his labours were greatly blessed," declared his brother William, "so that the place of public worship was unusually crowded with people of all ranks; and they seemed to hear generally as for their lives; yea, such as were wont to go to those places for their diversion, viz. to hear news or speak to their tradesmen and etc., even on the Lord's day, as they themselves have since confessed, were taken in the Gospel net; a solemn awe of God's majesty possessed

[1] B. Trumbull, *A Complete History of Connecticut*, Vol. II, p. 104.
[2] Gillies, *op. cit.*, p. 24.

many, so that they behaved themselves as at the bar while in His house. Many tears were usually shed when he preached, and sometimes the body of the congregation was moved or affected. . . . Religion was the general subject of discourse, though they did not all approve the power of it: the Holy Bible was searched by people on both sides of the question, and knowledge surprisingly increased: the terror of God fell generally upon the inhabitants of this place; so that wickedness, as ashamed in a great measure, hid itself."[1] The work continued with even more impressive effect during the ministry of William Tennent who occupied the pulpit for the last six months of his brother's life and was called to the church after his death.

However significant may be these successive though scattered manifestations as signs of what God was about to do in more abundant measure, it must be remembered that, as Trumbull suggests, they were but oases of spiritual concern in a desert of increasing indifference.[2] The Great Awakening was not yet. Not until 1740 did the fire descend in such a way as to produce a prairie blaze. But one further local Pentecost exceeded all others in intensity and influence. Although confined to a single town and its immediate environs, the fame of the Northampton revival was noised abroad throughout the American colonies and spanned the Atlantic to reach the shores of Britain. Chronologically speaking it was the precursor of the Evangelical Awakening in our land as well as in the continent of its origin, for it took place in the years 1734 and 1735, by which time Jonathan Edwards had succeeded Solomon Stoddart. After the latter's death there seems to have been something of a setback. What Edwards himself described as "a time of extraordinary dulness in religion" set in. "Licentiousness for some years prevailed among the youth of the town; they were many of them very much addicted to night walking, and frequenting the tavern, and lewd practices, wherein some, by their example, exceedingly corrupted others. It was their manner very frequently to get together in conventions of both sexes for mirth and jollity, which were called frolics; and they would often spend the greater part of the night in them, without regard to any order in the families they belonged to: and indeed family government did too much fail in the town. . . . There had also long prevailed . . . a spirit of contention between two parties, into which they had for many years been divided; by which they maintained

[1] *Op. cit.*, pp. 29-30.
[2] Cf. Gaustad, *op. cit.*, p. 17.

a jealousy one of the other, and were prepared to oppose one another in all public affairs."[1] Gradually, however, under the solemn preaching of Jonathan Edwards, the Holy Spirit began to deal with the laxity and frivolousness of youth and the frigid indifference of maturity. By 1733 the pastor was able to record with relief that the people "grew observably more decent in their attendance on public worship, and there were more who manifested a religious concern than there used to be."[2] In 1734 the whole town was brought to a serious concern for religion and a "fear that God was about to withdraw from the land" prevailed.[3] Edwards seized the opportunity to press home the evangelical gospel of justification by faith alone and to warn his people against heterodoxy. "It proved a word spoken in season here; and was most evidently attended with a very remarkable blessing of heaven to the souls of the people in this town. . . . Their minds were engaged the more earnestly to seek that they might come to be accepted of God, and saved in the way of the Gospel, which had been made evident to them to be the true and only way." "And then it was, in the latter part of December," the *Narrative* continues, "that the Spirit of God began extraordinarily to set in, and wonderfully to work amongst us; and there were, very suddenly, one after another, five or six persons, who were to all appearances savingly converted, and some of them wrought upon in a very remarkable manner."[4]

We can do no better than allow Edwards to complete the account himself:

Presently upon this, a great and earnest concern about the great things of religion and the eternal world, became universal in all parts of the town, and among persons of all degrees, and all ages. The noise among the dry bones waxed louder and louder; all other talk but about spiritual and eternal things, was soon thrown by; all the conversation, in all companies and upon all occasions, was upon these things only, unless so much as was necessary for people carrying on their ordinary secular business. Other discourse than of the things of religion would scarcely be tolerated in any company. The minds of people were wonderfully taken off from the world. . . . The only thing in their view was to get the Kingdom of heaven, and every one appeared pressing into it. The engagedness of their hearts in this great concern could not be hid, it appeared in their very countenances. It then was a dreadful thing amongst us to lie out of Christ, in danger every day of dropping into hell; and what persons" minds were intent upon, was to escape for their lives, and to fly from

[1] Edwards, *Works*, Vol. I, pp. 72-3.   [2] *Op. cit.*, p. 73.
[3] Ibid., p. 74.   [4] Ibid.

wrath to come. All would eagerly lay hold of opportunities for their souls, and were wont very often to meet together in private houses, for religious purposes: and such meetings when appointed were greatly thronged. . . . And the work of conversion was carried on in a most astonishing manner, and increased more and more: souls did as it were come by flocks to Jesus Christ. From day to day, for many months together, might be seen evident instances of sinners brought out of darkness into marvellous light, and delivered out of an horrible pit, and from the miry clay, and set upon a rock, with a new song of praise to God in their mouths. This work of God, as it was carried on, and the number of true saints multiplied, soon made a glorious alteration in the town, so that in the spring and summer following, *anno* 1735, the town seemed to be full of the presence of God. . . . The goings of God were then seen in His sanctuary, God's day was a delight, and His tabernacles were amiable. Our public assemblies were then beautiful: the congregation was alive in God's service, every one earnestly intent on the public worship, every hearer eager to drink in the words of the minister as they came from his mouth.[1]

It will be evident from the foregoing description from the pen of Edwards himself that all the unmistakable marks of revival were stamped upon this demonstration of the Spirit's power. As in the case of all genuine awakenings, it carries its own evidence of authenticity. The extent of this movement in a small town of not more than a couple of hundred families is nothing short of miraculous. Edwards sets down the incredible statistics. In the months of March and April 1735, when the work of God was at its peak, he estimates the number of attested conversions to have been at least four a day or nearly thirty a week. Over three hundred came to Christ in the space of six months, with an equal proportion of men and women.

Soon the fire began to spread throughout the district. This was something that could not be hid. Visitors to Northampton caught the blessing and returned to their homes to pass it on. The revival was carried to many other towns and villages in New Hampshire and even over into Connecticut. No wonder Isaac Watts and John Guyse, when they published Edwards's *Narrative* in England in 1737, spoke thus in the Preface: "Never did we hear or read, since the first ages of Christianity, any event of this kind so surprising as the present Narrative hath set before us." And then they pointed the moral as it applied to conditions in the United Kingdom:

Certainly it becomes us, who profess the religion of Christ, to take notice of such astonishing exercises of His power and mercy, and

[1] Ibid., pp. 75-6.

give Him the glory which is due, when He begins to accomplish any
of His promises concerning the latter days: and it gives us further
encouragement to pray, and wait, and hope for the like display of
His power in the midst of us. "The hand of God is not shortened
that it cannot save," but we have reason to fear that our iniquities,
our coolness in religion, and the general carnality of our spirits, have
raised a wall of separation between God and us: and we may add, the
pride and perverse humour of infidelity, degeneracy, and apostasy
from the Christian faith, which have of late years broken out
amongst us, seem to have provoked the Spirit of Christ to absent
Himself much from our nation. "Return, O Lord, and visit Thy
churches, and revive Thine own work in the midst of us."[1]

Edwards's account of the Northampton revival, first published by
Watts and Guyse and later by John Wesley, was widely read in·
Britain and played a prominent part in focusing the attention of
Christian people on the need for renewal. It was comparable to the
effect of William Arthur's *The Tongue of Fire* in the nineteenth
century. In his biography of Edwards, S. E. Dwight stresses the
significance of this publication:

> For a long period, revivals of religion had been chiefly unknown,
> both in Great Britain and on the continent of Europe. The church
> at large had grievously ceased to expect events of this nature; and
> appears to have entertained very imperfect views of their causes, their
> nature, and the manner in which they ought to be regarded. In no
> previous publication had these important subjects been adequately
> explained. . . . By the astonishing work of grace at Northampton, an
> impulse had been given to the churches of this whole western
> world, which could not soon be lost. The history of that event, hav-
> ing been extensively circulated, produced a general conviction in the
> minds of Christians, that the preaching of the gospel might be
> attended by effects, not less surprising than those which followed it
> in apostolic times. This conviction produced an important change
> in the views, and conduct, both of ministers and churches.[2]

It is in this sense that the awakening in America in 1734 and 1735
may be regarded as the initial spark of the Evangelical Revival in
Great Britain.

But at the time when the account of the Northampton manifestation was stimulating the churches of this country to new
activity, its own force was on the decline. The movement was
brought to a virtual halt with the same suddenness with which it
began. Benjamin Colman of Boston, to whom the *Narrative* was
originally addressed in the form of an extended letter, wrote to
Edwards to convey the sense of pleasure it had given him and

---

[1] Ibid., pp. 67-8.
[2] S. E. Dwight, *The Life of President Edwards*, p. 138.

many others to know that the Spirit of God had worked so sig-
nally. In reply, Edwards thanked Colman for his kindly interest,
but added: "Yet at the same time it is a great damp to that joy to
consider how we decline, and what decays that lively spirit in
religion suffers amongst us, while others are rejoicing and praising
God for us."[1] He could only conclude that "God is pleased to let
us see how entirely and immediately the great work lately wrought
was His, by withdrawing and letting us see how little we can do,
and how little effect great things have without Him."[2]

We have seen how in the plan of God the Northampton awakening of 1734 and 1735 was used to stir up concern in the home
country. The same visitation was also related to much wider
work in New England from 1740 to 1743. This is the American
Revival proper and is rightly entitled the Great Awakening.
Although by 1737 the Northampton signs had ceased and were
"very much at a stop,"[3] we cannot overlook the fact that in 1740
Northampton was once again a centre (though only one of
several) and Jonathan Edwards a key figure. But the major influence was that of George Whitefield, who had been invited to
New England after his successful tour of Georgia and South
Carolina. In order to present an abbreviated account of the climax
of revival in America we shall refer to Whitefield's American
visit before we introduce ourselves more fully to him in a subsequent chapter. It is quite impossible to calculate the full impact of
Whitefield's advent. Its effect was immediate, startling and far-
reaching. "With his coming," avers F. W. Hoffman, "the awakening, which had started in 1734, and then had partially subsided,
now burst again into full flame."[4]

It was in September 1740 that Whitefield first set foot on the
soil of New England. He preached in the parish church at Newport, Rhode Island. "It was more than filled in the afternoon," he
records in his *Journal*. "Persons of all denominations attended.
God assisted me much. I observed numbers affected, and had
great reason to believe the Word of the Lord had been sharper
than a two-edged sword in some of the hearer's souls."[5] This was
the prelude to the greatest single evangelistic tour in New
England's history and the most remarkable and widespread quickening the American colonies had known. News of the fruitfulness

[1] Gaustad, *op. cit.*, p. 22.
[2] Ibid.
[3] Ibid., p. 24.
[4] F. W. Hoffman, *Revival Times in America*, p. 50.
[5] G. Whitefield, *Seventh Journal*, p. 27.

of Whitefield's mission both in the old country and in the South had already reached New England and his arrival was anticipated with unusual eagerness. Indeed, in his standard history of the Great Awakening, Tracy goes so far as to say: "There is every reason to suspect that the manifestation of a revival, which was already secretly at work in men's hearts, was kept back for several months by the general feeling that it would take place when White-field came, and not before. In short, New England was ready and waiting to be moved by him."[1]

His appearance at Boston ignited the already kindled sparks. He preached in Colman's church in Brattle Street and at the Old South Church where Joseph Sewall had been pastor for fifty-six years. Then, when the crowds were too great to be housed in any ecclesiastical building, Whitefield took to the open air and addressed some five thousand people on the Common. By the following Sunday his congregation had increased to eight thousand and eventually to as many as fifteen thousand. The Spirit of God worked mightily and many were deeply moved by the message. "O how the Word did run," Whitefield wrote. "It rejoiced my heart to see such numbers greatly affected, so that some of them, I believe, could scarcely refrain from crying out, that the place was no other than a Bethel and the gate of heaven. Many wept exceedingly, and cried out under the Word, like persons that were hungering and thirsting after righteousness. The Spirit of the Lord was upon them all."[2]

Although Whitefield only spent a month in and around Boston, the results of his visit were phenomenal. Gilbert Tennent continued the work for four further months and all the signs of genuine revival were displayed. Pastors confessed that more people resorted to them in spiritual need within that short period than they had previously known throughout their entire ministry. William Cooper, Colman's associate, met about six hundred and John Webb, of New North church, received over a thousand. "There repaired to us boys and girls, young men and women, Indians and negroes, heads of families and aged persons," reported Thomas Prince, Sewall's colleague, "some in great distress for fear of being unconverted; others lest they had all along been building on a righteousness of their own, and more still in the gall of bitterness and bond of iniquity; some fearing lest the Holy Spirit should withdraw Himself; others in great anxiety lest He

[1] J. Tracy, *The Great Awakening*, pp. 83-4.
[2] *Seventh Journal*, p. 28.

should leave them for ever."[1] Other equally remarkable results ensued. No less than thirty religious societies were formed in the city. Churches were overcrowded. Ministers preached in private houses almost every evening. "Our lectures flourish," wrote Colman to Isaac Watts, "our sabbaths are joyous, our churches increase, our ministers have new life and spirit in their work."[2] It was said that the very face of Boston was strangely altered. Even the street loafers no longer made themselves objectionable and the taverns were well-nigh deserted.

On leaving Boston, Whitefield journeyed to Northampton, where for the first time he met Jonathan Edwards. It must have been a memorable encounter. Whitefield considered Edwards to be a "solid, excellent Christian. . . . I think I may say I have not seen his fellow in all New England." Of the Sunday worship he conducted there Whitefield wrote: "Dear Mr. Edwards wept during the whole time of the exercise. The people were equally affected; if not more affected, and my own soul was much lifted up towards God. In the afternoon the power increased yet more and more. Our Lord seemed to keep the good wine till the last. I have not seen four such gracious meetings together since my arrival. My soul was much knit to these dear people of God, and though I had not time to converse with them about their experiences, yet one might see, that for the most part they were a gracious tender people: and though their former fire might be greatly abated, yet it immediately appeared, when stirred up."[3] This visit served to fan the dying embers into a flame again. "The revival at first chiefly appeared among professors," wrote Edwards, "and those that had entertained the hope that they were in a state of grace, to whom Mr. Whitefield chiefly addressed himself; but in a very short time there appeared an awakening and deep concern among some young persons that looked upon themselves as in a Christless state; and there were some hopeful appearances of conversion, and some professors were greatly revived. In about a month or six weeks there was a great alteration in the town, both as to the revivals of professors, and awakenings of others. By the middle of December a very considerable work of God appeared among those that were very young; and the revival of religion continued to increase; so that in the spring, an engagedness of spirit about things of religion was become very general amongst young people

[1] Tyerman, *Whitefield*, Vol. I., p. 425.
[2] Gillies, *op. cit.*, p. 173.
[3] *Seventh Journal*, p. 47.

and children, and religious subjects almost wholly took up their conversation when they were together."[1] This gracious work continued for two whole years. Converts were numerous. Congregations often remained to pray and sing for hours after the public services were concluded. "The town seemed to be in a great and continued commotion, day and night."[2]

Whitefield's tour of New England had only covered six weeks before he returned to New York and thence to the South, but the Revival flourished long after his departure. Whereas the Awakening of 1734 and 1735 had been localized in the vicinity of Northampton this further outbreak was much more widespread. In three years it affected some one hundred and fifty churches, not only in New England, but also in New York, New Jersey and Pennsylvania, as well as in Maryland and Virginia. "By what I can understand," Edwards wrote in January 1742, "the work of God is greater at this day in the land than it has been at any time."[3] Whilst Whitefield had touched off the Revival, it was Edwards who proved to be its true leader. It is not without significance that this man of outstanding intellectual capacity, whom Principal Fairbairn hailed as "not only the greatest of all the thinkers that America has produced, but also the highest speculative genius of the eighteenth century,"[4] should be singled out by divine selection to guide the course of the evangelical movement in America in its formative period. Although he was aware that in this, as in every revival, there was an admixture of Satan's counterfeit, yet he remained its staunch champion against many critics. He brought to bear upon its defence all the powers of his sharply logical mind. In later years he expounded the message of the Awakening in his great books on the freedom of the will and original sin. Not only was Jonathan Edwards a signal instrument of the Revival: he was its foremost theologian. John Newton was once asked who he considered to be the greatest preacher he had ever heard. "Whitefield," he replied, without hesitation. And then he was further required to name the greatest divine of his time. "Edwards," he answered, with even greater alacrity. "There is as much in his little finger as in Whitefield altogether." Both as a promoter and expositor of evangelical life Edwards stands in the forefront of the eighteenth-century Awakening. No survey can afford to neglect him. Few could do him justice.

[1] Tyerman, *Whitefield*, Vol. I, p. 429.
[2] T. Prince, *Christian History*, No. 46.
[3] *Evangelical Library Bulletin*, No. 20, p. 5.
[4] A. M. Fairbairn, *Prophets of the Christian Faith*, p. 147.

CHAPTER V

THE MORAVIAN CONTRIBUTION

SEVEN YEARS BEFORE THE OUTBREAK OF REVIVAL IN NORTH-ampton, Massachusetts, under the ministry of Jonathan Edwards, another and perhaps even more significant visitation had occurred in Saxony. The events of 13th August, 1727, at Herrnhut, the newly established headquarters of the Moravian remnant, have rightly been described as a modern Pentecost. Certainly the repercussions of that quickening experience were to be felt throughout the West and far beyond. For the Moravians not only constituted, as Ronald Knox has expressed it, "the vital leaven of European Protestantism,"[1] but also, and no doubt as a consequence, blazed the trail of missionary enterprise. Scant justice has been done to the Moravian strand of the eighteenth-century Revival in most of the standard accounts, for reasons which will be made apparent later, and some sort of reassessment is needed. For, as Bishop Hassé has pointed out, "the Moravian influence was unquestionably one of the main factors in the early days of the Evangelical Revival; for a time it equalled that of the Methodists."[2]

Before we can proceed to an account of eighteenth-century Moravianism, a glimpse of its historical origin must be obtained. As the name implies, this Christian communion emerged in Moravia, now a province of Czechoslovakia. At first an independent state, Moravia was incorporated into Bohemia under the flag of the German Empire in 1029. It had already been evangelized by the Greek monks, Methodius and Cyril, despatched from Constantinople by the Empress Theodora, and was thus under the aegis of the Greek Church. Attempts to realign Bohemia with Rome were stoutly resisted and this hostility came to a head early in the fifteenth century under that reformer before the Reformation, John Huss. At his martyrdom in 1415 his followers separated into two contending parties. The more moderate group were

[1] R. A. Knox, *Enthusiasm*, p. 390.
[2] *E. R. E.*, Vol. VIII, p. 838.

eventually pacified by concessions and in 1437 formed the national church of Bohemia. But others were made of sterner stuff and, like the Puritans in England at a later date, held out for a more radical reform of doctrine and worship. They therefore withdrew from the establishment and settled at Kunwald to found a New Testament community. It was here in the year 1457 that they assumed the name of *Jednota Bratrská*—the church of the brother-hood. As they were afterwards joined by others of similar outlook in Bohemia their title became *Unitas Fratrum* (The Unity of the Brethren).

So rapid was their growth that by 1609, when Rudolph the Second granted them a Letter of Majesty ratifying the liberty they had already enjoyed under his predecessor, it was said that more than half the Protestants in Bohemia were attached to them. But this period of peace and expansion was destined to be brief. On the death of the Emperor the Roman Church set about enforcing the decrees of the Council of Trent insofar as they related to the treatment of Protestants and, not surprisingly, the Brethren found themselves in the front line of the onslaught. The eventual revolt of the Bohemians against their new King led to the Thirty Years' War and early in that struggle, at the battle of Weissenberg (1620), they were routed. The days of the Brethren in Bohemia were numbered. More than thirty-six thousand families fled. They were scattered all over Europe and the faith of many failed. But a remnant remained—the "hidden seed" preserved by God for which John Amos Comenius, first Bishop of the Brethren and their dauntless leader in these dark years, so earnestly prayed.

That prayer was to be answered in a most remarkable manner. In the year 1715 a spark of revival was kindled simultaneously at Fulneck, where Comenius had ministered, and at Lititz in Bohemia. Eventually the way opened up for a group of Moravian Brethren, led by Christian David, a convert from Roman Catholicism, to settle in Saxony. They were enabled to acquire these new headquarters through the good offices of Count Nicholas Zinzendorf, a Lutheran nobleman who held an important legal position in the court of Saxony. Already he had been aware that the divine hand was upon his life and it was with the intention of establishing some sort of religious fellowship that he had recently purchased the small estate of Berthelsdorf and installed John Andrew Rothe as pastor. The request of Christian David seemed to bear upon it the unmistakable stamp of providential direction and Zinzendorf gave immediate and unhesitating consent. So it came about that a band of Moravian exiles were able to form a Christian community similar to that in which they had their origin in Kunwald nearly three centuries previously. As Christian David struck his carpenter's axe into a tree on the site he quoted the words of the Psalmist: "Here hath the sparrow found an house, and the swallow a nest for herself, even Thine altars, O Lord of hosts." On 17th June, 1722, the task of building was begun. It was to be a city set on an hill, for the plot of land lay on the Hutberg or Watch Hill. This name was taken as a sign from God. So they christened it Herrnhut—the Lord's Watch. In the next few years it became the gathering-point of the dispersed Brethren and amongst those who made the pilgrimage and joined the community were five lineal descendants of the Ancient Church from Zauchenthal near Kunwald.

Meanwhile Zinzendorf himself was led to abandon his legal career and to devote himself unreservedly to the work of the Brethren. As a Lutheran he wished the colony to unite with the Lutheran Church, but as he came to understand the nature of their communion he was eventually prepared to suggest a compromise. Under this agreement, the Brethren undertook to share in the worship of the Lutheran Church and to place themselves under the pastoral care of Rothe on condition that they should be allowed to manage their own spiritual affairs as a distinct society within the Church. It was on 12th August, 1727, that these "Statutes, Injunctions and Prohibitions" were signed by all the members of the Herrnhut community. On the following afternoon they attended a Communion service at the parish church at Berthelsdorf in token of their concord. What precisely occurred none of the participants could fully describe. They experienced a veritable Pentecost of spiritual power. The fire of the Lord fell and they were lost in wonder, love and praise. They left the house of God "hardly knowing whether they belonged to earth or had already gone to heaven."[1] Zinzendorf's own account given several years later to an English audience will serve to depict the mood and atmosphere:

We needed to come to the Communion with a sense of the loving nearness of the Saviour. This was the great comfort which has made this day a generation ago to be a festival, because on this day twenty-seven years ago the Congregation of Herrnhut, assembled for Communion at the Berthelsdorf Church were all dissatisfied with themselves. They had quit judging each other because they had become

[1] J. Greenfield, *Power from on High*, p. 15.

convinced, each one, of his lack of worth in the sight of God and each felt himself at this Communion to be in view of the noble countenance of the Saviour.

> O head so full of bruises
> So full of pain and scorn,

In this view of the man of sorrows and acquainted with grief, their hearts told them that He would be their patron and their priest who was at once changing their tears into oil of gladness and their misery into happiness. This firm confidence changed them in a single moment into a happy people which they are to this day, and into their happiness they have since led many thousands of others through the memory and the help which the heavenly grace once given to themselves, so many thousand times confirmed to them since then.[1]

And amongst those who were to feel the impact of the Moravian Revival was the Church in England.

Within a year of these stirring events the first contact was made. Johann Töltschig was sent to this country in company with David Nitschmann and Wenzel Neisser to bear tidings of what had happened in Herrnhut. Letters from Zinzendorf were conveyed to the University of Oxford, the Society for Promoting Christian Knowledge, Ziegenhagen, chaplain to George I, and the Countess of Schaumberg Lippe, a Lady-in-Waiting to the Queen. This was more than a mission of goodwill. The deputation regarded themselves as ambassadors of revival and intended "to tell such as were not blinded by their lusts, but whose eyes God had opened, what God had wrought."[2] Their reception was mixed. The Countess was enthusiastic, but the chaplain was reserved and no opportunity was afforded of an introduction either to the King or at Oxford. A second visit proved to be more fruitful. In the spring of 1735 a team of ten Moravian missionaries bound for Georgia landed in London under the leadership of Töltschig. They had been preceded by August Gottlieb Spangenberg, a Professor at Jena University, who had attached himself to Zinzendorf and was commissioned to escort them to Georgia. Originally the Count had secured permission from the Governor, General Oglethorpe, for a group of Schwenckfeldters banished from Saxony to settle in Georgia. On arrival in Holland these descendants of the Anabaptists were persuaded instead to head for Pennsylvania. Spangenberg, who had been appointed to have spiritual charge of them, agreed to this alteration of plan but, in accordance with further instructions from Zinzendorf, sought the

[1] Ibid.
[2] Cf. C. W. Towlson, *Moravian and Methodist*, p. 35.

sanction of Oglethorpe for the establishment of a Moravian settlement in Georgia. Having made enquiries about the Brethren and being satisfied as to their doctrine and standing, Oglethorpe readily consented. Spangenberg therefore left England with the colonists in February, 1735, and superintended the establishment of a community near Savannah on the model of Herrnhut from which the evangelization of the Creek Indians was undertaken. These two contacts served to apprise at least certain circles in England of the Moravian Revival and its missionary outreach.

More significant still was the next step. The reception in Georgia was so favourable that in 1735 it was decided to despatch a further band of missionaries. Twenty-six of them left Herrnhut in the month of August, travelling once again via London. Here they joined the good ship *Simmonds* off Gravesend to take them across the stormy Atlantic. It is of the utmost significance for the subsequent course of the eighteenth-century Awakening in Great Britain that also on board the *Simmonds* were John and Charles Wesley, Benjamin Ingham and Charles Delamotte. It seems almost as if God were using this means to bring together some of His chosen instruments of blessing. As we shall see later, the influence of the Moravians upon the Wesleys was considerable, but our immediate concern is to trace the story of the Brethren themselves. So instead of following the vessel on its voyage to Georgia, we leave in the company of yet another key figure in the Revival who came to bid them farewell. He is a bookseller by the name of James Hutton who had been aroused under the preaching of John Wesley, according to Benham.[1] It was at his invitation that the Wesleys had lodged at his father's house in Westminster prior to embarkation. Hutton went aboard the *Simmonds* to speed the travellers on their way and thus came into contact for the first time with the Moravians. It was a momentous meeting, for Hutton was destined to become the original English member of the Moravian Church and, as Towlson describes him, a man "of exceptional importance in the early history of the Renewed Church of the Brethren."[2] He went home to ponder what he had witnessed. These strangely impressive apostles to the New World had moved him beyond measure. He felt he must know more about them. He kept in regular correspondence with the Wesleys and received remarkable accounts of the Moravian mission to the Indians. Inspired by what he had seen and heard, Hutton was led to form a small society for prayer and Bible study which met at

[1] D. Benham, *Memoirs of James Hutton*, p. 11. [2] Towlson, *op. cit.*, p. 49.

his bookshop in Little Wild Street. It was called a Vestry Society and consisted of earnest members of the established Church. At these informal gatherings Hutton would read the most recent letter from the Wesleys and heartfelt praise would be offered to Almighty God for the way in which He was working out His purpose in distant places. Similar societies sprang up elsewhere in London, some of which were attended by German exiles. A pattern which had already developed in Wales was taking shape now in the metropolis. The religious society was to prove a major item in the strategy of revival.

Meanwhile Zinzendorf and Wenzel Neisser arrived in London early in 1737 to confer with the Georgia Trustees about the Moravian colony there. They were greatly assisted by the return of Andrew Dober bearing informative letters from the missionaries. General Oglethorpe was favourably impressed with all that he heard and wholeheartedly encouraged the Brethren in their enterprise. A suggestion came from several members of the Society for the Propagation of the Gospel that the Moravians in Georgia would be the most suitable instruments for undertaking a mission to the negro slaves of South Carolina. The expanding work of the Brethren in the British Colonies of North America raised the whole question of the ecclesiastical status of the Moravian Church. Through the good offices of Dr. John Burton, of Corpus Christi College, Oxford, who had been a warm supporter of the Georgian mission, a series of interviews was arranged between Zinzendorf and Archbishop Potter of Canterbury. As a result a written declaration, dated 11th February, 1737, expressed His Grace's satisfaction with the claims of the Moravian Church and stated "that both from their writings and from personal interviews with the superintendent of the Brethren, he had been led to the conviction, that the Church of the Brethren is truly an apostolical and episcopal church, whose doctrines contain nothing whatever militating against the Thirty Nine Articles of the Established Church of England."[1] And when in May of the same year Zinzendorf was consecrated a Bishop he received a letter of warm congratulation from Dr. Potter. During the Count's stay in London the devotions of his household were attended by a number of Germans—no doubt those who already belonged to the societies mentioned above. Amongst them Zinzendorf organized an incipient congregation, appointing Andrew Ostroem and John Frederick Hintz as chief officers.

[1] Benham, *op. cit.*, p. 24; cf. E. Langton, *A History of the Moravian Church*, p. 94.

Another outstanding Moravian leader now makes his entrance upon the scene. In prosecution of the plan for an extension of missionary work into South Carolina, Zinzendorf ordained a young man who had only just joined the Moravians in Herrnhut. He had been reared in Pietistic circles and had undergone instantaneous conversion in Jena. His name was Peter Böhler. On his way to Carolina he waited in London for a suitable sailing. According to Taylor Hamilton, "with his arrival the more definite influence of the Moravian Church in the ecclesiastical life of Britain began."[1] On the very day of his landing Böhler made the acquaintance of John Wesley, who had returned from Georgia a dispirited and disillusioned man. They met in the house of Weinantz, a Dutch merchant, where Böhler was lodging. Wesley called with a letter from Töltschig and, as we know now, it was destined to be a meeting fraught with incalculable significance. But we are interested at the moment with its bearing upon the establishment of the Moravian Church in England rather than with the effect upon Wesley's religious experience, which will be treated in a later chapter.

From this point of view the meeting of Peter Böhler with James Hutton is of equal importance. As Hutton himself acknowledges, it was John Wesley who made the introduction, and so if Methodism was indebted to Moravianism, Moravianism was also indebted to Methodism. Both before and after his visit to Oxford with the Wesleys, Böhler addressed the several societies assembled by the Moravians. He swiftly acquired some fluency in the English language and when he was in difficulties either Hutton or Richard Viney, a tailor, acted as interpreters in the various meetings. Hutton has left an account of Böhler's preaching to his own society. For the first time they realized the full implications of that article of a standing or falling Church—justification by faith. "This truth came to us so acceptably," he writes, "that we obtained a sight of the only way of salvation. . . . It was with indescribable astonishment and joy, that we embraced the doctrine of the Saviour, of His merits and sufferings, of justification through faith in Him, and of freedom, by it, from the dominion and guilt of sin. This was something so very new to us, so universal, so penetrating,—for most of us had earnestly striven against sin without benefit or effect, and the preaching from pulpits in the churches was so constructed as though Christ and His merits, His walk upon earth, His becoming man, and the eternal redemption

[1] J. T. Hamilton, *A History of the Church known as the Moravian Church*, p. 85.

which through His bitter sufferings and death He had earned for us, were not the most essential matters—these alas! had been disregarded, and Pelagianism was the spirit of the pulpit,—a dry morality universally prevailed, and we who were the awakened, had been just as far from Christ as were the generality of the preachers. For we tried to help ourselves; we dreamt not, we heard not, and knew not that our eternal welfare lay solely in Christ. Here therefore the evangelic period commenced in England."[1] We must not forget that George Whitefield had been preaching the evangelical message since 1735, as had others of the awakened clergy of the Church of England, but nevertheless, when we consider the way in which the sparks were kindled into a spreading flame in this epochal year of Böhler's visit, we cannot accuse Hutton of overstatement.

Four days before Böhler left for Carolina he and Wesley together drew up the statutes of the Fetter Lane Society, which was to become the centre of Moravian activities in Britain. But in its inception it was by no means exclusively Moravian. Its precursor was, as we have seen, James Hutton's Anglican group. Whitefield directed converts into this and other societies. Wesley, as Towlson thinks, probably drafted the eleven rules listed by him in his *Journal* and Böhler expanded them to the thirty-three contained in the final version. A Committee set up by the Moravian Synod held in Herrnhaag in 1747 to consider the Revival in England states that "John Wesley was the beginner of the Fetter Lane Society," but a second Committee, meeting a day or two afterwards, corrects this by adding that "the taking Fetter Lane Society Room . . . cannot so positively be ascribed to John Wesley, it being probable that it was done by P. Böhler's advice and with the concurrence of many other Methodist brethren."[2] The document itself does not mention Wesley, but is headed: "Orders of a Religious Society meeting in Fetter Lane. In Obedience to the Command of God by St. James, and by the advice of Peter Böhler, May 1, 1738." There were obviously several strands in this united society, but in it the Moravians took a prominent part and eventually assumed sole control. As J. E. Hutton, the distinguished historian of the movement, put it: "Although no one suspected it, that Society was the beginning of the Moravian Church in England."[3]

[1] Benham, *op. cit.*, pp. 27-8.
[3] Towlson, *op. cit.*, p. 63.
[2] J. E. Hutton, *A Short History of the Moravian Church*, p. 186.

The members, however, still regarded themselves in every way as belonging to the Church of England. They traced their lineage, consciously or otherwise, to the religious societies described by Woodward. They agreed to meet weekly for mutual confession and prayer. They divided themselves into small bands, each with a leader. They maintained an unceasing apostolate of intercession. They held regular fasts and Love-feasts. They submitted to the discipline of the Society, "that no particular person be allowed to act in any Thing contrary to any Order of this Society, but that every one, without Distinction, submit to the Determination of his Brethren; and that if any Person or Persons, do not, after being thrice admonished, conform to the Society, they be not esteemed any longer as Members."[1] When Böhler sailed for America the Wesleys were responsible for its oversight and maintained the preaching. Meanwhile Hutton had written to Zinzendorf requesting that Böhler might be retained as pastor on his return.

The year 1739 was to prove one of astonishing expansion as the Evangelical Revival got under way and it is not without significance that in its earliest hours we find its leaders experiencing a signal visitation of God following upon the observance of a Love-feast at Fetter Lane. "About three in the morning," Wesley records in his *Journal*, "as we were continuing instant in prayer, the power of God came mightily upon us, insomuch that many cried out for exceeding joy, and many fell to the ground. As soon as we were recovered a little from the awe and amazement at the presence of His Majesty, we broke out with one voice, 'We praise Thee, O God; we acknowledge Thee to be the Lord!' "[2] This Pentecost at New Year, as it has been called, constituted a turning point in the progress of the Awakening and prefaced a period of swift and striking growth. The Revival was really gathering strength. And the Moravian contribution was considerable and central.

But dissension and disruption lay ahead of the Fetter Lane Society. As Towlson observes, "the Love-feast of 1st January 1739 was the high-water mark of Methodist and Moravian fellowship," and there followed a steep decline.[3] The principal factors in the disintegration were Molther's doctrine of "stillness" and the temperamental incompatibility of Zinzendorf and Wesley. Philip Henry Molther was an Alsatian who had been greatly influenced

---

[1] Benham, *op. cit.*, p. 32.
[2] *The Journal of John Wesley*, ed. N. Curnock, Vol. II, pp. 121-5.
[3] Towlson, *op. cit.*, p. 77.

by Zinzendorf. He was called to work in Pennsylvania but remained for several months in London awaiting transport. He
arrived in October, 1739, and was soon asked by the Fetter Lane
Society to conduct some of their meetings. This he consented to
do, despite his imperfect acquaintance with the English tongue.
He records that the obvious eagerness of the congregation to hear
his message encouraged him and gave him added confidence. "My
stammering testimony of the free grace in the blood of Jesus was
so eagerly received as to create a greater hunger after the bread of
life, although I often addressed them for hours. Each one told his
acquaintances of these meetings, so that in a short time not only
our place of meeting but the adjoining courtyard was entirely
crowded with hearers, and thenceforward I had so much to do
that the days and hours appeared too short to me. During the day-
time I visited from house to house, and the evenings were employed at the public and band meetings, upon which, by granting
His grace, our Saviour laid His rich blessing."[1]

But along with this earnest gospel preaching Molther, in a
mistaken attempt to safeguard the Lutheran doctrine of justification by faith alone, and in order to calm the hysterical behaviour of
some of the members, warned the society against an undue stress
upon ordinances. It was this teaching of "stillness" (which was no
part of official Moravian belief and was no doubt the product of
Molther's Pietist background) that precipitated a rift with Wesley
that had already been pending. Matters came to an unfortunate
head in July 1740 when at a Sunday evening Love-feast Wesley
withdrew with eighteen or nineteen followers. Henceforth, says
Addison, "Moravian and Methodist went separately on their
several ways, to attempt to forward the revival through the
organization of societies within the framework of the National
Church. Each carried over into the new crusade much of what
they had learned together in the brief period of their alliance."[2]

Two more years were to elapse before the Fetter Lane Society
actually became a Moravian congregation. As we have already
seen, though the Moravian influence was predominant, it was
nevertheless ostensibly an Anglican group, and such it was to
remain until 1742. Its Moravian character, however, became more
marked, especially after Spangenberg's arrival in 1741. He came
with a commission from the Synod at Marienborn and under his·
direction the Moravian work was furthered on two fronts.

[1] Benham, *op. cit.*, pp. 53-4.
[2] Addison, *op. cit.*, pp. 84-5.

Characteristically, that which concerned the extension of the work overseas came first. The Society for the Furtherance of the Gospel had its birth at a Love-feast on 27th April, 1741. Its purpose was to afford a rallying-point for all sympathizers with the Brethren's missionary enterprises. The solid core of support came from the Fetter Lane Society itself. In September of the same year a Synodal Conference was held in London, under the presidency of Zinzendorf himself, which, as Addison remarks, "must rank as the crucial constitutional event in this period of transition."[1] A full and representative assembly of "labourers," both English and German, was convened, and the progress of the renewed Church of the Brethren over nineteen years was reviewed and "the best mode of governing the same" decided.[1] As a result the English headquarters were transferred to Fulneck, in Yorkshire, and the London work was directed from that remote establishment. And eventually in October 1742 the Fetter Lane Society was constituted "a congregation of the Unity of the Brethren" and organized in accordance with the customary Moravian regulations. But there was no suggestion of separation from the Church of England. "These men had but one idea," wrote Benham, "which Spangenberg himself fostered, namely, 'that as members of the Moravian Church of the Brethren they continued to remain members of the Episcopal English Church, both being sister churches,' and they had sought reception into the Church of the Brethren under the impression of this conviction."[3] The licensing of the Fetter Lane Chapel under the designation "Moravian Brethren, formerly of the English communion," tended to obscure the issue and convey an impression of dissent. In a letter to the Archbishop of Canterbury Zinzendorf and David Nitschmann sought to clarify the position, by repudiating the titles both of Moravian and dissenter.

With the metamorphosis of James Hutton's religious society into the first recognized congregation of the United Brethren in Britain we must close this survey of the Moravian contribution to the Evangelical Revival in its initial phase. Already the work was beginning to expand. Not only was there much activity in Yorkshire, but missions were held in East Anglia, the Midlands and in the West country. This was but the beginning of a great and growing witness which must be recounted as we proceed to review the second stage of the Revival.

[1] Ibid., p. 88.   [2] Ibid.   [3] Benham, *op. cit.*, p. 89.

CHAPTER VI

THE TRUMPET VOICE

HAVING TRACED THE ORIGINS OF THE EIGHTEENTH-CENTURY Awakening in Wales and America and examined the Moravian contribution to its beginnings in England, we now proceed to sketch its earliest course as reflected in the lives of its principal promoters. It is often assumed and asserted that the Evangelical Revival started in Oxford. It has been classed amongst the great Oxford movements in the history of English Christianity. But whilst several of the most prominent figures in the Revival were members of that university, it is to be noticed that it was not during their terms of residence that there descended upon them that dynamic of the Holy Spirit which alone kindles the passion for evangelism and equips the servant of God to revolutionize the life of the Church and the morals of a nation. As Dr. John S. Simon properly points out, "the cleansing fire did not fall on John and Charles Wesley at Oxford. It came amidst other surroundings; and it was only after that baptism that they went out with the message of salvation to the people of England."[1] The same was true of other pioneers.

There is, however, one significant exception. George Whitefield, the prophet of the movement, entered into the experience of conversion and received the fiery touch of Pentecost whilst at Oxford. It was in the very year when the Welsh Revival had come to a head and the first American outbreak was flowing freely. The precise date is not recorded, but "about seven weeks after Easter"[2] in 1735 Whitefield was born again. In the following year he was ordained deacon and began his notable preaching ministry. In point of time, therefore, Whitefield was the foremost leader of the Evangelical Revival in England. It is well to recall his priority and the astonishing extent of his influence in a generation that tends to subordinate his work to that of the Wesleys. There is, of course, no necessity to set one great servant of God over against another or to

---

[1] Simon, *op. cit.*, p. 150.
[2] Tyerman, *Whitefield*, Vol. I, p. 25.

arrange an order of merit. But the time is overdue for a balanced
and just assessment of the part played by Whitefield in the eighteenth-century Awakening. In an introduction to a welcome re-
publication of Whitefield's sermons Dr. Martyn Lloyd-Jones by
no means exaggerates when he declares that "of all the men of the
eighteenth century whom God raised up to do that marvellous
work called 'the Evangelical Awakening,' none was more remarkable than George Whitefield. Of few men can it be said that his
preaching was 'apostolic' in character; but it certainly can be said
of Whitefield. His whole career from beginning to end was an
amazing phenomenon and his Herculean labours both in Great
Britain and America can only be explained by the power of the
Holy Ghost."[1] If the historians of our own time are beginning to
realize the primary significance of Whitefield in the Revival, we
must remind ourselves that there have always been those who
discounted the attempt to write him off, as Dr. Johnson did, as a
spiritual mountebank. In a justly celebrated essay, published in
mid-nineteenth century, J. C. Ryle, later Bishop of Liverpool, did
not hesitate to name Whitefield as the foremost of the Christian
leaders in the previous century. "Though not the first in order, if
we look at the date of his birth, I place him first in the order of
merit, without any hesitation. Of all the spiritual heroes of a
hundred years ago none saw so soon as Whitefield what the times
demanded, and none were so forward in the great work of
spiritual aggression. I should think I committed an act of injustice
if I placed any name before his."[2] We must, then, be prepared to
hail him at least as the first among equals.

A scrutiny of the contemporary records will reveal that in the
eighteenth century itself the name of Whitefield figures most
prominently of all. In the letters of Horace Walpole, for example,
Wesley is hardly mentioned, whereas Whitefield appears re-
peatedly. This may of course be explained to some extent by the
fact that Whitefield was found more frequently than Wesley in
fashionable circles and that his was the more spectacular ministry
and thus more likely to catch the eye of publicity. Whatever may
be the ulterior reason for the estimate, it is unquestionable that in
the popular view Whitefield was regarded as the primate of the
new movement and even as the founder of Methodism. This is
reflected not only in periodical literature but also in the serious
histories of the age. J. A. Mosheim, the distinguished German

[1] G. Whitefield, *Select Sermons*, p. 5.
[2] Ibid., p. 11.

scholar, added "A Brief Sketch of the Eighteenth Century" to the revised edition of his *Institutes of Ecclesiastical History* in 1755, and noted that "at this present time, one George Whitefield is collecting a party and contemplates the formation of a Christian community more perfect than all others, nor is he altogether unsuccessful."[1] Archibald Maclaine, the first English translator of Mosheim, placed Whitefield at the head of his table of "Heretics and Sectarians" of the century, with Wesley running second—a circumstance which the latter noted when compiling his own *Ecclesiastical History*, no doubt, as Brigden surmises, "with a twinkling eye."[2]

If diligence be a criterion, no man contributed more to the Revival than Whitefield in sheer bulk of service. "A true faith in Christ Jesus will not suffer us to be idle," he himself declared. And then in a passage reminiscent of Luther's classic definition of faith, he added: "No: it is an active, lively restless principle; it fills the heart so that it cannot be easy till it is doing something for Jesus Christ."[3] For thirty-four strenuous years following upon his conversion Whitefield strove to redeem the time in profitable Christian employment. Before he reached the age of fifty his life of ceaseless toil and strain, combined with the continual neglect of his health, began to affect him seriously. But unless in a state of physical collapse he refused to rest from his multifarious labours. "I had rather wear out than rust out," he said. "No nestling, no nestling on this side eternity."[4] It has been calculated that he regularly preached for between forty and sixty hours a week and in the course of his career delivered over eighteen thousand sermons. In an age of incredibly slow and laborious travel he crossed to Ireland twice, visited Scotland fifteen times and penetrated almost every nook and cranny of England and Wales. But no tight little island could contain him. The Atlantic was traversed in all thirteen times and in a fashion it was fitting that he should breathe his last on American soil. For, as F. W. Boreham has put it in one of his essays, he was "the first man who treated Great Britain and America as if they both belonged to him. He passed from the one to the other as though they were a pair of rural villages, and he was minister in charge of the parish. George Whitefield took a couple of continents under his wing; and the

---

[1] J. A. Mosheim, *Institutes of Ecclesiastical History*, p. 873.
[2] *A New History of Methodism*, ed. W. J. Townsend, H. B. Workman and G. Eayrs, Vol. I, p. 163.
[3] Cf. J. R. Andrews, *George Whitefield*, p. 70.
[4] Ibid., p. 29.

wing proved capacious enough for the task."[1] The purely physical achievement of Whitefield is staggering in itself.

But he was not only a pioneer in the ground he covered. He was first in the field in half a dozen enterprises inseparably associated with the Revival. It was Whitefield who first set regeneration at the heart of the evangelical message in this era. It was Whitefield who first realized the need to evangelize according to what Thomas Chalmers later called "the aggressive system." It was Whitefield who first ventured into the open air to proclaim the gospel in the fields of England. It was Whitefield who first saw the converts gathered in shoals. It was Whitefield who first employed lay preachers. It was Whitefield who first itinerated as "one of God's run-abouts," as he described himself. It was Whitefield who held the first Conference, in Wales in 1743. It was Whitefield who first missioned in Scotland. It was Whitefield who first made contact with the American Awakening. And, as A. D. Belden justifiably points out, "it is to the pioneer that we owe the launching of the grand effort. Whilst it was through Charles Wesley that George Whitefield found conversion, and by John Wesley that he was drawn into the Holy Club at Oxford, it is nevertheless doubtful if there would have been any Evangelical Revival at all if Whitefield had been other than he was—the master-evangelist of all time, and if he had not discovered the grace and the audacity to initiate out-of-church preaching. It was the bringing of the gospel into the open air that gave to it the contagion, as it were, of the very atmosphere itself—that freed it from the artificialities and intolerable stuffiness of a dull and dead ecclesiasticism and made it again part of the vital experience of mankind."[2] It is, then, to a thumb-nail sketch of the pioneer, preacher and prophet of the eighteenth-century Revival that we must now give our attention.

George Whitefield was born in Gloucester in 1714—the year Queen Anne died. He enjoyed no advantages in his birth, either social or financial. How often God calls men from the lowliest walks of life to do His mighty work! Martin Luther the son of a poor German miner, William Carey a village cobbler, David Livingstone a Scottish mill worker. George Whitefield's father kept the Bell Inn in Southgate Street, Gloucester. It was there that "the great awakener", as he has been called, was born. Sometimes it has been noted as a curious coincidence that Henry Phill-

---

[1] F. W. Boreham, *A Casket of Cameos*, p. 44.
[2] *London Quarterly Review*, July 1954, p. 217.

potts, who became Bishop of Exeter in the next century, was also born in the same hostelry, but this was not so.[1] Although White-field's parents were of lowly social status he nevertheless had clerical blood in his veins, so to speak. His great-grandfather, Samuel Whitefield, was Rector of Liddiard and afterwards of Rockhampton, in Gloucestershire. Whitefield learned to read a special providence in the circumstances of his birth and the premature death of his father. "My father and mother kept the Bell Inn. The former died when I was two years old; the latter is now alive, and has often told me how she endured fourteen weeks' sickness after she brought me into the world, but was used to say, even when I was an infant, that she expected more comfort from me than any other of her children. This, with the circumstance of my being born in an inn, has been often of service to me in exciting my endeavours to make good my mother's expectations, and so follow the example of my dear Saviour, who was born in a manger belonging to an inn."[2]

Little is known of Whitefield's childhood other than his own rather highly coloured account. He tells us that he can remember "such early stirrings of corruption in my heart, as abundantly con-vinces me that I was conceived and born in sin—that in me dwell-eth no good thing by nature, and that if God had not freely pre-vented me by His grace, I must have been for ever banished from His presence."[3] He adds: "I can truly say, I was froward from my mother's womb," and then proceeds to catalogue his juvenile de-linquencies after the manner of the age—impurity, bad temper, lying, swearing, stealing, Sabbath breaking, card playing and novel reading.[4] It is possible that, like Augustine in his *Confessions* and John Bunyan in *Grace Abounding*, he made himself out to be worse than he actually was under a mistaken impression that somehow the glory of God would be promoted in inverse ratio to the heinousness of his sins. On the other hand, as Stuart C. Henry reminds us in the most recent biographical study of Whitefield, a child exposed to the coarse and vicious environment of an eighteenth-century inn may well have been perverted in tender years.[5]

---

[1] Cf. G. C. B. Davies, *Henry Phillpotts*, p. 15. Bishop Phillpotts was born at Bridgwater, Somerset, in 1778: his father became landlord of the Bell in 1782.
[2] G. Whitefield, *A Short Account of God's Dealings*, p. 8.
[3] Ibid., p. 9.   [4] Ibid., pp. 9, 10.
[5] Stuart C. Henry, *George Whitefield: Wayfaring Witness*, p. 17. Henry quotes a con-temporary description from Thomas Brown which begins: "A tavern is a little Sodom, where as many vices are daily practised as ever were known in the great one."

Nevertheless, the God who never leaves Himself without witness was already beginning to draw this wayward youth to Himself, for he was a chosen vessel. "But such was the free grace of God to me," he testified, "that though corruption worked so strongly in my soul, and produced such early and bitter fruits, yet I can recollect very early movings of the blessed Spirit upon my heart, sufficient to satisfy me that God loved me with an everlasting love and separated me even from my mother's womb for the work to which He afterwards was pleased to call me."[1] It would appear that from an unusually early age he had a premonition of his future vocation. "I was always fond of being a clergyman," he confessed, "and used frequently to imitate the minister's reading prayers etc. Part of the money I used to steal from my parent I gave to the poor, and some books I privately took from others, for which I have since restored fourfold, I remember were books of devotion."[2] Even his love of the theatre and his marked ability as an actor were to be capitalized in the interests of the Gospel. It is evident that from his schooldays at the Grammar School of St. Mary-le-Crypt Whitefield was a born orator, and in this the child was father to the man.

Whitefield was compelled to cut short his education at the age of fifteen because of his mother's reduced circumstances, and he began to assist her in the running of the public house. "I put on my blue apron and my snuffers," he was not ashamed to acknowledge, "washed mops, cleaned rooms, and in one word, became professed and common drawer for nigh a year and a half."[3] Eventually his mother, who had remarried, left the inn, which was then taken over by one of her sons. George soon left, too, and, after a brief stay in Bristol, was back in Gloucester leading a careless and useless life. "Much of my time I spent in reading plays, and in sauntering from place to place. I was careful to adorn my body, but took little pains to deck and beautify my soul. Evil communications with my old school fellows soon corrupted my good manners. By seeing their evil practices, the sense of the divine presence I had vouchsafed unto me insensibly wore off my mind, and I at length fell into abominable secret sin, the dismal effects of which I have felt, and groaned under ever since."[4]

It was at this unlikely moment, when Satan was finding work for his idle hands to do, that God began more obviously and urgently to lead him towards his spiritual destiny. The first intimation was afforded whilst he was actually engaged in reading a play.

[1] *Short Account*, p. 10.   [2] Ibid., p. 11.   [3] Ibid., p. 14.   [4] Ibid., p. 17.

He suddenly broke off to confide in his sister. "God intends some-thing for me which we know not of," he told her. "As I have been diligent in business, I believe many would gladly have me for an apprentice, but every way seems to be barred up, so that I think God will provide for me some way or other that we cannot appre-hend."[1] How he came to such a conclusion remained a mystery to him until, in the light of after events, he realized that he was prompted by the Almighty. Immediately an unexpected door was opened for him to complete his education by proceeding to the University of Oxford. It so happened that a young undergraduate, who was a servitor at Pembroke College, came to visit White-field's mother. He told them how it was possible for a matriculant to earn his expenses. "This will do for my son," exclaimed Mrs. Whitefield. And, turning to him, she pleaded, "Will you go to Oxford, George?" And he replied, "With all my heart." Thus, with dramatic suddenness and finality, the matter was settled. Within a week George Whitefield was back at school: within a year he had entered an Oxford college.

He went up in the Hilary term of 1732. Pembroke was his choice. Samuel Johnson had left just twelve months previously and the poet Shenstone was enrolled at the same time. So many of the English poets eventually passed through Pembroke that Dr. Johnson used to say, "Sir, we are a nest of singing birds." White-field spent four years at Oxford. Balleine describes him as "a shy, retiring, shabbily-dressed lad, with dark blue eyes and a singularly beautiful face."[2] In return for performing the duties of a servitor, or "fag", to a number of more affluent undergraduates—a task for which he had been admirably prepared by his experience at the Bell Inn—he was excused his class fees and was thus enabled to proceed to graduation without cost. Whitefield now had no doubt that God was calling him to some special service, but as to what it might be he had no conception as yet. His conversion was to resolve that dilemma, but meanwhile he presents himself to us in the guise of an earnest seeker. "To be a seeker," wrote Oliver Cromwell, "is to be of the best sect next to a finder, and such an one shall every humble seeker be in the end."[3] It was to this next best sect that Whitefield apparently belonged at this spiritually plastic period. In the wise providence of God he came up to Oxford at the time when the brothers John and Charles Wesley, together with their devout and earnest friends, had formed the Holy Club and were zealously striving after the Christian ideal.

[1] Ibid., p. 18.   [2] Balleine, op. cit., p. 8.   [3] J. Buchan, Oliver Cromwell, p. 51

Not unnaturally they were much talked about at Oxford and Whitefield soon heard of them. He says he defended them so strenuously when others reviled them that his colleagues forecast that before long he too would become a Methodist.

It was, however, almost a year before the path was opened. A seemingly trivial circumstance facilitated the introduction. An unhappy wretch in the workhouse had attempted to cut her throat. Fortunately she was prevented from taking her own life in this drastic manner, but it was obvious that she needed counsel and help. Whitefield heard of the case and believed that the Wesleys would be the very men to assist her. He therefore sent a message to Charles Wesley, then a tutor at Christ Church, through an old apple woman, who was instructed not to disclose Whitefield's name. She, however, inadvertently betrayed her trust and Charles Wesley thereupon invited Whitefield to breakfast the following morning. Whitefield "thankfully embraced the opportunity" which, he added, proved to be "one of the most profitable visits" he ever made in his life.[1] Henceforward he was associated with the Methodists in the Holy Club and "began, like them, to live by rule."[2]

Meanwhile Charles Wesley undertook to guide his devotional reading. On the first encounter he had presented him with a treatise against the *Fear of Man* by A. H. Francke, the German Pietist leader, and *The Country Parson's advice to his Parishioners* from the choice pen of George Herbert. But the most influential of all was Henry Scougal's *The Life of God in the Soul of Man.* "I never knew what true religion was," he wrote, "till God sent me that excellent treatise by the hands of my never-to-be-forgotten friend."[3] He learned that true religion is a vital union of the soul with God through Christ formed within the heart. As he read, he testified that "a ray of divine light was instantaneously darted in upon my soul, and, from that moment, but not till then, did I know that I must be a new creature."[4] Whitefield was the first of the Holy Club to gain a clear understanding of the gospel. His realization of the need for regeneration was akin to Luther's discovery of a gracious God. He wrote excited letters to his relations and friends announcing that there was such a thing as the new birth.

George Whitefield was not far from the kingdom. He saw the need for conversion. He recognized the fact of conversion. All he

[1] *Short Account*, p. 27.
[2] Ibid., p. 29. [3] Ibid., p. 21. [4] Ibid.

lacked was the experience of conversion. It was not long delayed. Yet in the interim Whitefield endured all the onslaughts of a chagrined Satan who saw his prey slipping from his clutches. What the mystics call "the dark night of the soul" engulfed him prior to his eventual illumination. It culminated in a prostrating illness, but through it all the Lord was bringing him to full surrender. Even of his sickness, which continued for seven weeks, he could write: "A glorious visitation it was! The blessed Spirit was all this time purifying my soul. All my former gross and notorious, and even my heart sins also, were now set home upon me, of which I wrote down some remembrance immediately, and confessed them to God morning and evening."[1] In the 1756 revision of his *Short Account* Whitefield supplied a fuller record of his conversion than had appeared in 1740. We must hear him tell of the determinative experience in his own enraptured language:

> After having undergone innumerable buffetings of Satan, and many months inexpressible trials by night and day under the spirit of bondage, God was pleased at length to remove the heavy load, to enable me to lay hold on His dear Son by a living faith, and, by giving me the Spirit of adoption, to seal me as I humbly hope, even to the day of everlasting redemption. But oh! with what joy—joy unspeakable—even joy that was full of, and big with glory, was my soul filled, when the weight of sin went off, and an abiding sense of the pardoning love of God, and a full assurance of faith broke in on my disconsolate soul! Surely it was the day of my espousals,—a day to be had in everlasting remembrance. At first my joys were like a spring tide and, as it were, overflowed the banks; afterwards it became more settled—and, blessed be God, saving a few casual intervals, has abode and increased in my soul ever since.[2]

The days of his mourning were ended. The long night of desertion and temptation had passed, and the Daystar arose in his heart. Henceforward the very site of his conversion was sacred to him.

> I know the place; it may perhaps be superstitious, but, whenever I go to Oxford, I cannot help running to the spot where Jesus Christ first revealed Himself to me, and gave me the new birth.[3]

Two immediate consequences of Whitefield's conversion are worthy of note. One was that he now laid aside all other books to allow priority to the Word of God. The Bible came alive for him. Whereas before it seemed obscure and hard to be understood, now it was as clear as the sun at noon. "When God was pleased to shine with power on my soul," he said, "I could no longer be contented to feed on husks or what the swine did eat; the Bible

[1] Ibid., p. 48.   [2] Ibid., pp. 48-9.   [3] G. Whitefield, *Seventy-Five Sermons*, p. 755.

then was my food; there, and there only I took delight."[1] He read
the Scripture as it should be read—upon his knees. He endeavoured to pray over every line and word. "I got more true
knowledge from reading the Book of God in one month," he
claimed, "than I could ever have acquired from all the writings of
men!"[2] The other consequence of Whitefield's conversion was
that prayer became his vital breath and native air. "Oh, what
sweet communion had I daily vouchsafed with God in prayer!"
he exclaimed. "How often have I been carried out beyond myself
when sweetly meditating in the fields!"[3]

In the period following his conversion Whitefield discovered
that as his inward strength increased so his outward sphère of
action expanded accordingly. He eagerly seized every opportunity
for witness and service. He began to visit the sick and the poor in
his native town of Gloucester, where he spent his protracted convalescence, and to read the Scriptures with them. He also expounded the Word at several religious societies and was the means
of leading many to the Saviour. It was on his return to Oxford
that he became more acutely aware of a vocation to the Christian
ministry. Many of his friends urged him towards this goal, but
Whitefield himself was not completely convinced and resolved to
wait further upon God. In the end, the decision was virtually
made for him. Lady Selwyn happened to meet the Bishop of
Gloucester, Martin Benson, as he was walking alone, and took the
opportunity to recommend Whitefield for ordination. Shortly
afterwards, as Whitefield was leaving Evensong at the cathedral,
one of the vergers summoned him to speak with his Lordship.
The kindly father in God met him at the head of the stairs, held
him by the hand and told him how glad he was to see him. He said
that he had heard about him and was impressed with his demean-
our in worship. He enquired his age and then announced, "Notwithstanding I have declared I would not ordain anyone under
three and twenty, yet I shall think it my duty to ordain you whenever you come for holy orders." The Bishop thereupon pulled
out his purse and presented the astonished Whitefield with five
guineas. This incident confirms the report of Beilby Porteus on
Benson that "his purity, though awfully strict, was inexpressibly
amiable."[4]

Whitefield went home to reflect upon this unexpected turn of
events. His previous scruples were based on his unfitness for the

[1] *Short Account*, p. 37.   [2] Ibid.,   [3] Ibid., p. 38.
[4] C. J. Abbey, *The English Church and its Bishops*, 1700-1800, Vol. II, p. 62.

work and the fear that it might not be God's will. "God knows how deep a concern entering the ministry and preaching was to me!" he could affirm in later years. "I have prayed a thousand times till the sweat has dropped from my face like rain, that God of His infinite mercy would not let me enter the Church before He called me and thrust me forth in His work."[1] He wrote to his many friends urging them to pray against this step, but they were unanimous in advising him to accept the Bishop's offer. "I began to think to myself," he concluded, "that if I held out any longer I should fight against God. At length I came to a resolution, by God's leave to offer myself for holy orders the next Ember days."[2] In view of these circumstances it can hardly be said that Whitefield coveted the ministry as an advancement in social status. He viewed it entirely as a vocation from God and his sole concern was to avoid the error of Ahimaaz the son of Zadok who ran without being called.

Whitefield was ordained deacon in 1736 at the early age of twenty-one in Gloucester Cathedral, the imposing edifice founded by Osric, subregulus of Ethelred, King of Mercia. As he went to the altar he could "think of nothing but Samuel's standing a little child before the Lord," and when the Bishop laid hands upon his head, his "heart melted down."[3] I have thrown myself blindfold, and I trust without reserve into His almighty hands," he wrote in a letter to a friend. "I hope the good of souls will be my only principle of action."[4] That same afternoon he preached his first sermon in the church of St. Mary-le-Crypt to a crowded and no doubt curious congregation, who wondered how the boy they had seen behind the bar would fare in a pulpit. His subject was "The Necessity and Benefit of Religious Society" and in one passage he had the courage to speak out against the secular assemblies then so popular in Bristol. What was to prove his life-long theme—the new birth—was handled even in this maiden effort.

I remember when I first began to speak against baptismal regeneration—in my first sermon, printed when I was about twenty-two years old, or a little more—the first quarrel many had with me was because I did not say that all people who were baptized were born again. I would as soon believe the doctrine of transubstantiation. Can I believe that a person who, from the time of his baptism

[1] *Seventy-Five Sermons*, p. 787.
[2] *Short Account*, p. 44.
[3] Ibid., p. 47.
[4] Tyerman, *Whitefield*, Vol. I, p. 48.

to the time, perhaps, of his death, never fights against the world, the flesh, and the devil, and never minds one word of what his god-fathers and godmothers promised for him, is a real Christian? No, I can as soon believe that a little wafer in the hands of a priest is the very blood and bones of Jesus Christ.[1]

At the outset of his ministry the basic note was struck which was to characterize the message of the entire evangelical movement. "By his preaching," averred Dr. Simon, "he lifted into the light the most conspicuous doctrine of the Methodist Reformation, a doctrine without which that Reformation would have been impossible."[2]

Bishop Benson had reserved two small livings for Whitefield, but after returning to Oxford to take his degree he preferred to fill a temporary vacancy at the Tower Chapel in London whilst the curate, Thomas Broughton, one of the original Holy Club, was on duty elsewhere. Doors opened everywhere for his preaching and for a spell of four months he took the city by storm. Large congregations assembled to hear him and there were many converts. These were the first fruits of the great ingathering. Whilst the Wesleys were still away in Georgia on their frustratingly ineffectual mission, Whitefield not only superintended the work at Oxford but sounded the opening trumpet blast within the metropolis itself. After a brief stay at Dunmer in Hampshire supplying for Charles Kinchin—yet another Holy Club member—and having refused a lucrative curacy in London, Whitefield responded to the call of America.

Charles Wesley had by now returned from Georgia to enlist volunteers for the transatlantic mission. He wrote to Whitefield informing him of this purpose, but adding: "I dare not prevent God's nomination."[3] A few days later another letter came from John Wesley in Savannah. It pleaded with the young evangelist to come to America.

> Only Mr. Delamotte is with me, till God shall stir up the hearts of some of His servants, who, putting their lives in His hands, shall come over and help us, where the harvest is so great and the labourers so few. What if thou art the man, Mr. Whitefield?[4]

A further appeal proved irresistible.

> Who will rise up with me against the wicked? Who will take God's part against the evil doers? Whose spirit is moved within him

---

[1] G. Whitefield, *Eighteen Sermons*, p. 351.
[2] Simon, *op. cit.*, p. 156.
[3] Tyerman, *Whitefield*, Vol. I, p. 60.
[4] Wesley, *Letters*, Vol. I, p. 204.

to prepare himself for publishing glad tidings to those on whom the Sun of righteousness never yet arose, by labouring first for those his countrymen who are else without hope as well as without God in the world. Do you ask what you shall have? Why, all you desire: food to eat, raiment to put on, a place where to lay your head (such as your Lord had not), and a crown of life that fadeth not away![1]

Whitefield has left it on record that when he read this Macedonian plea, his heart leapt within him and echoed to the call. The intervening months before he could obtain a passage were occupied with continuous and fruitful preaching both in London and the West country, until he sailed from Purfleet at the end of the year.

Whitefield's first visit to America was brief but triumphant. His fame had preceded him. As Stuart Henry shows, he was virtually accepted in Georgia even before he landed there.[2] Although his first congregation only numbered seventeen adults and twenty-five children, he soon began to attract considerable companies. Very soon he was reported as having delivered a sermon "to the most thronged congregation" ever seen in the colony, which captivated "many loose livers, who heard him gladly and seemed to give due attention."[3] When he left in August 1737, his departure was very different from that of John Wesley eight months previously. "I who went to America to convert others, was never myself converted to God," confessed the latter.[4] Whitefield, on the other hand, was eager to leave America only that he might the sooner return with more funds to continue the work and build an orphan house.

When he disembarked in England he found himself faced with a quite different situation from the one he had left. No longer was he welcomed to the pulpits of London and Bristol. No longer did the Bishops regard him with a lenient eye. It was evident that every attempt was being made to circumscribe his movements and curb his zeal. A number of reasons may have combined to produce this altered attitude. The crowds that had flocked to hear him had left their own churches empty to the annoyance of the clergy. Moreover, the regular worshippers in the places where he preached protested that they were debarred from their own sittings by the same thronging multitudes. Furthermore, Whitefield's doctrine of regeneration was clearly incompatible with current views of baptismal grace. He was looked upon as a fanatic and an enthusiast. His readiness to preach the Word not only in

---

[1] Ibid., p. 205.   [2] Henry, *op. cit.*, p. 35.
[3] W. Stephens, *A Journal of the Proceedings in Georgia*, Vol. I, pp. 204, 222.
[4] Wesley, *Journal*, Vol. II, p. 12.

the authorized pulpits but in private houses was regarded as a breach of ecclesiastical decorum. The publication of his *Journal* describing his American tour aroused a strong prejudice against him amongst those who were unsympathetic towards his evangelical fervour. None of these factors, however, stood in the way of his ordination as priest at Oxford in January 1739.

The inhibitions he encountered in the diocese of Bristol inadvertently paved the way for the step which more than any other served to promote the interests of the Revival. When the Chancellor had refused him permission to preach in any of the churches until the Bishop had given a ruling on the matter, Whitefield resorted first to the Newgate Prison, until he was forbidden by the authorities, and then to Kingswood Hill. This latter spot was to prove a veritable mount of the Lord. Whitefield had thought long and prayed much before this about the Kingswood colliers whose labours provided the city with its coal and fuel, but who lived in a poor and neglected area without church or school. One Saturday afternoon, 17th February, 1739, the evangelist walked out to the village. He climbed a hill and addressed about two hundred. "Blessed be God that I have now broken the ice!" he wrote. "I believe I was never more acceptable to my Master than when I was standing to teach these hearers in the open fields. Some may censure me; but if I thus pleased men I should not be the servant of Christ."[1] Within a month the numbers had grown from two hundred to twenty thousand and Whitefield was convinced that the seal of God lay upon this novel method of reaching the masses of the people with the gospel of life. The hearers were so affected that the preacher could never forget "the white gutters made by their tears, which plentifully fell down their black cheeks as they came out of their coal pits."[2] "Blessed be God!" he cried, "all things happen for the furtherance of the Gospel. I now preach to ten times more people than I should if I had been confined to the churches. Surely the devil is blind, and so are his emissaries, or otherwise they would not thus confound themselves. Every day I am invited to fresh places. I will go to as many as I can; the rest I must leave unvisited until it shall please God to bring me back from Georgia."[3]

His second trip to America was made, as we have noticed already, in 1739. "My Master makes me more than a conqueror,"

[1] *Third Journal*, p. 28.
[2] J. Gillies, *Memoirs of the Life of George Whitefield*, pp. 37-8.
[3] *Third Journal*, p. 45.

he wrote from the departing *Elizabeth*.[1] It was a prophetic affirmation. In the providence of God Whitefield was to be an instrument of spiritual blessing on both sides of the Atlantic. Having shared in the first fine careless rapture of the Revival in England he now took his divinely appointed place as the awakener in the colonies. His first sermon was addressed to six thousand people blocking the street in Philadelphia as he stood in the gallery of the Court House, and it seemed as if the prospects were bright indeed. But the response was not to be immediate. As he made his way to Georgia he found little to encourage him. In Virginia and Maryland the tide of the Spirit was at a low ebb. Arrived in Savannah he saw the foundation stone of the orphan house laid before setting out yet again on his restless itinerancy. This brought him into New England and to the triumphs outlined in Chapter IV. Although Jonathan Edwards was the initiator of awakening in 1734 and its consolidator in 1740, it was nevertheless under the spellbinding oratory of Whitefield that the fires of revival blazed and spread. His prophetic messages were used by the Spirit of God to produce a white heat of religious fervour. The judgment of Dr. Wesley Gewehr by no means exceeds the truth:

> Whitefield was the greatest single factor in the Awakening of 1740. He zealously carried the work up and down the colonies from New England to Georgia. Among the revivalists, his influence alone touched every section of the country and every denomination. Everywhere he supplemented and augmented the work with his wonderful eloquence. He literally preached to thousands as he passed from place to place. He was the one preacher to whom people everywhere listened—the great undying agency in the Awakening, the great moulding force among the denominations.[2]

Whitefield reached London again in the spring of 1741. He had returned to find someone to superintend the Savannah orphan house. Success had not turned his head. No man was less likely to be unbalanced by adulation. "Lean thou on His sacred bosom night and day," he had written in the midst of his triumphal progress. "Keep close to Him, and be what I long to become—a little child. . . . The more the Lord honours me, the more I feel my unworthiness. I am sometimes sick of love, and often, often sick of self."[3] He was to fulfil two short missions in Bristol and then in Essex before heading north for Scotland. But of this we shall hear later.

---

[1] G. Whitefield, *Works*, Vol. I, p. 63.
[2] W. M. Gewehr, *The Great Awakening in Virginia*, pp. 8-9.
[3] *Works*, Vol. I, p. 224.

CHAPTER VII

THE CONVERSION OF THE WESLEYS

REVIVAL AND CONVERSIONS CANNOT BE DISSOCIATED. THEY go together. Whenever the Church experiences the renewal of Pentecost, conversions invariably ensue. And the means God employs to usher in such seasons of refreshing is usually through the conversion of His chosen leaders. Such was clearly the case in the eighteenth century. That is why so much of our story is occupied with the spiritual biography of keymen like Griffith Jones and Daniel Rowland, Howell Harris and Jonathan Edwards, Count Zinzendorf and George Whitefield. Now it is time for us to turn to the most significant of all the conversions of the eighteenth-century Awakening, the twofold miracle which really set the movement alight, namely, the conversion of the brothers Wesley. John and Charles Wesley were led into the fullness of Christ within three days of each other in the memorable month of May 1738, and we shall treat this momentous double event as part of a single stroke of the Holy Spirit. Indeed, so closely were these remarkable brothers associated in the cause of the Kingdom that it is tempting to emulate Dr. Franz Hildebrandt in his book *From Luther to Wesley* and treat them throughout as one Wesley. The twin profiles on the medallion affixed to the walls of Westminster Abbey serve to remind us that as they were called together to the task of evangelizing Britain, so they laboured actively together until after his marriage Charles gradually relinquished his itinerant ministry. John Wesley always assumes a joint work. "My brother and I" is his constant expression. "So closely were the two brothers connected," writes Dr. J. E. Rattenbury, "that, if they had lived a few centuries earlier, Dr. Rendel Harris might have used them as another illustration of the Dioscuri and called them 'Heavenly Twins.' "[1]

Tributes to the incalculable influence and importance of John Wesley are legion. He is increasingly appreciated as multiplied research presents him more fully to our view. He was always

[1] J. E. Rattenbury, *Wesley's Legacy to the World*, p. 61.

recognized as great. Nowadays we are realizing the measure of his greatness. The judgment of Augustine Birrell that he was "the greatest force of the eighteenth century"[1] is widely accepted today. Nor is this recognition confined to these shores. His fame is gone out into all lands and his praise unto the ends of the earth. In the language of Gladstone, his "life and acts have taken their place in the religious history not only of England, but of Christendom."[2] Even those of communions far removed from Methodism and Anglicanism add their meed of acclamation. Lord Acton, a Roman Catholic, hailed Wesley along with Baxter as the most eminent of English Protestants. Father Maximin Piette concludes his fascinating study of *John Wesley in the Evolution of Protestantism* by comparing him to St. Benedict for his liturgical sense and piety, to St. Dominic for his apostolic zeal, to St. Francis of Assisi for his love of Christ and detachment from the world, and to St. Ignatius of Loyola for his organizing genius.[3] Monsignor Ronald Knox provided "A Profile of John Wesley" in his *Enthusiasm* and most recently of all a Roman layman, John M. Todd, interprets him as an ecumenical figure occupying "a providential middle position."[4]

The secular historians take up the tale of these ecclesiastical writers. Dealing with the age of Walpole and the Pelhams in the *Cambridge Modern History*, Professor H. W. V. Temperley names as outstanding figures Chatham among politicians, Thomson among poets, Berkeley among philosophers and Law among divines. "But more important than any of these in universality of influence, and in range of achievement," he concludes, "were John Wesley and the religious revival to which he gave his name and life."[5] W. E. H. Lecky linked Wesley with the elder Pitt as the foremost men of the time and Sir Charles Grant Robertson wrote that "his gifts for command stamp him as probably the most striking of eighteenth-century figures, and leave him in the select division of the first class of the great leaders of all ages."[6]

The importance of John Wesley to the Revival movement cannot be exaggerated. Even before his evangelical conversion he exerted a considerable influence. His strange heart-warming on 24th May, 1738, proved to be the crucial occurrence in the entire operation of the Spirit in this period. It was here, unquestionably,

[1] A. Birrell, *Miscellanies*, p. 34.
[2] W. E. Gladstone, *Gleanings of Past Years*, Vol. VII, p. 205
[3] Piette, *op. cit.*, p. 480.
[4] J. M. Todd, *John Wesley and the Catholic Church*, p. 22.
[5] *Cambridge Modern History*, Vol. VI, p. 77.
[6] *A History of England*, ed. C. Oman, Vol. VI, p. 386.

that the eighteenth-century Awakening received its vital stimulus. The flames ignited by Whitefield were now blown into a blaze. And once the Revival was under way, it was the organizing flair of Wesley which secured the conservation of its gains. Whitefield was no planner. He could gather souls, but he had no scheme for keeping them. Much of his work might well have been undone had not Wesley's follow-up programme been put into action. And, of course, Wesley's own evangelistic itinerations, covering an extensive stretch of over fifty years, rivalled those of Whitefield himself. In Wesley the Revival found its real genius. "Take him all for all," wrote Canon Overton, "he towers far above all the leaders of the Evangelical Revival, not so much in saintliness, or in intellectual power, or in eloquence, or in sound judgment, or in singleness of purpose, but in general force. If one man had to be picked out as the Reviver, that man's name assuredly would be John Wesley."[1] We must be careful, however, not to elevate Wesley to any grey eminence of lonely greatness. He was by no means the only agent of revival. He was simply the most outstanding member of a remarkable team. As Knox discerningly insisted, "he is not a solitary peak but the summit of a range."[2]

Such an estimation of John Wesley enables us to find a more equitable niche for his brother Charles than has sometimes been awarded him. Too often he has appeared as the subordinate Andrew to a dominating Peter. But Charles Wesley has a title to recognition in his own right. He is something more than John's shadow. No doubt Overton went too far when he claimed that his contribution was far more effective and permanent than Whitefield's, but the part played by Charles not only as a hymn-writer but also as a preacher and evangelist, to say nothing of his rôle as an intermediary between John and George, was much more considerable than has sometimes been supposed. "His least praise," wrote his brother after his death, "was his talent for poetry."[3] This was not said in disparagement of his achievement as a sacred bard, but in appreciation of his other pre-eminent gifts and attainments. When these are taken fully into account it will be seen that, so far from being the creation of a single genius, Methodism is the product of a fraternal collaboration. The narrative of its inception and increase is, to borrow the title of Miss Brailsford's provocative volume, *A Tale of Two Brothers*.

Before rehearsing the events culminating in their evangelical

---

[1] Overton, *op. cit.*, p. 29.   [2] R. A. Knox, *op. cit.*, p. 483.
[3] *Minutes of Conference* 1788.

conversion we must sketch in the background of the Wesleys' early life. The facts are sufficiently familiar to excuse more than a cursory glance. The brothers Wesley were sons of the Church. Their father was Rector of Epworth in Lincolnshire. Saints and scholars stood prominently in the family line. Bartholomew Wesley was ousted from his Dorset incumbency in advance of the general ejection of 1662 and became a Nonconformist. His son, John, even more brilliant than his father, was imprisoned at the same time for refusing to use the Book of Common Prayer and was subsequently removed from his living and died a virtual martyr to the troubled times in which his lot was cast. Samuel, father of the Wesleys, was trained at a Dissenting Academy, but, disgusted at the bigotry and immorality he found there, trudged to Oxford to enter Exeter College as a poor scholar and take holy orders in the Established Church. As has often been noted, this must be taken as an apt instance of reversion to type. After holding a London curacy and two chaplaincies, Samuel Wesley was instituted to Epworth in 1695. His wife was Susannah Annesley, whose father had been expelled from St. Giles', Cripplegate, where Cromwell was married and Milton buried, by the Act of Uniformity. At the age of thirteen, when she was already conversant with the Greek, Latin and French languages and read the early Christian Fathers, she solemnly reviewed "the whole issue in dispute between Dissent and the Church" and thereupon "clomb into the fold" of Anglicanism.[1] As William Wakinshaw has commented, "it is one of the ironies of history that this pair of converts from Nonconformity should give to the human race the founder of the largest Protestant Church, either Free or Established, in the Anglo-Saxon world."[2]

As the same writer observes, neither Samuel nor Susannah suffered from spinal complaint. Each of them was endowed with inflexible resolution. In the most notorious disagreement of their marriage, Susannah refused to subscribe a confirmatory Amen to the family prayers for King William III. Her allegiance lay immovably with the King across the water of the Stuart line. When Samuel issued his ultimatum of "Two kings and two beds" she still remained unyielding, and Samuel left for London. Only the speedy accession of Queen Anne opened the door for a reconciliation. Apropos this illuminating episode, Augustine Birrell enquired pertinently, "If John Wesley was occasionally a little pigheaded, need we wonder?"[3]

---

[1] Fitchett, *op. cit.*, p. 16.   [2] W. Wakinshaw, *John Wesley*, p. 10.
[3] A. Birrell, *op cit.*, p. 18.

It was in the great gaunt Rectory at Epworth that the Wesley brothers were born—John in 1703 and Charles four years later. In their earliest training their mother was their mentor. As a domestic educator she was in a category by herself. It has been said that for her own purpose she raised pedagogy to a science and her methods of instruction were amply vindicated in the careers of at least two of her sons. The discipline may appear to be Spartan judged by modern standards, but its effectiveness is its justification and behind the forbidding regimen we must always picture the tender, long-suffering figure of Susannah herself. On one occasion when he was an interested and admiring onlooker, Samuel counted the number of times she repeated the same thing to one of the children. At length he could restrain himself no longer. "I wonder at your patience," he exclaimed. "You have told that child twenty times the same thing." The reply was swift and shrewd. "If I had satisfied myself with mentioning it only nineteen times I should have lost all my labour. It was the twentieth time that crowned it." We may well conclude with Dr. Maldwyn Edwards: "Educational theory and practice have advanced greatly in the two hundred odd years that separate us from Susannah and her domestic school. There is much to criticize in her views which were so largely those of her age. But is not the final verdict one of complete admiration for a woman who against such odds accomplished so much?"[1]

Childhood years passed uneventfully enough, apart from the disastrous fire at the Rectory in 1709, which left an indelible mark on John Wesley's memory. He himself was snatched at the last minute from an upper room and afterwards it was impressed upon him that God had a particular purpose in thus sparing his life. He made this entry in his *Journal* on 9th February, 1750, concerning a Watch Night service in West Street Chapel, London. "About eleven o'clock it came into my mind that this was the very day and hour on which forty years ago I was taken out of the flames. I stopped and gave a short account of that wonderful providence. The voice of praise and thanksgiving went up on high, and great was our rejoicing before the Lord."[2] And his self-composed epitaph prepared in 1753, when he believed his end to be near, begins: "Here lieth the body of John Wesley, a brand plucked out of the burning." Charles quotes this in his *Journal*, but links the boyhood deliverance more specifically with the consequent spiritual conver-

[1] M. Edwards, *Family Circle*, p. 66.
[2] Wesley, *Journal*, Vol. III, pp. 453-4.

sion by making the phrase run: "A brand, not once only, plucked out of the fire."[1] Throughout his long life John Wesley was convinced that he had been preserved by providential care in order to fulfil a special mission. As Fitchett explains, the incident became a mystic picture of the condition of the whole world and the part he was to play in it. "His theology translated itself into the terms of that night scene. The burning house was the symbol of a perishing world. Each human soul, in Wesley's thought, was represented by that fire-girt child, with the flames of sin, and of that divine and eternal anger which unrepentant sin kindles, closing round it. He who had been plucked from the burning house at midnight must pluck men from the flames of a more dreadful fire. That remembered peril coloured Wesley's imagination to his dying day."[2] It would appear that Susannah also sensed the portentous significance of this escape, for she recorded this resolve two years later: "I do intend to be more particularly careful of the soul of this child, that Thou hast so mercifully provided for, than I have ever been, that I may do my endeavour to instil into his mind the principles of true religion and virtue. Lord, give me grace to do it sincerely and prudently, and bless my attempts with good success!"[3]

Though not comparably spectacular, there was nevertheless an element of divine intervention in the life of Charles Wesley and that at its very outset. He was born prematurely and appeared to be dead rather than alive, neither crying nor opening his eyes. He was kept wrapped in soft wool before the fire until the time when he should have been born and then, so it is said, he opened his eyes and made himself heard. Thus he barely escaped the fate of so many of his infant contemporaries in an age of tragically high mortality. So it seemed that for each of these notable brothers there was a divine work to do and that God Himself had ensured that they should live to undertake it.

Many years were to elapse before that call was clarified in their hearts and they embarked upon the mighty mission. John passed from Charterhouse to Oxford in 1720 and Charles followed from Westminster in 1726. John's description of his schoolboy faith is a sufficient indication of his spiritual state. He may perhaps have been rather severe on himself when he said that he was "almost continually guilty of outward sins,"[4] which he knew to be such,

[1] *Journal of Charles Wesley*, ed. T. Jackson, Vol. II, p. 97.   [2] Fitchett, *op. cit.*, p. 33.
[3] H. Moore, *Life of John Wesley*, Vol. I, p. 116.
[4] Wesley, *Journal*, Vol. I, p. 466.

though they were not scandalous in the eyes of the world. He still read a Scripture portion, however, and observed a time of prayer both morning and evening. "And what I now hoped to be saved by was, (1) not being so bad as other people, (2) having still a kindness for religion, and (3) reading the Bible, going to church and saying my prayers."[1] We have no parallel disclosure from Charles. In a biographical letter of 28th April, 1785, he simply records that he was placed under the care of his eldest brother, Samuel, a strict Churchman, who brought him up in his own principles.[2] But another incident is recorded which must take its place in the chain of providential preparation for his life work. His kinsman, Garrett Wesley, a wealthy landowner in Ireland, helped to pay for Charles's education and wanted to adopt him as his heir. It was an attractive offer. But after consulting his father, Charles declined. The estates were thereupon bequeathed to Richard Colley, who assumed the name of his benefactor and whose grandson was the Duke of Wellington. It is one of the fascinating ifs of history. As Southey comments: "Had Charles made a different choice, there might have been no Methodists, the British Empire in India might still have been menaced from Seringapatam, and the undisputed tyrant of Europe might at this time have insulted and endangered us on our own shores."[3] John Wesley called this "a fair escape" and such we recognize it to have been from the standpoint of the divine purpose.

John Wesley had been in residence at Oxford for some five years before he became conscious of his spiritual need. He presented to the world the appearance of an irreproachable life, yet he himself was aware of its deficiency. "I cannot well tell what I hoped to be saved by now, when I was continually sinning against that little light I had; unless by those transient fits of what many divines taught me to call repentance."[4] Although he adhered to the devotional programme which he had been taught in the Epworth home, he confessed that he "had not all this while so much as a notion of inward holiness."[5] The first indication of awakening seems to have been given in 1725. He had graduated during the previous year and was concerned about his career. His father urged him to take orders. Naturally he was led to question his fitness for such a calling and it was this consideration that brought a deeper seriousness into his life. His mother wrote:

[1] Ibid. [2] F. Baker, *Charles Wesley as Revealed by his Letters*, p. 7.
[3] R. Southey, *The Life of Wesley*, p. 30.
[4] Wesley, *Journal*, Vol. I, p. 466. [5] Ibid.

The alteration of your temper has occasioned me much speculation. I, who am apt to be sanguine, hope it may proceed from the operations of God's Holy Spirit, that by taking away your relish of sensual enjoyments, He may prepare and dispose your mind for a more serious and close application to things of a more sublime and spiritual nature. . . . I heartily wish you would now enter upon a serious examination of yourself, that you may know whether you have a reasonable hope of salvation: that is, whether you are in a state of faith and repentance or not, which you know are the conditions of the gospel covenant on our part.[1]

Meanwhile, a conversation he had late one night with the porter of his college deeply impressed him and convinced him that there was more in religion than as yet he had found. Wesley discovered that the man had only one coat and that nothing had passed his lips that day save a drink of water, and yet his heart was full of gratitude to God. "You thank God when you have nothing to wear, nothing to eat, and no bed to lie upon. What else do you thank him for?" "I thank him," answered the porter, "that He has given me my life and being, and a heart to love Him, and a desire to serve Him."

It is characteristic of the scholar in Wesley that books should contribute to the change that came over his life. From Thomas à Kempis he "began to see, that true religion was seated in the heart, and that God's law extended to all our thoughts as well as our words and actions."[2] He read Jeremy Taylor's *Holy Living and Holy Dying*, and, on his mother's recommendation, Henry Scougal's *Life of God in the Soul of Man*. He also had the advantage of "a religious friend," whom Curnock surmised to be identical with Varanese—the cryptic name of Sarah Kirkham.[3] "I watched against all sin, whether in word or deed," he tells us. "I began to aim at, and pray for, inward holiness. So that now, 'doing so much and living so good a life,' I doubted not but I was a good Christian."[4] It is evident from this account that although Wesley was earnestly seeking the truth of the gospel, he had not yet entered into the transforming experience. This is the period in which Father Piette wishes to place Wesley's conversion. But what more can we find here that an agonized striving after righteousness? The language of Wesley is not that of a man who has arrived. The year 1725 may rightly be said to inaugurate a quest, but surely not to signalize a discovery.

---

[1] L. Tyerman, *The Life and Times of John Wesley*, Vol. I, p. 32.
[2] Wesley, *Journal*, Vol. I, p. 466.
[3] Not Betty, as Dr. Frank Baker has conclusively shown.
[4] Wesley, *Journal*, Vol. I, p. 467.

This is sufficiently reflected in the barrenness of his ministry. "From the year 1725 to 1729 I preached much," he confessed, "but saw no fruit of my labour. Indeed, it could not be that I should; for I neither laid the foundation of repentance, nor of believing the gospel; taking it for granted that all to whom I preached were believers, and that many of them 'needed no repentance'."[1] His first sermon had been delivered at the little village of South Leigh. Afterwards he occupied the pulpit from time to time in neighbouring Oxfordshire parishes and for two terms acted as curate to his father at Wroot, near Epworth. In his invaluable introduction to John Wesley's *Journal* Curnock paints a picture of the young clergyman at Wroot, describing him as "a better sort of country parson in times degenerate."[2] He is gentlemanly, cultured, conversant with current literature, a congenial companion. Still to a certain degree worldly, he avoids grossness, though not what he so frequently calls "levity." He seeks to bring himself under the iron rule of law and resolution and honestly strives to prove himself "an Israelite indeed, in whom there is no guile." But, asks Curnock pertinently, "Could such a man ever have aroused a whole country to religious enthusiasm? Could such a scheme of morality and religion ever have forged Methodism, with the world as its parish and baptisms of fire as its normal experience? We follow this handsome, clean-living parson as he rides about the fen lands in immaculate attire—cheery, conservative, adored by his sisters, the ever-welcome companion of his scholarly mother; and, apart from miracle, we have difficulty in realizing that this man, a few years hence, will be one of the Church's greatest evangelists."[3] "Apart from miracle": the miracle is to be performed, but the time is not yet.

Charles Wesley had come up to Oxford in 1726 as a member of Christ Church with a scholarship worth a hundred pounds a year. At first he lived a gay and carefree undergraduate life, intent only on having a good time—an attitude not unusual in one of his age. When his brother John remonstrated with him and broached the subject of religion, Charles would answer with some warmth, "What! would you have me to be a saint all at once?" and refuse to pursue the matter. In later years he himself regretted his "misspent moments past" and declared that "harmless diversions" had kept him "dead to God, and asleep in the arms of Satan for eighteen

[1] Wesley, *Works*, Vol. VIII, p. 468.
[2] Wesley, *Journal*, Vol. I, p. 22.
[3] Ibid., pp. 22-3.

years."[1] No doubt Charles was relieved when John quitted Oxford
to serve the curacy at Wroot, but it would appear that when the
latter returned in the summer of 1728 to be ordained priest by
John Potter, there had been a change of heart. During that brief
absence of his brother, something happened to Charles, as Dr.
Frank Baker elucidates. "The prospect of being a saint seemed
more attractive, though little nearer. His spiritual pilgrimage had
begun, though not for another ten years did he come within sight
of the Promised Land."[2] On 22nd January, 1729, he wrote to
John: "God has thought fit (it may be to increase my wariness) to
deny me at present your company and assistance. 'Tis through
Him strengthening me I trust to maintain my ground till we meet,
and neither before or after that time shall I, I hope, relapse into
my former state of insensibility. 'Tis through your means, I firmly
believe, that God will establish what He has begun in me, and
there is no one person I would so willingly have to be the instrument of good to me as you."[3] Charles himself was at a loss to
account for this greater susceptibility to the touch of the Spirit.
He says he was not ashamed to request John's prayers, for " 'tis
owing in great measure to somebody's (my mother's most likely)
that I am come to think as I do, for I cannot tell myself how or
when I first awoke out of my lethargy—only that it was not long
after you went away."[4]

It was out of this quickening of Charles Wesley's spiritual aspirations that the Holy Club grew. In May 1729 Charles had been
able to rescue a young undergraduate from falling into the wrong
sort of company. He and his friends therefore banded together for
mutual protection and encouragement, since Oxford was such an
unpropitious place for the profession and practice of genuine
Christianity. They gathered to observe the method of study prescribed by the statutes of the University and to partake of a weekly
sacrament. No one was more conscious of need than Charles
Wesley himself. "I earnestly long for and desire the blessing God
is about to send me in you," he told John, shortly before he came
back to Oxford as a tutor. "I am sensible this is my day of grace,
and that upon my employing the time before our next meeting
and next parting will in great measure depend my condition for
eternity."[5] It was to this little group of earnest seekers that what

[1] M. R. Brailsford, *A Tale of Two Brothers*, p. 55.
[2] Baker, *op. cit.*, p. 10.
[3] Ibid.
[4] Ibid., p. 11.
[5] T. Jackson, *The Life of Charles Wesley*, Vol. I, p. 15.

Charles calls "the harmless nickname of Methodist"[1] was first applied. The scope of the Holy Club was widened when John Wesley joined it a few weeks after its inception. Characteristically he began to mould it to his own notions, so that it virtually became his club rather than his brother's. Here is an early instance of his flair for seizing upon what others had initiated and developing it in a way that the originators could never have contrived. The semi-educational purpose of the Holy Club soon gave place to that of concentrated spiritual improvement. Searching the Scriptures superseded the study of the Greek classics. Prayer and self-examination followed. Fasting was observed on Wednesdays and Fridays. And to the devotional exercises were added works of mercy and charitable relief. Prisons and workhouses were visited. The sick and poor were helped with money, food and clothing. Here was not indeed the inauguration of the Revival itself, but the beginning of what A. W. Harrison aptly christened "The Quest."[2] The part played by the Holy Club in paving the path for the Awakening and the continued usefulness of the society as it proceeded represents a significant link with the groups formed during the Restoration era under Horneck and Smythies. Its influence was out of all proportion to its size, for there were but four in the little band when it was formed in 1729 and six years later, as Wesley left for Georgia, there were only fourteen. With such a despised minority of men called Methodists God was planning to launch a mighty revival. As yet none of them had tasted the experience of evangelical conversion. George Whitefield, the last recruit, was the only one to enter into blessing whilst still a member of the Holy Club. But the remainder were sincerely seeking and God is always a rewarder of such. They did not separate themselves because they entertained any Pharisaical misconceptions of moral pre-eminence. It was not their intention to advertise themselves as paragons of holiness. "The Oxford Methodists," wrote Tyerman, "had no desire to aggrandise themselves. They had not the slightest wish to be considered superior to their fellow mortals. They were sincere and earnest enquirers after truth, and in the study of the Holy Bible, in prayer to God, and in other devotional exercises, were an example worthy of imitation. God rarely leaves such enquirers in the dark. Wesley and most of his Oxford friends were brought to a knowledge of 'the truth as it is in Jesus;' and being so, their faith, their energy, their prayers, their toils, and

[1] Baker, *op. cit.*, p. 14.
[2] Harrison, *op. cit.*, p. 14.

their cheerfully endured sufferings resulted in one of the most
glorious revivals of the work of God recorded in the history of
the Christian Church."[1]

Before the Wesleys were led to such a saving acquaintance with
Christ they were to undergo a further chastening experience of
fruitless ministry. So little success attended their efforts in this
country that they determined to seek their spiritual fortune in the
colonies. In 1735 they sailed for Georgia with two others of the
Oxford Club, Ingham and Delamotte. John Wesley went as a
missionary of the Society for the Propagation of the Gospel and
Charles as secretary to the Governor, General James Oglethorpe.
A mother's generous benediction rested upon them. "Had I
twenty sons," she declared with typical prodigality, "I should rejoice that they were all so employed, though I should never see
them more." John Wesley's analysis of his motives affords an
instructive glimpse into his spiritual condition at this juncture as
well as betraying anticipations of a cult which was to reach its
peak of fashionability in the late eighteenth century through the
sponsorship of the philosopher Rousseau and the explorer
Bougainville, namely that of the noble savage.

> My chief motive . . . is the hope of saving my own soul, I hope to
> learn the true sense of the gospel by preaching it to the heathen. They
> have no comments to construe away the text; no vain philosophy to
> corrupt it; no luxurious, sensual, covetous, ambitious expounders to
> soften its unpleasing truths. . . . They have no party, no interest to
> serve, and are therefore fit to receive the gospel in its simplicity.
> They are as little children, humble, willing to learn, and eager to do
> the will of God.[2]

It was in such a spirit that John Wesley, with his brother, "exchanged the religion of a hermit for that of a frontiersman," as
Cell has neatly put it.[3]

Disillusionment set in with remorseless rapidity. Life in the
idealized colony was no more conducive to holiness than anywhere else in this present evil world. The Wesleys began to learn
that salvation lies not in external environment but in inward
transformation. The Indians proved far from docile. Few of them
matched John's optimistic description. The Wesleys returned
from Georgia sadder and wiser men. John wrote:

> I went to America to convert the Indians; but, oh, who shall con-

[1] L. Tyerman, *The Oxford Methodists*, p. vii.
[2] Wesley, *Letters*, Vol. I, p. 188.
[3] Cell, *op. cit.*, p. 99.

vert me? . . . I have a fair summer religion. I can talk well; but let
death look me in the face, and my spirit is troubled. . . . Oh! who
will deliver me from this fear of death? . . . A wise man advised me
some time since, "Be still and go on." Perhaps this is best, to look
upon it as my cross.[1]

And again, at the close of his Georgia journal:

It is now two years and almost four months since I left my native
country in order to teach the Georgian Indians the nature of
Christianity. But what have I learned myself in the meantime? Why
(what I the least of all suspected) that I, who went to America to
convert others, was never myself converted to God.[2]

We must beware, however, of accepting these emphatic statements
uncritically. A note added at a later date perhaps more accurately
summarizes Wesley's condition. "I had even then the faith of a
servant, though not that of a *son*."[3] Nor must we entirely write off
the mission to Georgia. Later in the same year George Whitefield
arrived in the colony and bore this unstinted testimony to his
friend's achievements.

The good Mr. John Wesley has done in America is inexpressible.
His name is very precious among the people, and he has laid a
foundation that I hope neither men nor devils will ever be able to
shake. Oh that I may follow him as he has followed Christ![4]

Unsatisfactory as the Georgian venture may have appeared to
the Wesleys themselves, it nevertheless established a relationship
which was to prove decisive in their conversion to the fullness of
Christ. We have already examined the Moravian contribution to
the Revival up to 1742. The Moravians, however, not only themselves played a vital part in the advancement of the evangelical
cause, but were also instrumental in leading the Wesleys to an
understanding of salvation-faith. The contact was made aboard
the *Simmonds* which carried the Wesleys to Georgia. Twenty-
six Moravian missionaries—the second instalment—also occupied berths on the same vessel and their behaviour in an
Atlantic storm, which broke whilst they were holding a service,
was destined to exert an immeasurable influence upon the
Wesleys. As "a terrible screaming began among the English,"
John Wesley records, "the Germans looked up, and without inter-
mission calmly sang on. I asked one of them afterwards, 'Were
you not afraid?' He answered, 'I thank God no.' I asked, 'But

[1] Wesley, *Journal*, Vol. I, p. 418.
[2] Ibid., pp. 421-2.
[3] Ibid., p. 422n.
[4] *Second Journal*, p. 4.

were not your women and children afraid?' He replied mildly,
'No; our women and children are not afraid to die'."[1] What per-
turbed Wesley was not that the English yielded to hysteria whilst
the Germans retained their nerve. It was rather that he himself,
who had been zealously endeavouring to teach others on board
the way of life, was now weighed in the balances and found wanting. For he knew himself afraid to die: he, with all his advantages
—the outstanding personality amongst the entire company—
lacked what these unlearned Moravians possessed. Wesley's
rational temperament could not overlook the evidence of plain
fact; nor could he fail to enquire into the reason for the contrast.
Curnock's footnote to his edition of the *Journal* at this point is
worth pondering.

> The student who traces the sequence of events will see that the
> storm was one of the crucial facts in the history of early Methodism.
> It shook the nerve of all on board, passengers and seamen—of all
> except the Moravians. It was their great peacefulness when the sea
> split the mainsail, and the joy of their singing, that brought Wesley's
> incipient friendship to maturity. It may be said to have made Ingham
> a Moravian, and no doubt it influenced Delamotte in the same
> direction.[2]

On the first Sunday in Georgia, John Wesley sought out the
Moravian leader, Spangenberg, who had already commenced
work in the colony, and asked for advice with regard to his own
conduct. This was evidently a direct consequence of Wesley's contact with Moravian piety on board the *Simmonds*. The interview
was to prove pivotal, although we have not time to accompany
Curnock as he questions whether Wesley did not owe even more
to Spangenberg than to Böhler.[3] Wesley submitted to searching
interrogation. "Do you know yourself?" asked Spangenberg.
"Have you the witness within yourself? Does the Spirit of God
bear witness with your spirit that you are a child of God?" Wesley
was taken aback at such directness and scarcely knew what to
say. His interlocutor noticed his hesitancy and discomfiture and
so pressed an even more pertinently personal enquiry: "Do you
know Jesus Christ?" Wesley hedged. "I know He is the Saviour
of the world." "True, but do you know He has saved you?"
Thoroughly at a loss, Wesley stammered feebly, "I hope He has
died to save me." But Spangenberg insisted, "Do you know yourself?" In order to extricate himself from a most embarrassing

[1] Wesley, *Journal*, Vol. I, pp. 142-3.
[2] Ibid., p. 141n.
[3] Ibid., Vol. II, p. 60n.

situation Wesley unconvincingly said he did. "But," he adds with endearing honesty, "I fear they were vain words."[1] Spangenberg's own impression is perhaps a little surprising yet replete with almost prophetic discernment. "I noticed that true grace reigns and dwells within him."[2] Throughout their stay in Georgia the Wesleys were to come into regular contact with the Moravians and were increasingly affected by them.

On his return to England in February 1738 John Wesley wrote:

> If it be said, that I have faith (for many such things have I heard, from many miserable comforters), I answer, So have the devils—a sort of faith; but still they are strangers to the covenant of promise. So the apostles had even at Cana of Galilee, when Jesus first "manifested forth His glory"; even then they, in a sort "believed on Him," but they had not then "the faith that overcometh the world." The faith I want is "a sure trust and confidence in God, that through the merits of Christ, my sins are forgiven, and I reconciled to the favour of God." I want that faith which St. Paul recommends to all the world, especially in his Epistle to the Romans: that faith which enables every one that hath it to cry out, "I live not; but Christ liveth in me; and the life that I now live, I live by faith in the Son of God Who loved me and gave Himself for me"; I want that faith which none can have without knowing he hath it.[3]

Wesley knew what he sought and it was this very assurance which at length he found.

It was through the influence of another Moravian that both the Wesleys were to be brought into this experience. John Wesley lost no time in seeking out Peter Böhler, for the time being the leader of the London Moravians. As Towlson remarks, "this was the man to whom, more than to any other single person, John and Charles Wesley owed that change of mind and heart which brought about the Methodist Revival."[4] John Wesley described 7th February, 1738, as a "day much to be remembered"[5] for it was then that he met Böhler on his way to Carolina, and found him lodgings in Westminster near to James Hutton, where he himself was staying. Ten days later the Wesleys set out for Oxford with Böhler and we can now read the latter's own account of the journey and his companions. "The elder, John," he told Zinzendorf, "is an amiable man; he acknowledges that he does not yet rightly know the Saviour and suffers himself to be instructed. He

[1] Ibid., Vol. I, p. 151.
[2] Diary: cf. C. W. Towlson, *Moravian and Methodist*, p. 41.
[3] Wesley, *Journal*, Vol. I, p. 424.
[4] Towlson, *op. cit.*, p. 48.
[5] Wesley, *Journal*, Vol. I, p. 436.

loves us sincerely. His brother, with whom you conversed frequently in London a year ago, is greatly troubled in spirit and
knows not how he shall begin to know the Saviour."[1]

It seems that at first Böhler's conversation had a more marked
effect upon Charles Wesley than upon John. As Towlson explains,
this may have been because the latter was more argumentative and
the former was in poor health and in more immediate need of
comfort. It was in the midst of this aggravated illness, when he
appeared almost about to die, that Böhler, after having prayed
with him and assured him that he would live, embarked upon a
colloquy with him that bears a singular resemblance to that of
Spangenberg with John. Böhler asked, "Do you hope to be
saved?" When Charles assured him that he did, he enquired further, "For what reason do you hope it?" "Because I have used my
best endeavours to serve God," returned Charles. At such an inadequate response Böhler shook his head sadly and said no more.
Charles admitted later that he considered his interrogator to be
most uncharitable and thought, rebelliously, "What, are not my
endeavours a sufficient ground of hope? Would he rob me of my
endeavours? I have nothing else to trust to."[2] At that moment
what he said was tragically true and there lay the pathos of his
predicament.

Meanwhile John Wesley's friendship with Böhler began to
ripen. He had already talked with him, but confessed that he
failed to grasp his meaning when he said, "*Mi frater, mi frater,
excoquenda est ista tua philosophia*—My brother, my brother, that
philosophy of yours must be purged away." But he sets it down
that on Sunday, 5th March, he was "clearly convinced of unbelief,
of the want of faith whereby alone we are saved," and this he
attributed to the intervention of Böhler in the hand of the great
God.[3] He asked whether he ought to leave off preaching and
received the classic reply: "Preach faith *till* you have it; and then,
because you have it, you will preach faith." Dr. Rattenbury correctly
emphasizes the significance of these interviews. "The period from
March 5 to 7 is only less important than May 24. They are the
days of his *intellectual* conversion to Protestant truth, or rather. of
the beginning of it, for that was a process."[4] Henceforward
Wesley went out to preach what to him was a totally new doctrine.
Now he accepted the truth with his mind and, on Böhler's sound

[1] *World Parish*, Vol. II, No. 1, p. 3.
[2] C. Wesley, *Journal*, Vol. I, p. 82.
[3] Wesley, *Journal*, Vol. I, p. 442.
[4] J. E. Rattenbury, *The Conversion of the Wesleys*, p. 70.

advice, proceeded to expound it until it became his spiritual conviction.

The experience itself was not long delayed. But it came to Charles
first. Like Jacob, he claimed his birthright before his brother.
Another of the Moravians, William Holland, came upon Luther's
commentary on Galatians and took it to Charles Wesley, who was
lying ill at the house of John Bray in Little Britain. He himself
recorded in his Journal for 17th May "Today I first saw Luther on
the Galatians, which Mr. Holland had accidentally lit upon. We
began, and found him nobly full of faith." Later in the day, he
added, "I spent some hours this evening in private with Martin
Luther, who was greatly blessed to me, especially his conclusion
of the second chapter. I laboured, waited, and prayed to feel 'Who
loved *me* and gave Himself for *me*'."[1] It was Luther himself who
once said that the whole of religion could be expressed in terms of
personal pronouns. Here in his comment on the second chapter of
Galatians he urged his readers to "put a great emphasis on those
words me and for me."[2] "Not Peter and Paul, but me"—and so
the Reformation was born. And so first Charles Wesley and then
John was enabled in the same way to say "Not Peter and Paul,
but me"—and so the Evangelical Revival was born.

It was not, however, until Whit Sunday, 21st May, that the great
transaction was completed. John visited Charles in his sick room
at nine in the morning and the brothers mingled their voices in a
hymn of praise. When John had left, Charles resorted to prayer.
"O Jesus," he cried, "Thou hast said, 'I will come unto you.' . . .
Thou art God who canst not lie; I wholly rely upon Thy most
true promise; accomplish it in Thy time and manner." Then he
tells us, "I was composing myself to sleep in quietness and
peace, when I heard one come in and say, 'In the name of
Jesus of Nazareth, arise, and believe, and thou shalt be healed of
thy infirmities'."[3] It was Bray's sister, a Mrs. Turner, who had
been commanded by the Lord in a dream to convey this message.
"I never heard words uttered with such solemnity," continues
Charles.

> The sound of her voice was entirely changed. . . . I arose and looked
> into the Scripture. The words that first presented were, "And now,
> Lord, what is my hope? Truly my hope is even in Thee". I then cast
> down my eye and met, "He hath put a new song in my mouth, even
> a thanksgiving unto our God. Many shall see it, and fear, and shall
> put their trust in the Lord." Afterwards I opened upon Isaiah 40 : 1,

[1] For the precise passage in Luther, see Bett, *op. cit.*, pp. 18-19.
[2] Ibid.   [3] C. Wesley, *Journal*, Vol. I, p. 90.

"Comfort ye, comfort ye My People, saith your God; speak ye com-
fortably to Jerusalem, and cry unto her, that her warfare is accomplished, and that her iniquity is pardoned; for she hath received of
the Lord's hand double for all her sins." I now found myself at peace
with God, and rejoiced in hope of loving Christ.[1]

As Rattenbury comments, this is a strangely different record from
John's account of 24th May. "Almost, the critic might say, 'a
jumble of superstitions and emotions.' . . . Well, God's ways with
critics and poets are different. There are twelve gates to the city,
and they are all beautiful as pearls."[2]

After hearing John Heylyn, the popular Rector of St. Mary-le-
Strand, preach "a truly Christian sermon" on Acts 2, and assisting
him at Holy Communion, John Wesley received the glad and surprising news that his brother "had found rest to his soul."[3] Three
days later a similar experience came to him. It was on Wednesday,
24th May, 1738—an ever-memorable day. He has left us a careful
and detailed report. It seems that throughout each hour he was
attuned to the voice divine. An air of intense expectancy pervades
his attitude from the first. When he opened his Greek Testament
at five o'clock in the morning his eyes fell on the comforting words
of 2 Peter 1 : 4, "There are given unto us exceeding great and
precious promises, even that ye should be partakers of the divine
nature." Just as he left his room he resorted to the Word again,
and received the prophetic assurance, "Thou art not far from the
kingdom of God." In the afternoon he attended evensong at St.
Paul's Cathedral and the words of the anthem, set to Purcell's
music, taken from Psalm 130, seemed to express his own agoniz-
ing quest. But that *cri de coeur* was followed by the reassurance of
the closing verses, "O Israel, trust in the Lord; for with the Lord
there is mercy, and with Him is plenteous redemption. And He
shall redeem Israel from all his sins." But it was not until the
shadows were gathering that light and warmth came to his soul.
His own immortal language shall depict the scene which more than
any other stands at the centre of the eighteenth-century Revival:

> In the evening I went very unwillingly to a society in Aldersgate
> Street, where one was reading Luther's preface to the Epistle to the
> Romans. About a quarter before nine, while he was describing the
> change which God works in the heart through faith in Christ, I felt
> my heart strangely warmed. I felt I did trust in Christ, Christ alone,
> for my salvation; and an assurance was given me that He had taken
> away my sins, even *mine*, and saved *me* from the law of sin and

[1] Ibid., pp. 91-2. .   [2] Rattenbury, *Conversion of Wesleys*, pp. 89-90.
[3] Wesley, *Journal*, Vol. I, p. 464.

death. I then testified to all there what I first felt in my heart.[1]

Charles Wesley was still lying in his sick room, though his cure had been wrought. He wrote: "Towards ten my brother was brought in triumph by a troop of friends, and declared 'I believe!' We sang a hymn with great joy, and parted with prayer."[2] The hymn was "Where shall my wondering soul begin?" which Charles had composed two days before. The second verse epitomizes their joint testimony.

> O how shall I the goodness tell
>   Father, which Thou to me hast showed?
> That I, a child of wrath and hell,
>   I should be called a child of God,
> Should know, should feel my sins forgiven,
> Blest with this antepast of heaven!

The links between the Evangelical Revival and the Protestant Reformation are strong and obvious. The name of Martin Luther was prominent in the conversions of each of the Wesleys. In the case of Charles it was the commentary on Galatians: in that of John it was the Preface to Romans. Dr. Henry Bett has traced the very words from the latter, which he surmises were read in Latin.

> Wherefore let us conclude that faith alone justifies, and that faith alone fulfilleth the Law. For faith through the merit of Christ obtaineth the Holy Spirit, which Spirit doth make us new hearts, doth exhilarate us, doth excite and inflame our heart, that it may do those things willingly of love, which the Law commandeth; and so, at the last, good works indeed do proceed freely from the faith which worketh so mightily, and which is so lively in our hearts.[3]

Whatever the language, there can be little doubt that this was the passage. Not only does the exposition of Scriptural faith exactly match the need of Wesley for the assurance of forgiveness, but there is a remarkable verbal parallel between Wesley's own words, "I felt my heart strangely warmed," and Luther's phrase, "*Hic Spiritus cor novat, exhilarat, et excitat et inflammat.*" Wesley's new-found faith was swiftly subjected to the outraged onslaught of Satan.

> After my return home, I was much buffeted with temptations; but cried out, and they fled away. They returned again and again. I as often lifted up my eyes, and He "sent me help from His holy place". And herein I found the difference between this and my former state chiefly consisted. I was striving, yea fighting with all my might

---

[1] Ibid., p. 475-6. [2] C. Wesley, *Journal*, Vol. I, p. 95.
[3] Bett, *op. cit.*, pp. 21-2.

under the law, as well as under grace. But then I was sometimes, if not often, conquered; now, I was always conqueror.[1]

Despite recent and learnedly ingenious attempts to play down the determinative significance of this experience and to dismiss it, with Piette, as "the official Wesleyan legend," there can be little doubt that Wesley himself regarded it as the turning-point in his ministry. It may be true that both 1725 and 1729 represent important stages in his spiritual pilgrimage, but in his own estimate 1738 stands out as unique. Writing to his brother Samuel in October 1738 Wesley declared:

> With regard to my own character, and my doctrine likewise, I shall answer you very plainly. By a Christian I mean one who so believes in Christ as that sin hath no more dominion over him; and in this obvious sense of the word I was not a Christian till May 24th last past. For till then sin had the dominion over me, although I fought with it continually; but surely then, from that time to this it hath not, such is the free grace of Christ. What sins they were which till then reigned over me, and from which by the grace of God I am now free I am ready to declare on the house-top, if it may be for the glory of God. If you ask by what means I was made free (though not perfect, neither infallibly sure of my perseverance), I answer, By faith in Christ; by such a sort of degree of faith as I had not till that day.[2]

Seven years later, when the emotional dust could be said to have settled and he could view the matter dispassionately, he told Archbishop Secker of Canterbury:

> It is true that from May 24 1738, whenever I was desired to preach, salvation by faith was my only theme. . . And it is equally true that it was for preaching the love of God and man that several of the clergy forbade me their pulpits before that time, before May 24, before I either preached or knew salvation by faith.[3]

And these are not isolated references. There are many similar allusions to this crucial date, all indicative of its centrality in Wesley's religious development. Nor was he loth to give his testimony. In 1759 we come upon him comforting a sinner under conviction by telling him how he himself had passed through the purging fires. "I have often found," he observed, "that nothing I can say makes so much impression on myself or others, as thus repeating my own conversion."

If John Wesley was certain that the experience of 24th May,

[1] Wesley, *Journal*, Vol. I, pp. 476-7.   [2] Wesley, *Letters*, Vol. I, pp. 262-3.
[3] Piette, Vol. II, p. 65.

1738, constituted the fulcrum of his spiritual career, he is equally confident in dating the commencement of revival power in his ministry from this same day. "Then it pleased God," he said, "to kindle a fire which I trust shall never be extinguished." The inextinguishable blaze which burned so brightly throughout the remainder of the century and beyond was nourished in the warmed heart of this one man at Aldersgate Street. "As soon as I saw clearly the nature of saving faith and made it the standing topic of my preaching," he informs us, "God then began to work by my ministry as He never had done before."[1] He lists the several stages of his growth in grace and the consequent effect upon his preaching. From 1725 to 1729 he saw no fruit whatsoever: from 1729 to 1734 as he laid a deeper foundation of repentance he saw a little: from 1734 to 1738 speaking more of faith in Christ he saw more.

> From 1738 to this time—speaking continually of Jesus Christ; laying Him only for the foundation of the whole building, making Him all in all, the first and the last; preaching only on this plan, "the kingdom of God is at hand, repent ye and believe the Gospel", the Word of God ran as fire among the stubble; it was glorified more and more; multitudes crying out, "What must we do to be saved?" and, afterwards witnessed, "By grace we are saved through faith".[2]

The ultimate vindication of this interpretation lies in the immediate consequences of Wesley's conversion. There was a twofold outcome: great achievement and great opposition. It was only after 1738 that the authorities began to object to Wesley's preaching, and it was in this same period that his message was attended by multiplied conversions. The pragmatic test is final. Dr. Bett quite legitimately enquired, "Does anyone think for a moment that the Wesley of 1725, even if he had been older at the time, could have done the work that the Wesley of 1738 did? No one could imagine such a thing. Whatever you call the experience of 1738, then, it was that which made Wesley the man he was and enabled him to do the work he did. It does not really matter whether you call it his conversion or not. On any and every possible interpretation of it, it was a spiritual event that gave Wesley quite a new sort of religious experience, with an assurance and a power and a peace and a joy he had never known before, and it was this change that made him into the Apostle of England."[3] But of this apostolic mission we must speak in a later chapter.

[1] Cf. Wesley, *Works*, Vol. VIII, pp. 28-9, 349-50.
[2] Wesley, *Letters*, Vol. II, p. 264.   [3] Bett, *op. cit.*, p. 25.

CHAPTER VIII

THE REVIVAL IN SCOTLAND

THOMAS CHALMERS ONCE DESCRIBED THE EIGHTEENTH CEN-
tury as "the Dark Age of the Scottish Church." Certainly
the period extending from the Restoration in 1689 to the
Disruption of 1843 was disturbed in the extreme. But those selfsame years witnessed the revival and resurgence of the Evangelical
party and its rise to a position of strength and strategic importance. A genuine visitation of the Spirit occurred in the fourth
decade when much of Scotland caught its share of the revival
flame.

Before outlining the events associated with that gracious
awakening it is necessary briefly to indicate the condition of the
Church prior to its inception. In the first part of the eighteenth
century religious life in Scotland had sunk to a sadly low ebb. For
this the patronage controversy was largely responsible, since it
sapped the vitality of the Church and left it effete and ineffective to
meet the more serious challenge of scepticism. At the Union of
1707 care was taken to safeguard the privileges and liberties of the
Scottish Church. An Act of Security was passed by which the
Confession of Faith and the Presbyterian form of ecclesiastical
government were ratified and guaranteed "to continue without
any alteration to the people of this land in all succeeding generations."[1] It was further declared that "with the establishment contained therein, shall be held and observed in all times coming as a
fundamental and essential condition of any treaty of Union to be
concluded betwixt the two kingdoms, without any alteration
thereof or derogation thereto in any sort for ever."[2] These stipu-
lations were eventually included in the Articles of Union and the
Church of Scotland entered the new régime under the impression
that no infringement of her rights was now possible.

Hopes of such an amicable and enduring agreement were frus-

---

[1] N. L. Walker, *Scottish Church History*, p. 102.
[2] Ibid.: cf. *English Constitutional Documents*, ed. G. B. Adams and H. M. Stephens,
pp. 482-3.

trated within five years when the passing of two further bills clearly interfered with the privileges of the Scottish Church. The Toleration Act allowed legal protection for Episcopalians in Scotland to use the Prayer Book and at the same time repealed those enactments of the Scottish Parliament by which they were subjected to the discipline of the Presbyterian Church courts. But it was the subsequent Patronage Act which really roused the ire of the Scots and ushered in a lengthy period of controversy. From early times it had been the practice that the landowners who assumed the responsibility of erecting the churches and providing for the clergy should also select the men who were to do the work. The Church merely required that the choice should be made from amongst those whom it approved as being duly qualified. At the same time it was always conceded that the consent of the congregation, either directly or indirectly, was a necessary element in the process of election. Democratic ideas which are a commonplace today were hardly mooted then. But there was nevertheless an increasing body of opinion which held it as a matter of solemn principle that "the Christian people or society of believers who join in full communion together are the persons who, according to the New Testament, have a right to elect their minister."[1] Patronage had actually been abolished in 1649, restored in 1660, and again abolished in 1690. In these instances, as in 1712, the determinative factor was political.

The effect of this reimposition was disastrous. It was described without undue exaggeration as having "rendered Christianity inefficient in well-nigh half her parishes."[2] It caused some of the best ministers to leave the Church and some of the best people to repudiate those who remained. As a consequence what was known as the Moderate party gained the ascendency and exercised a dominant influence. Its origin may be traced to the admission after the Revolution settlement of conforming Episcopalians. A Laodicean spirit was introduced which paralysed the Church of the early eighteenth century. Richard Hill's jibe was not unjustified: "A moderate divine is one who has a very moderate share of zeal for God. Consequently, a moderate divine contents himself with a moderate degree of labour in his Master's vineyard."[3] John Witherspoon indulged in a similar satire at their expense, crediting them with having preached good works but left others to practise

---

[1] R. Buchanan, *The Ten Years' Conflict*, Vol. 1, p. 150.
[2] Letter to Lord Brougham.
[3] Buchanan, *op. cit.*, p. 150.

them.[1] The Moderate party aligned itself with the patronage policy, seeing in it the only hope of preferment. A youthful disciple of the school declared in the General Assembly that he gave God thanks for the law of patronage. "Moderator," intervened an old Evangelical minister, "this must needs be a singularly pious youth—he is thankful for very small mercies."

The successive secessions from the Church of Scotland in 1733 and 1761 were the tragic entail of the insistence on patronage and the theological ineptitude of the Moderates. The Evangelical group within the Auld Kirk was too feeble to prevent these unfortunate and indeed unnecessary defections. Neither the Erskines nor Gillespie claimed more than belonged to the ancient rights of the Presbyterian Church. But it must be added that once the separations had taken place, a certain hardening of attitude is to be observed which closed the door to any overtures of reconciliation and even to co-operation with the Evangelicals within the Church.

In the ripening purpose of God it was almost exclusively through the Church Evangelicals that revival was to come. When the spreading flame reached the Scottish border it by-passed the splinter groups as well as the Moderate strongholds and found its fullest scope in the Evangelical parishes. Many of these faithful ministers must have been sorely tempted to follow in the train of the seceders. But they could not bring themselves to believe that the Church they loved so well could best be served by their departure. They longed for the opportunity to reform from within. And as they waited on the will of God, that opportunity came. Their decision to remain within the fold proved crucial in paving the way for revival. "Why, it may be asked, did not these other evangelical brethren rather retire along with them?" enquired Robert Buchanan, referring to the Original Secession of 1733. "Their reasons were equally simple and strong. The constitution of the Church was sound. As the seceders allowed, the grievances complained of resulted from the maladministration of the prevailing party in Church courts. In this state of affairs, both principle and policy appeared to the evangelical minority to dictate and require that they should abide at their post, and endeavour to rescue an institution which they honoured and loved, from the hands of those by whom it was for the time misgoverned."[2] Men like John Willison of Dundee, John Bonar of Torpichen and John McLaurin of Glasgow, who all played a prominent part in

[1] D. Maclean, *Aspects of Scottish Church History*, p. 89.
[2] Buchanan, *op. cit.*, p. 153.

the subsequent Awakening, lived and ministered through the barren years, but held fast to the Church of their fathers in the hope that a better day would dawn, as indeed it did.

Tokens of coming revival were not wanting even in the blackest years. "From almost the very commencement of the century there were in Scotland indications of returning power," wrote Donald MacFarlane in his classic account. "The habitations of horrid cruelty abroad, and the abominations of immorality at home, being both glaring, began to engage the public mind. The country was not so far gone as not to feel, at least in many places, a want of gospel light and gospel warmth in the pulpit, and the tyranny of ecclesiastical moderation in the Church courts; and for a time the few strove against the many, in seeking to arrest the downward progress in both: the secession broke the strength of the reclaiming party within the Church, and their attention was perhaps all the more directed to other and brighter scenes."[1] As early as 1724 the first stirrings of revival in Easter Ross began to manifest themselves, and it was from this source that the subsequent movement in the Northern Highlands sprang.[2] Wodrow, writing in 1728, on the authority of Walter Ross, minister of Kilmour Easter, speaks of unusual visitations at the communion seasons in Sutherland, when people would travel as far as fifty miles to share the blessing.[3] In 1730 John Balfour was inducted to the Parish of Nigg and from that date onward became the recognized leader of revival in the Highlands. There was a gradual quickening, "with stops and intermissions," in the spiritual life of the people, which reached its climax in 1739.[4] This was a year of definite awakening. Only a few were under concern at the same time, "nor was it attended," added Balfour, "at all with such bodily symptoms, as were in sundry instances the effect of awakenings in some other parts."[5] But he was able to report with satisfaction that not one in forty of the converts had lapsed. A prayer meeting had to be started some years previously, but so great was the increase of numbers that this had to be divided into two societies, led by the minister. In addition, ten other societies met each Saturday. Balfour described the blessed effects of this revival in a letter to James Robe of Kilsyth:

Worship is kept in all the families of the parish except three or

---

[1] D. MacFarlane, *The Revivals of the Eighteenth Century*, p. 31.
[2] J. MacInnes, *The Evangelical Movement in the Highlands of Scotland*, p. 156.
[3] R. Wodrow, *Analecta*, Vol. IV, p. 4.
[4] MacInnes, *op. cit.*, p. 156.
[5] Gillies, *op. cit.*, p. 453.

four. The Lord's Day is very solemnly observed. After public worship is over, there are meetings in all parts where neighbouring
families join in prayer, reading and repetition of sermons . . . the
ordinary diets of worship are punctually attended . . . diets of cate-
chising are much crowded with people from other parts . . . no
crimes . . . the Kirk Session had little to do but to inform and con-
sult about the religious concerns of the parish . . . the people are
more forward in the business of their husbandry than their neighbours in other parts of the country.[1]

It is significant that these initial stirrings took place before the
Revival had really got under way in England and prior to the
arrival of George Whitefield in Scotland. He is usually regarded
as the harbinger of the Scottish Awakening, but the Spirit had
already been at work. As in America, Whitefield came to a land
prepared. It was at the invitation of Ralph Erskine and the
Associate Presbytery that the great evangelist crossed the Scottish
border in July 1741. From the start he made it clear that he could
not be confined to the Secession in his ministrations.

I come only as an occasional preacher to preach the simple Gospel
to all who are willing to hear me, of whatever denomination. It will
be wrong in me to join in a reformation as to church government
any further than I have light given me from above. If I am quite
neuter as to that in my preaching, I cannot see how it can hinder or
retard any design you may have on foot. My business seems to be to
evangelise, to be a Presbyter at large.[2]

Although he was strongly urged to preach in Edinburgh, Whitefield determined to reserve his first sermon in Scotland for Ralph
Erskine's meeting house in Dunfermline. It was here, when he
announced his text, that he was pleasantly surprised to hear "the
rustling made by opening the Bibles all at once."[3] His association
with the Seceders was short-lived, however. He was required to
confine his preaching within the bounds of the Secession churches.
When Whitefield asked, why only for them? Erskine replied that
they were the Lord's people. "I then asked," Whitefield tells us,
"whether there were no other Lord's people but themselves; and,
supposing all others were the devil's people, they certainly had
more need to be preached to; and, therefore, I was more and more
determined to go out into the highways and hedges; and that, if
the Pope himself would lend me his pulpit, I would gladly proclaim the righteousness of Christ therein."[4]

[1] Ibid.   [2] Tyerman, *Whitefield*, Vol. I, p. 505.
[3] Ibid., p. 508.
[4] Ibid., pp. 510-11. J. McKerrow, *The History of the Secession Church*, p. 158n., tries
to excuse the Associate Presbytery.

This breach with the Secession, despite the vituperation which emanated from that body, opened a great door and effectual to Whitefield within the Church of Scotland. He received a warm welcome from many of the ministers and laymen of the Auld Kirk and many pulpits were opened to him, besides opportunities for open-air preaching. He paid fourteen visits in all and left an indelible impression upon the Church life of Scotland. He refused to be drawn into sectarian wrangling. "I find it best to preach the pure Gospel, and not to meddle at all with controversy," he told Ogilvie of Aberdeen. "The present divisions are a sore judgment to Scotland. This is my comfort, Jesus is King. . . . O that the power of religion may revive! Nothing but that can break down the partition wall of bigotry."[1] Wherever he went the multitudes congregated and a trail of spiritual blessing was left behind. "Since you left Scotland numbers in different places have been awakened," wrote an Edinburgh minister when Whitefield's first visit had concluded. "Religion in this sinful city revives and flourishes. Ordinances are more punctually attended. People hear the Word with gladness, and receive it in faith and love. New meetings for prayer and spiritual conference are being begun everywhere. Religious conversation has banished slander and calumny from several tea-tables. Prais is perfected out of the mouths of babes and sucklings. Some stout-hearted sinners are captivated to the obedience of Christ."[2] Another Edinburgh minister, Dr. Muir, spoke of twenty praying societies started in the city. Similar reports came from Glasgow, Dundee and Aberdeen. The wider effect of Whitefield's ministry is suggested by an extract from some early biographical *Sketches*.

> The dead cold Moderatism of the predominant body in the Church, was pervaded by the electric influence of a style of preaching that commanded and compelled attention: the Evangelical Party was encouraged and strengthened: and the Secession itself, although he refused to shut himself up within its pale, found its best religious principles enforced by so effective and yet so disinterested an advocate. It was the commencement of a better day in the religious history of Scotland, the blessings of which we still continue to enjoy.[3]

Such, then, was the impact of Whitefield's first tour of Scotland in 1741. It is hard to realize that it only lasted thirteen weeks. But it was the second visit in 1742 that was to prove even more revo-

[1] Tyerman, *Whitefield*, Vol. I, p. 515.
[2] Ibid., p. 528.
[3] *Sketches of the Life and Labours of George Whitefield*, p. 86.

lutionary and was linked with the outbreak of revival. After spending twelve days in Edinburgh, preaching twice daily and expounding the Scriptures each evening, he set out for the West of Scotland. In a letter of 19th June he reported:

> Yesterday morning I preached at Glasgow to a large congregation. At mid-day I came to Cambuslang, and preached at two to a vast body of people; again at six and again at nine at night. Such commotions, surely, were never heard of, especially at eleven o'clock at night. For an hour and a half there was much weeping, and so many falling into such deep distress, expressed in various ways, as cannot be described. The people seemed to be slain in scores. Their agonies and cries were exceedingly affecting. Mr. M'Culloch preached, after I had done, till past one in the morning; and then could not persuade the people to depart. In the fields all night might be heard the voices of prayer and of praise.[1]

This was the beginning of the Revival. It had been prepared for by the faithful evangelical ministry of William McCulloch who had been ordained to the parish in 1731. He was an able and judicious preacher without being in any way outstanding in eloquence. His manner of speech was slow and cautious—far removed from the style of the popular orator. We reach the vital core of this man's ministry when we learn that "he spent much time in secret prayer, waiting with humble patience for a favourable return. He greatly encouraged private Christians to meet for social prayer, and particularly that God would revive His work everywhere."[2] Soon the church was found to be too small to hold the crowds and McCulloch resorted to the open fields. "The place chosen was well adapted for the purpose," according to Clason. "It is a green brae on the east side of a deep ravine near the church, scooped out by nature in the form of an amphitheatre. At present it is sprinkled over with broom, furze, and sloe-bushes, and two aged thorns in twin-embrace are seen growing side by side near the borders of the meandering rivulet which murmurs below. In this retired and romantic spot Mr. McCulloch, for about a year before 'the work' began, preached to crowded congregations, and on the Sabbath evenings, after sermon, detailed to the listening multitudes the astonishing effects produced by the ministrations of Mr. Whitefield in England and America; and urged, with great energy, the doctrine of regeneration and newness of life."[3]

Towards the end of 1741 he noticed a distinct change in his

---

[1] Tyerman, *Whitefield*, Vol. II, pp. 5-6.
[2] MacFarlane, *op. cit.*, p. 36.
[3] *Statistical Account.*

congregation. They began to display a more than ordinary concern for things spiritual. Early in the new year he received a petition pleading for a weekly Bible lecture. At the same time what became known as the concert of prayer commenced. Three prayer meetings were already being held and soon another dozen sprang up. But they not only met separately in the homes of their leaders but gathered together in the manse. As yet there was no sign of multiplied conversions, but after sermon on 18th February, "a considerable number of people, reckoned by some present to be about fifty, came together to the minister's house, under conviction and alarming apprehensions about the state of their souls and desiring to speak with him."[1] So acute was their spiritual hunger that McCulloch had to arrange for a daily service followed by a time of prayer and exhortation. Within the space of a few months there were over two hundred converts and many more were awakened to their soul's need. The transforming effects of revival began to evidence themselves. "There is a visible reformation of the lives of some who were formerly notorious sinners," runs a contemporary account, "particularly in the laying aside cursing and swearing and drinking to excess among persons addicted to these practices; remorse for acts of injustice and the violation of relative duties, confessed to the persons wronged, joined to new endeavours after a conscientious discharge of the duties previously neglected; restitution, which has more than once been distinctly inculcated in public since this work began; forgiving of injuries; all desirable evidence of fervent love to one another, to all men, and even to those who speak evil of them; and among those people, both in Cambuslang and other parishes, more affectionate expressions of regard than ever to their own ministers, and to the ordinances dispensed by them."[2]

It was to a people thus prepared that Whitefield came at the earnest invitation of William McCulloch. He returned in July to share in the Communion season. He was astonished above measure at what he saw.

On the Sabbath, scarce ever was such a sight seen in Scotland. Two tents were set up, and the holy sacrament was administered in the fields. When I began to serve a table, the people crowded so upon me, that I was obliged to desist, and go to preach in one of the tents, whilst the ministers served the rest of the tables. There was preaching all day, by one or another; and in the evening, when the sacrament was over, at the request of the ministers, I preached to the whole congregation of upwards of twenty thousand persons. I

[1] MacFarlane, *op. cit.*, p. 48. [2] Ibid., p. 49.

preached about an hour and a half. It was a time much to be remembered. On Monday morning I preached again to near as many. I never before saw such a universal stir. The motion fled, as swift as lightning, from one end of the auditory to the other. Thousands were bathed in tears—some wringing their hands, others almost swooning, and others crying out and mourning over a pierced Saviour. In the afternoon, the concern was again very great. Much prayer had been previously put up to the Lord. All night, in different companies, persons were praying to God, and praising Him. The children of God came from all quarters. It was like the passover in Josiah's time.[1]

So great was the effect that it was agreed to convene another Communion assembly in August. Meanwhile, the concert of prayer was intensified. The objective of sustained supplication was, according to McCulloch himself, "that the Lord would continue and increase the blessed work of conviction and conversion, and eminently countenance the dispensing of the holy sacrament of the supper a second time in this place, and thereby make the glory of this latter solemnity to exceed that of the former."[2]

The prayer of faith was heard and answered. The second Cambuslang Communion was a time of even more remarkable visitation than the first and, as visitors had come from near and far, was the means of spreading the fire into many other parishes. There were some three thousand communicants and it was estimated that crowds of up to forty thousand heard Whitefield preach. "But what was most remarkable," said McCulloch, "was the spiritual glory of this solemnity; I mean the gracious and sensible presence of God. Not a few were awakened to a sense of sin, and their lost and perishing condition without a Saviour. Others had their bands loosed, and were brought into the glorious liberty of the sons of God. Many of God's dear children have declared, that it was a happy time to their souls, wherein they were abundantly satisfied with the goodness of God in His ordinances, and filled with joy and peace in believing."[3]

The Revival could not now be contained within the bounds of a single parish. It fanned out into the Presbytery of Hamilton and beyond. The ministers of East Kilbride, Blantyre, Bothwell and Cathcart all shared the Communions. William McKnight of Irvine was a close friend of McCulloch and readily attested the lasting results of the Awakening. John McLaurin and John Gillies from Glasgow were also associated with the work and John Hamilton of the Barony received a hundred new communicants that summer.

[1] Tyerman, *Whitefield*, Vol. II, pp. 6-7.   [2] *Revivals of Religion*, No. 1, p. 3.
[3] Ibid., p. 6.

Alexander Webster of the Tolbooth, Edinburgh, and the aged John Bonar of Torpichen, were of the company too, with many of their congregations. All these places shared a measure of the quickening influence.

But it was at Kilsyth that the next outbreak was to occur. The parish minister, James Robe, had witnessed the scenes of memorable visitation at Cambuslang and returned to his own sphere determined to watch and pray until a similar token appeared. He had laboured for over thirty years without seeing any sign of such renewal. Despite his fearless preaching and constant intercession, his people seemed to grow even more careless. in the year 1740 he embarked upon a series of sermons dealing with the doctrine of regeneration. Although he expounded the relevant Scriptures and applied them with all the earnestness he could command, there seemed to be no response. After the barriers had yielded to the spate of revival power, he realized that more had been accomplished in the apparently barren years than he had supposed.

> I sometimes could observe that the doctrine of these sermons was acceptable to the Lord's people, and that there was more than ordinary seriousness in hearing them: yet I could see no farther fruit. But now I find that the Lord, who is infinitely wise, and knoweth the end from the beginning, was preparing some for this uncommon dispensation of the Spirit, which we looked not for; and that others were brought under convictions issuing, by the power of the Highest, in their real conversion, and in a silent way.[1]

It was on 16th May, 1742, that the first indications of a season of refreshing were given. Robe preached, as he had done several times before, on Galatians 4 : 19—"My little children, of whom I travail in birth until Christ be formed in you." His own account describes the consequences:

> While pressing all the unregenerate to seek to have Christ formed within them, an extraordinary power of the Divine Spirit accompanied the word preached. There was great mourning in the congregation, as for an only son. Many cried out, and these not only women, but some strong and stout-hearted young men. After the congregation was dismissed, an attempt was made to get the distressed into my barn, but their number being so great this was impossible, and I was obliged to convene them in the kirk. I sung a psalm and prayed with them, but when I essayed to speak to them I could not be heard, so great were their bitter cries, groans and the voice of their weeping. After this I requested that they might come into my closet one by one. I sent for the Rev. Mr. John Oughterson,

---

[1] J. Robe, *Narrative of the Revival of Religion at Kilsyth*, pp. 31-2.

minister of Cumbernauld, who immediately came to assist me in dealing with the distressed. In the meantime, I appointed psalms to be sung with those in the kirk, and that the precentor and two or three of the elders should pray with them.[1]

On the following Wednesday, when Warden of Campsie and McLaurin of Glasgow preached, there were similar scenes, and throughout the years 1742 and 1743 they continued. As at Cambuslang, it was found necessary to institute a weekday Bible lecture. Prayer meetings abounded. Seekers were continually brought to the minister. A notable change came over the life of Kilsyth. "In social meetings, edifying conversation has taken the place of what was frothy, foolish, or censorious," reported Robe. "Instead of worldly and common discourse on the Lord's Day, there is that which is spiritual and to the use of edifying. There is little of what was formerly common, strolling about the fields, or sitting idle at the doors of their house on that holy day. There is a general desire after public ordinances. . . . The worship of God is set up and maintained in many families who formerly neglected it. . . . Former feuds and animosities are in a great measure laid aside and forgot, and this hath been the most peaceable summer amongst neighbours that was ever known in this parish. I have heard little or nothing of that pilfering and stealing that was so frequent before this work began. Yea, there have been several instances of restitution, and some of these showing consciences of more than ordinary tenderness. . . . The change is observed by every one who formerly knew the parish. One observing person said to me, that if there was no more gained by this wonderful work of the Spirit, there was at least a great increase of morality."[2]

The revival at Kilsyth inevitably affected adjoining parishes and we hear of similar quickening at Campsie and Calder, at Kirkintilloch and Gargunnoch, at Baldernock and Killearn. Meanwhile the flame had spread into Perthshire and Muthill and Crieff are mentioned amongst the parishes awakened. Nor must the continuing movement in the Highlands be overlooked. The 1739 revival in Nigg was but the beginning. In the nearby parish of Rosskeen "there came a surprising revival and stir among the people" in 1742 and 1743 under Daniel Beton.[3] In 1744 Rosemarkie was touched in the same way. Before this the minister, John Wood, had found the spiritual condition of his people discouraging in the extreme. It was in his district catechizings that he noticed the first evidences of quickened interest. Soon he was

[1] Ibid., pp. 38-9.   [2] Ibid., pp. 73-4.   [3] Gillies, op. cit., p. 384.

overwhelmed by the numbers of those who came to him for counsel. Rogart was also a centre of renewal. In 1743 John Sutherland, minister of Golspie, went to Cambusland, Kilsyth and Muthill to see for himself the gracious effects of the Revival. On his return he told his people of his experiences. Three praying societies were formed but little seemed to happen. Then in 1745, when he had almost despaired of seeing any fruit, "the great and bountiful God . . . was mercifully pleased to breathe upon a number of the dry bones, and visit them with his salvation."[1]

No account of the Revival in Scotland would be complete without a reference to John Wesley's twenty-two visits north of the border. The first was not paid until 1751 and his contribution was one of consolidation, especially in the face of Arian and Socinian tendencies amongst the Moderate leaders of the Church. He met with comparatively little success so far as establishing Methodist societies was concerned, but his impact upon the Church was permanent. "If the John Wesley of Scottish history founded no extensive organization on Scottish soil, the John Wesley *in* Scottish religion has been an influence of the deepest and most pervading kind," wrote Butler. "In Scotland, assuredly, Wesley's work has been a victory; the spirit of his movement within the Church has been an expansive force."[1] The full flowering of the eighteenth-century Revival in Scotland was not seen until early years of the following century under men like Andrew Thomson and Thomas Chalmers. In this development the influence of Wesley is unmistakable and considerable, both in the realms of belief and practice.

The immediate effects of the Revival were not unimportant, however. The Scottish pulpit was recalled to doctrinal orthodoxy. The inroads of rationalism were resolutely resisted. Sir Henry Moncreiff Wellwood could claim in 1818 that "for more than half a century neither Hutcheson nor Shaftesbury has found his way into a pulpit in Scotland."[2] Whilst such an assertion may well be too sweeping, it nevertheless remains true that the Revival profoundly affected Scottish preaching and ensured that the evangelical emphases should not be overlooked. The formation of prayer societies represented a spiritual force in Scotland the ultimate repercussions of which can hardly be calculated. A new devotion to the Lord's Day and the ordinances of the Church, not

[1] Ibid., p. 388.
[1] D. Butler, *Wesley and Whitefield in Scotland*, p. 221.
[2] H. M. Wellwood, *The Life of John Erskine*, p. 62.

least the Holy Communion, was a further consequence of the Revival. As Professor Donald Maclean has observed, "While the effects of the revivals flowed far beyond the Church's ecclesiastical boundaries, within the Church they were a powerful factor in re-forming the character of ministers and people, in enthroning Christ, and in vitalizing what Ebenezer Erskine called 'the carcase of worship,' all of which helped to mould the history of the Church."[1]

Perhaps the most significant contribution of the Evangelical movement to the continuing history of the Scottish Church lay in the impetus it supplied to the missionary awakening. Although it was not until 1824·that the General Assembly agreed to the estab-lishment of missions to the heathen, the Evangelicals had pleaded for such a step in 1796 and since that time had been actively spon-soring missionary work. At the General Assembly of 1796 there took place a debate which Hugh Miller described as "the most extraordinary, perhaps, and the richest in character that ever originated in the Courts of a Protestant Church."[2] The Synods of Fife and Moray petitioned the Assembly to consider the most effective means by which the Church might "contribute to the diffusion of the gospel over the world" and urged it "to aid the several societies for propagating the gospel among the heathen nations."[3] After the suggestion had been received with scant sym-pathy by a succession of Moderate speakers, the doyen of the Evangelicals, John Erskine of Greyfriars, Edinburgh, rose to support the overtures. The scene has been depicted in Scott's *Guy Mannering*. He poured scorn on the pusillanimous argument that the perils of the times precluded such a venture. Then, with a dramatic gesture, Erskine appealed to the Word of God. "Rax me that Bible," he cried, and from Romans 1 : 14 he urged the need to fulfil the missionary commission of the New Testament. By a vote of 58 against 44 the overtures were dismissed, but a stand had been made and, though delayed, the eventual outcome was assured. Incidentally, it was from this moment that Moderatism began to decline as the dominant force in the Assembly. When in 1824 the ban was lifted and the way opened for Alexander Duff to sail to India, the missionary implications of the Revival were realized within the Church and its influence was eventually ex-tended to the uttermost parts of the earth.

---

[1] Maclean, *op. cit.*, p. 92.
[2] H. Miller, *The Church of Scotland, Missionary and Anti-Missionary*, p. 3.
[3] Maclean, *op. cit.*, p. 86.

THE
YEARS OF EVANGELIZATION
1742—1800

CHAPTER IX

THE RISE OF ANGLICAN EVANGELICALISM

B Y THE YEAR 1742 THE REVIVAL WAS WELL UNDER WAY. GOD'S river was in full spate. The evangelists were covering the counties of eighteenth-century Britain. The vital matter of organization and follow-up was being canvassed. It was only as the tide flowed that it was seen to be composed of several streams. The departure of Wesley from the Moravians indicated that it was possible for divergent views to accentuate differences unobserved before. The parting of Wesley and Whitefield marked out a further stratification. But the most noticeable of all divisions within the forces of the Revival was undoubtedly that which distinguished the Methodists from the Anglican Evangelicals.

A clear definition of terms is essential if we are to unravel this tangled skein of relationship and ultimate differentiation. In the eighteenth century the name Methodist was employed indiscriminately to denote all sympathizers with the Awakening. Writing in 1778, Thomas Scott explained that "Methodist as a stigma of reproach was first applied to Mr. Wesley, Mr. Whitefield and their followers; and to those who, professing an attachment to our Established Church, and disclaiming the name of Dissenters, were not conformists in point of parochial order, but had separate seasons, places and assemblies for worship. The term has since been extended by many to all persons, whether clergy or laity, who preach or profess the doctrines of the Reformation, as expressed in the Articles and Liturgy of our Church."[1] Sidney Smith, as late as 1808, lumped together "Arminian and Calvinistic Methodists and the Evangelical clergymen of the Church of England" and added, not without a touch of sarcasm, "we shall use the general term of Methodism to designate those three classes of fanatics, not troubling ourselves to point out the finer shades and nicer discriminations of lunacy, but treating them all as in one general conspiracy against common sense and rational orthodoxy."[2] Thus,

---

[1] T. Scott, *The Force of Truth*, p. 13n.
[2] *Edinburgh Review*, 1808, pp. 341-2.

although the name Methodist in its strict connotation ought only to be applied to those adherents of John Wesley who eventually emerged as a separate denomination, and might perhaps be extended to include those disciples of Whitefield and Lady Huntingdon who owed no permanent allegiance to the Church of England, it came nevertheless to be attached inexactly and uncritically to all supporters of the Revival.

The term Evangelical, as representing a party designation, refers specifically to those within the Church of England who embraced such views but who refused to countenance or emulate the irregularities of an itinerant ministry. The divergence was not primarily theological. It is an over-simplification to regard Evangelicalism as merely the Calvinist wing of the Revival. As we shall learn, the Calvinist-Arminian controversy cut right across the division between Methodists and Evangelicals, for some Methodists were Calvinistic and some Evangelicals were Arminian. Doctrinally speaking, the Anglican Evangelicals represent a sort of third race, usually comprehended under the name of "Moderate Calvinists." The crucial issue, then, was not dogmatic. As Canon Charles Smyth has so effectively demonstrated, "the fundamental divergence between Evangelicals and Methodism came over the problem of Church order."[1] The Evangelicals sought to carry out the mission of the Revival strictly within the framework of the existing ecclesiastical structure. The Methodists broke through the restraints imposed by tradition and adopted a new technique to meet the demands of a new age.

The term "Evangelical", of course, reaches the eighteenth century with an accumulation of colouring. It had been applied to Wyclif and his followers as well as to the Reformers, both on the Continent and here in England. As early as 1531 Sir Thomas More declared that "these Evaungelicalles theimself cease not to pursue and punish their bretherne."[2] When it was first used in the eighteenth century to denote those clergy who preached the doctrines of the Revival is uncertain. Pearson, in his life of Hey, states that "to men thus orthodox do a certain number of their clerical brethren apply the epithet of Evangelical ministers as a term of reproach."[3] As soon as 1759 Thomas Haweis wrote to Samuel Walker of Truro concerning the Vicar of Kineton: "Talbot took his living with a view to do good, before he could be at all said to be evangelical."[4] This may well prove to be the earliest use of the

---

[1] C. Smyth, *Simeon and Church Order*, p. 255.   [2] Cf. Balleine, *op. cit.*, p. 40n.
[3] Ibid.   [4] E. Sidney, *The Life and Ministry of Samuel Walker*, p. 479.

term with reference to the eighteenth-century Revival within the Establishment, although Canon Elliott-Binns wonders whether it means anything more than a recognition that Talbot was acting in conformity with the Gospel.[1] In this doctrinal sense the term Evangelical was applicable to all adherents of the Awakening, Methodist and Anglican alike. And it is in this sense, too, that we speak comprehensively of the Evangelical Revival. But gradually Evangelical came to denote a member of that growing party within the Church of England, distinct from those Methodists (whether Wesleyan, Whitefieldite, or what) who eventually seceded from the Establishment. It would appear that this demarcation had been effected by 1770 when Toplady could refer to Wesley's complaint "that the Evangelical clergy are leaving no stone unturned to raise John Calvin's ghost."[2] Certainly by the turn of the century the great gulf had been fixed. The question of adherence to or separation from the Establishment constituted the determinative principle. The issue will therefore be clarified if this distinction be applied retrospectively.

If it is necessary to avoid confusion between Evangelicals and Methodists, it is equally essential not to identify Evangelicals with Low Churchmen. However similar they may seem today, they were very different in the eighteenth century. Indeed, the Low Churchmen were the bitterest opponents of the Revival. They continued the Latitudinarian tradition of the previous century and whilst, as Abbey seeks to show, they had a useful task of comprehension to perform, they were unanimously inimical to the Evangelical Awakening. Henry Sacheverell, the High Church pamphleteer, pilloried their attitude:

> We will sum up the articles of a Low Churchman's Creed. . . . He believes very little or no revelation, and had rather lay his faith upon the substantial evidence of his own reason than the precarious evidence of divine testimony. . . . He had rather be a Deist, Socinian, or Nestorian than affront his own understanding with believing what is incomprehensible, or be so rude as to obtrude on others what he himself cannot explain. He thinks the Articles of the Church too stiff, formal, and strait-laced a rule to confine his faith in. . . . He looks upon the censuring of false doctrine as a dogmatical usurpation, an intrusion upon that human liberty which he sets up as the measure and extent of his belief. He makes the most of this world, being not over-confident of any other.[3]

[1] Elliott-Binns, *Early Evangelicals*, p. 132.
[2] Cf. Balleine, *op. cit.*, p. 40.
[3] H. Sacheverell, *The Character of a Low Churchman*, p. 5.

It is sufficiently obvious that such an outlook, even allowing for the licence of satire, could not possibly be mistaken for that of an Evangelical.

Although it is true that the advance of Methodism stimulated a healthy reaction within the Church of England towards a more evangelical standpoint, it must not be supposed that the Evangelical party was simply a by-product of the Wesleyan Revival. It had an independent origin. In his earlier book on *The Evangelical Movement in the English Church*, published in 1928, Elliott-Binns falls into this misconception of regarding Evangelicalism as "one of the offshoots of the great Methodist Revival of the eighteenth century."[1] It is interesting to see how he corrects himself in his more recent and comprehensive examination of *The Early Evangelicals*, where he actually writes: "It is often taken for granted that the Evangelical Movement was merely one of the offshoots of the Methodist Revival; but such an opinion requires considerable modification."[2] Then he proceeds to quote from Abbey and Overton: "The two movements were far from being identical. They were often warmly opposed. . . . Evangelicalism, or something nearly akin to it, would certainly have arisen about the same period, even if Methodism had never existed."[3] Two nations were, in fact, struggling to be born in the womb of the eighteenth-century Revival. Though related, they were nevertheless quite distinct.

That Evangelicalism was by no means a mere ancillary of Methodism will become clear as we now proceed to review the lives of some of the pioneers. Few of them owed any direct inspiration to the Methodist movement as such. They were raised up, as were the Wesleys themselves, by the immediate operation of the Holy Spirit. Not only did they commence their evangelical witness with little or no pressure from the Methodist wing of the Revival, but their work grew and prospered under the normal parochial system. It even extended beyond the bounds of the original parish to the surrounding areas in many cases. Gradually clusters of Evangelical influence and activity sprang up in the West Country, in the Midlands, in Yorkshire, and elsewhere. But there was no overall organization. There was no concerted action on a national scale. The leaders knew and at times met one another, but there was no constitutional cohesion about the movement as

[1] Elliott-Binns, *Evangelical Movement*, p. 3; Bready, *op. cit.*, p. 289, treats Methodism and Evangelicalism almost as cause and effect.

[2] Elliott-Binns, *Early Evangelicals*, p. 133.

[3] Abbey and Overton, *op. cit.*, Vol. I, p. 417.

such. It was content to flourish within the time-honoured boundaries of the Established Church. For this reason its impact appears to be less spectacular than that of Methodism. The progress of Anglican Evangelicalism cannot be measured in terms of the growth of societies or the development of a system. It can best be assessed through the impact of its leaders upon the Church as a whole. It has been said that "the history of the Evangelical Revival is essentially a history of personalities rather than of opinions"[1] and this is particularly apposite in the case of the Anglican group. Our purpose will be to consider some of those personalities and to trace the influence of the movement through them. It is in the main a story of single parishes from which a widening impression was made upon a district. Whereas the Methodists made the world their parish, the Evangelicals tended to make the parish their world. They rated the effectiveness of a fixed ministry higher than that of the vagrant evangelist. "I wish well to irregulars and itinerants," wrote Newton to Cadogan. "I am content that they should labour in that way who have not talents to support the character of a parochial minister; but I think you are qualified for more important service."[2]

In point of time the father of the Church Evangelicals was George Thomson, who was presented to the benefice of St. Gennys in Cornwall as early as 1732. At that date he was an unconverted man. An Oxford graduate in Laws, he had served for a spell as chaplain of the *Tiger*, bound for America. He was of a gay and worldly disposition, like so many of the contemporary clergy. But shortly after his installation at St. Gennys, God spoke to him in a dream thrice repeated in a single night with mounting terrors. Its admonition halted him in his careless course. He was solemnly informed that in a month he would die and be brought to judgment. He called together his friends and the principal people of the parish, and related his experience. He asked them to give him relief from his duties whilst he searched his own soul. He locked himself away and turned to the Book of God, to find some peace of mind. Instead, he could read nothing but condemnation. The sanctions of the law and the just punishment which awaited offenders gripped his heart. After a fortnight of deep distress, he fell upon the Third Chapter of Romans and his fears were gradually allayed as he came to hope and trust in Him "whom God hath set forth to be a propitiation through faith in His blood,

[1] Smyth, *op. cit.*, p. 6.
[2] J. Newton, *Works*, ed. R. Cecil, Vol. II, p. 168.

to declare His righteousness for the remission of sins that are past." He still remained in "unassisted solitude" and eventually entered into salvation by faith alone.[1] According to a notice in *The Christian Observer* for 1877, Thomson's conversion antedated that of the Wesleys by some five or six years, which would place it sometime in 1732 or 1733.[2]

Thomson's regeneration and call to exercise an evangelical ministry was thus entirely independent of the Methodist wing of the Revival and indeed prior to it. He seems to have known White-field before Wesley. In 1738 he subscribed to the Georgia fund and in 1739 went to Bath to meet the mighty preacher. Describing this encounter, Tyerman said that Whitefield "was introduced to the Rev. George Thompson (*sic*), Vicar of St. Gennys, Cornwall, from the first a hearty friend of the Oxford Methodists."[3] It would rather appear that Thomson and Whitefield had already been introduced, though perhaps only by correspondence. On White-field's first visit to Cornwall in 1743 he reached Bideford on 11th November and was met by Thomson, who took him back to St. Gennys, where he remained for a fortnight. "I am glad that the Lord inclined my heart to come hither," Whitefield wrote. "He has been with us of a truth. How did His stately steps appear in the sanctuary last Lord's day! Many, many prayers were put up, by the worthy rector and others, for an outpouring of God's blessed Spirit. They were answered. Arrows of conviction fled so thick and so fast, and such a universal weeping prevailed from one end of the congregation to the other, that good Mr. Thompson could not help going from seat to seat, to encourage and comfort the wounded souls."[4]

A fellow-labourer had evidently been raised up to share the witness with Thomson. Whitefield spoke of "another clergyman about eighty years of age, but not above one year old in the school of Christ. He lately preached three times and rode forty miles on the same day."[5] This was doubtless John Bennett, incumbent of Tamerton with Laneast and Tresmere. He seems to have been a typical eighteenth-century sporting parson, fond of the hunt and its subsequent revels. Charles Wesley tells us in his *Journal* that Bennett was a convert of Thomson. "I met an aged clergyman

---

[1] G. C. B. Davies, *The Early Cornish Evangelicals*, p. 31.
[2] A letter to Isaac Watts dated 17 January 1736 requesting prayer suggests that by then Thomson was an Evangelical: cf. T. Gibbon, *Memories of Isaac Watts*, p. 433.
[3] Tyerman, *Whitefield*, Vol. I, p. 184.
[4] Ibid., Vol. II, p. 79.   [5] Ibid., p. 78.

whom Mr. Thomson had sent to meet us, and found in conversing, that he had been an acquaintance and contemporary with my
father. Upon Mr. Thomson's preaching salvation by faith, he had
received the kingdom as a little child, and has ever since owned
the truth and its followers."[1] Preaching in Laneast church later,
Charles was bold to warn his hearers against the hindrance of even
harmless diversions. When he testified that through them he had
been kept dead to God, asleep in the devil's arms and secure in a
state of damnation for eighteen years, John Meriton (a clergyman
from the Isle of Man associated with the Wesleys) added aloud,
"And I for twenty-five." "And I," cried Thomson, "for thirty-
five." To cap it all, Bennett confessed, "And I above seventy."

Afterwards Charles Wesley preached at St. Gennys and recorded that one of his auditors was a neighbouring cleric who
had been with him at Christ Church, Oxford, and who invited
him back to his house. This was probably John Turner of Week
St. Mary, who makes up the third in a faithful trio of evangelical
pathfinders in Cornwall. John Wesley preached in Turner's
church in 1745 and on several subsequent occasions. This inaugurated an association which continued over a period of some
five years, punctuated by regular visits from the founder of
Methodism. A distinct cooling off is apparent after the death of
Bennett in 1750. Wesley visited St. Gennys for the last time in
1753. "I never saw so many people in this church," he noted in his
Journal, "nor did I ever speak so plainly to them. They hear; but
when will they feel? Oh what can man do toward raising either
dead bodies or dead souls!"[2] It seems probable, as Professor
G. C. B. Davies thinks, that Wesley's doctrinal views occasioned
this hardness. It is significant that on his next and final visit to
Week St. Mary he preached in the open air and there is no mention of John Turner, though he remained in the cure until his
death in 1772. It would therefore appear that, after supporting
Wesley for a time and indeed accompanying him round the duchy,
these Anglican Evangelical pioneers remained true to type in
concentrating on a parish ministry. It has been said that the
separation was caused by Thomson's adoption of Moravian
opinions. A notice in *The Evangelical Magazine* states that "he
joined the society of the *Unitas Fratrum* . . . many years before he
died, although he still held his living and resided upon it."[3]

[1] C. Wesley, *Journal*, Vol. I, p. 369.
[2] Wesley, *Journal*, Vol. IV, p. 79.
[3] *Evangelical Magazine*, 1800, p. 318.

Whether this report is based on fact or otherwise it is not easy to determine, although one would have hardly supposed that had his connexion with the Moravians been openly advertised he would have been permitted to retain his benefice when such a zealot for rectitude as George Lavington was his Bishop.

Another prominent Evangelical figure was also linked with this early work in Cornwall. James Hervey—"the literary parish priest,"[1] as Tyerman dubs him—came in 1738 to recuperate after a serious illness at the house of his friend Paul Orchard at Stoke Abbey near Hartland, on the north Devon coast. Whilst staying there he preached for Thomson at St. Gennys. It was during this period that he was brought to his evangelical conversion. Already as a member of the Holy Club at Oxford he had been roused from carelessness. In after-years he paid his tribute to the influence of John Wesley. "I can never forget the tender-hearted and generous Fellow of Lincoln, who condescended to take such compassionate notice of a poor undergraduate, whom almost everybody condemned, and when no man cared for my soul."[2] But, like Wesley himself, Hervey was still a stranger to the evangelical faith and it was only during his convalescence in Devon that he was finally led to the new birth. It was under the guidance of Whitefield and through a lengthy correspondence that the transformation took place. Hervey had been puzzled by the doctrine of justification and thought it irreconcilable with James 2 : 24 which, he said, he dare not blot out of his Bible. In November 1739 Whitefield wrote from America: "Let me advise dear Mr. Hervey, laying aside all prejudices, to read and pray over St. Paul's Epistles to the Romans and Galatians, and then tell me what he thinks of the doctrine."[3] This application to the Word brought the desired result. A letter later reproduced in *The Evangelical Magazine* contains Hervey's own version of what happened. Whitefield had evidently enquired how at length he had been brought to conviction.

You are pleased to ask, How the Holy Ghost convinced me of self righteousness, and drove me out of my false rests? Indeed, sir, I cannot precisely tell. The light was not instantaneous, but gradual. It did not flash upon my soul, but arose like the dawning day. A little book, wrote by Jenks, upon *Submission to the Righteousness of God*, was made serviceable to me. Your Journals, dear sir, and sermons, and especially that sweet sermon on "What think ye of

[1] Tyerman, *Oxford Methodists*, p. 201.
[2] *London Quarterly Review*, January 1957, p. 62.
[3] Elliott-Binns, *Early Evangelicals* ,p. 144.

Christ ?" were a means of bringing me to a knowledge of the truth.[1]

No longer relying on his own righteousness he cast himself upon
the only sufficient righteousness of Christ, and thus entered into
his inheritance of salvation. From this juncture his whole attitude
was altered.

> I now desire to work in my blessed Master's service, not *for*, but
> *from* salvation. I believe that Jesus Christ, the incarnate God, is my
> Saviour; that He has done all which I was bound to perform; and
> suffered all I was condemned to sustain; and so has procured a full,
> final and everlasting salvation for a poor damnable sinner. I would
> now fain *serve* Him who has *saved* me. I would glorify Him before
> *men*, who has justified me before *God*. I would study to please Him in
> holiness and righteousness all the days of my life. I seek this blessing,
> not as a *condition* but as a *part*—a choice and inestimable part—of that
> complete salvation, which Jesus has purchased for me.[2]

By 1739 Hervey's health was sufficiently restored for him to
undertake the curacy of Bideford on his ordination at Exeter. His
stipend was small but his congregation large as he proclaimed the
fundamentals which had laid hold upon his own soul. He preached
twice each Sunday. On Tuesdays and Fridays he gave Bible readings on the appointed Lessons. He examined the children and expounded the Church Catechism. Most significant of all, he formed
a religious society, "by no means in contradistinction to the
Established Church, but in conformity to her."[3] The rules laid
down by Woodward were observed. His exhortations were read
and his prayers employed. In place of religious conference was
substituted the reading of some edifying book. It was now that
Hervey mapped out and began to compose two of his most
popular literary efforts—*Meditations among the Tombs* and *Reflections
on a Flower Garden*. In 1743 he was dismissed by a new Rector who
disapproved of his evangelical message. For the remainder of his
ministry he served first as curate and then as Vicar of Weston
Favell in Northamptonshire. His contribution to the Revival lay
largely in the realm of literature. His style—"prose run mad," as
a witty critic called it[4]—may not appeal much today, but it
must not be forgotten that it was designed to reach the polite
eighteenth-century ear with the message of Christ. As Hervey
confessed to John Ryland, "I have not a strong mind; I have not

---

[1] Tyerman, *Oxford Methodists*, p. 223.
[2] *Evangelical Magazine*, 1794, p. 503.
[3] Tyerman, *Oxford Methodists*, p. 227n.
[4] It was "a judicious friend" of Samuel Richardson, Hervey's publisher, cf.
London Quarterly Review, January 1957, p. 67.

powers fitted for arduous researches; but I think I have a power of writing somewhat in a striking manner, so far as to please mankind and to recommend my dear Redeemer."[1] That was his sole concern. He utilized his flair for elegant fancies to confront his genteel audience with the Word of truth. "Let us endeavour to catch men by guile," he declared, "turn even a foible to their advantage; and bait the gospel hook agreeably to the prevailing taste."[2]

These men, however, were but the precursors of the real prophet of Evangelicalism in the West, Samuel Walker. It was not the habit of the Evangelicals to range themselves under a party leader, but if any single figure in these pioneering days could be regarded as the chief it would surely be Walker. Yet his importance has all too often been overlooked by historians. Speaking of such neglected heroes Professor Davies adds:

> Amongst these Samuel Walker of Truro must take an eminent place. He refused to commit irregularities, and so attract the notice of the authorities as did Berridge; he did not possess the greater scholarship of others, such as Romaine and Venn; the geographical isolation of Cornwall two centuries ago, together with his views and early death, prevented his ever rising beyond a curacy-in-charge to occupy a position more fitted to his particular gifts. But few men exercised a greater or more lasting spiritual influence in a sphere limited to his own parish and immediate neighbourhood. As a pastor, teacher, and faithful servant of Christ, and the leader of the "awakened" clergy in that part of the county, his life and work can bear comparison with that of any incumbent of his day.[3]

To this encomium there might well have been appended the fact that in this early period Evangelical clergymen everywhere looked to Walker for a lead, as his correspondence shows. Moreover he represents the purest type of Anglican Evangelical who refused to overstep his own parish boundaries or to resist the authority of the Church. John Wesley recognized in Walker the solitary exception to his somewhat arbitrary and indefensible rule that the regular clergymen could not possibly exercise a fruitful ministry.[4] That Wesley acknowledged Walker as the head of the Evangelicals in 1761—the year of the latter's death—is evident from a letter he wrote to James Rouquet in which he roundly declared, "The grand breach is now between the irregular and the regular clergy" and continued, "The latter say: Stand by yourselves; we are better than you! And a good man is continually exhorting

[1] Ibid., p. 65.   [2] Ibid., p. 66.
[3] Davies, *op. cit.*, p. 53.   [4] Wesley, *Letters*, Vol. III, p. 151.

them so to do, whose steady advice is so very *civil* to the Methodists. But we have nothing to do with them. And this man of war is a dying man—it is poor, honest Mr. Walker."[1]

Walker was born, curiously enough, on the same day as Whitefield. From Exeter Grammar School he passed to Exeter College, Oxford, where he counted William Talbot, afterwards the Evangelical Vicar of Kineton, amongst his friends. Though he was a contemporary of the Wesleys, there is no hint that he was affected by them. He can hardly have been unaware, however, of the stir they created in the University. It is possible that his acquaintance with James Hervey began in these undergraduate days. Disappointed in failing to gain a Fellowship, Walker turned to the ministry with little or no sense of call. The week prior to his ordination he had spent with the other candidates "in a very light, indecent manner; dining, supping, and laughing together, when God knows we should have been all on our knees, and warning each other to fear for our souls in the view of what we were about to put our hands to."[2] After serving several curacies, Walker came to Truro in 1746 to assist an absentee Rector, St. John Elliott, and, on his own admission, in order to be near the Assembly Rooms, for he was passionately fond of card playing and dancing. In a town that was notorious for its worldliness and dissipation, Walker aimed, as Balleine puts it, to lead the life of a fashionable Abbé.[3] But God had other designs for him and within a year of his arrival he was led into the experience of conversion. The instrument was a Scotsman, George Conon, who had been headmaster of the local Grammar School since 1729.[4] Nicholas Carlisle describes him as "a sound grammarian" and "a Christian both in faith and practice."[5] Walker substantiates the second part of that judgment by saying that Conon was "verily the first person I had met with truly possessed of the mind of Christ."[6] It was the scrupulous honesty of Conon in going out of his way to pay customs duty which first commended him to Walker and led to the friendship which culminated in his conversion. For this we must turn to a contemporary account, from the pen of James Stillingfleet. Walker was conversing with some of his friends and Conon was doubtless amongst them.

---

[1] Ibid., Vol. IV, p. 143.   [2] Sidney, *op. cit.*, p. 4.   [3] Balleine, *op. cit.*, p. 74.
[4] Davies, *op. cit.*, p. 58, has 1728, but an entry in the Truro Account Book is decisive.
[5] N. Carlisle, *A Concise Description of the Endowed Grammar Schools of England and Wales*, Vol. II, p. 149.
[6] E. Middleton, *Biographia Evangelica*, Vol. IV, p. 358.

The subject of their conversation turned upon the nature of justifying and saving faith; he, as he freely owned afterwards, became sensible that he was totally unacquainted with that faith which had been the topic of the discourse, and also convinced that he was destitute of something which was of the greatest importance to his own as well as to the salvation of the people committed to his charge. He said nothing at that time of the concern he was brought under to any one of the company, but was ever afterwards, as opportunity offered, ready to enter upon the subject. He began to discover that all had been wrong both within and without. Upon this discovery, he applied himself with diligence and fervent prayer to the study of the Holy Scriptures, and having by these means gained a farther insight into the nature of man's spiritual disorder, and of the remedy afforded in the gospel, this necessarily led him to make a considerable alteration in his preaching, both as to the choice of his subjects and the manner of his address.[1]

Walker's denunciation of sin and proclamation of the new birth, combined with the striking revolution in his own habits, produced a remarkable effect in the town. Although he was decried as an enthusiast, a killjoy and even a lunatic, his fearless championship of the gospel truth began to gain converts. His sincerity and devotion made an indelible impression and even those who did not hear him in the pulpit feared and respected him out of it. On the Lord's day the loiterers and absentees from Church would slink away at his approach, saying, "Let us go; here comes Walker." Such recalcitrants grew fewer and fewer, until at length it was said "you might fire a cannon down every street in Truro in church time, without a chance of killing a single human being."[2] The frivolity and moral looseness of former days disappeared. The playhouse and the cockpit were each compelled to close down for lack of patrons. Walker's first convert was a dissolute soldier and his subsequent consistency of life under much provocation greatly encouraged his minister. Shortly afterwards the young man died and the event produced many enquiries after salvation, so much so that Walker had to rent two rooms for the purpose of counselling. Writing to his friend Thomas Adam in 1754, Walker said, "The number of those who have made particular application to me enquiring what they must do to be saved cannot have been less than eight hundred."[3] As Balleine points out, this in a town of sixteen hundred inhabitants meant very nearly the whole adult population.[4] Walker's converts were gathered into classes and

---

[1] Life of Walker by James Stillingfleet, prefaced to *Fifty-Two Sermons*, p. xix.
[2] Sidney, *op. cit.*, p. 15.
[3] *Christian Observer*, 1802, p. 566.
[4] Balleine, *op. cit.*, p. 76.

nurtured with the utmost care. Several evenings each week were devoted to their instruction. The depth and quality of this guidance can be measured by an examination of his published *Lectures on the Church Catechism*. It has been said that after more than twenty years of hard and prayerful work, Walker left Truro the most Christian town in England.

Nor was his influence confined to his own parish, though he himself never left it. The fire of revival spread to surrounding areas and in 1750 he was able to found a Clerical Club attended by a growing group of Evangelical incumbents in the diocese. It is a remarkable circumstance that in this remote corner of England the work of the Revival should have progressed so far and so favourably. Referring to these combined operations, Walker wrote, "Through much evil report we all gain ground; and I suppose there are not less than ten thousand to whom we preach the Gospel, one or another of us."[1]

We have spent a considerable amount of time in dealing with Cornwall, for it was the cradle of Anglican Evangelicalism in England. George Conon—a Presbyterian by birth, but confirmed in the Established Church—may rightly be described as the first Evangelical layman and George Thomson the first Evangelical cleric. The separate origin of the Evangelical movement as distinct from Methodism is apparent from the fact that the work in Cornwall was well established before the conversion of either Whitefield or the Wesleys.

We shall now glance more briefly at the rise of Anglican Evangelicalism in two further pioneering areas—namely, London and Yorkshire. The first real leader in London was William Romaine. It is true, of course, that a number of clergy sympathetic to the Revival opened their pulpits to Whitefield and the Wesleys, but Romaine was the first of the regulars to gain a settled hearing in the city.[2] He came to be recognized as one of the major figures in the Evangelical section of the eighteenth-century Awakening. Bishop Loane refers to him as "that iron pillar of the truth"[3] and Canon Overton went even further and concluded: "Take him for all in all, William Romaine was the strongest man connected with the Evangelical branch of the revival."[4] His conversion took place after he had come to London as "a very, very vain young

---

[1] Sidney, *op. cit.*, p. 79.
[2] J. W. Middelton, *An Ecclesiastical Memoir of the First Four Decades of the Reign of George III*, p. 43.
[3] M. L. Loane, *Oxford and the Evangelical Succession*, p. 128.
[4] Overton, *op. cit.*, p. 68.

man,"[1] seeking honours in the Church. He had already attracted
attention as a preacher in St. Paul's and as the editor of Calasio's
Hebrew Concordance in its English version. He confessed afterwards that in his intellectual arrogance "he knew almost everything but himself, and met many disappointments to his pride,
till the Lord was pleased to let him see the plague of his own
heart."[2] Although the precise circumstances of his spiritual transformation are not recorded we must not therefore conclude with
some authorities that he never experienced such a crisis.[3] He himself clearly implies it. He says he found no help in human counsel,
not even from some of the leaders of the Revival, for his Saviour
"would not let him learn of man."[4] He went everywhere to listen
to preachers, but none of them appealed to his condition. He
hoped to be saved by his devotions—"sweet food to a proud
heart" he later admitted.[5] It would seem that he was finally drawn
to search the Scriptures and it was as he bowed before the Word of
God that the saving truth dawned upon his soul. He says that the
Bible became a new and precious book to him and his self-conceit
was crushed.[6] His sense of emancipation is reflected in the auto-
biographical extract on his memorial plaque in St. Hilda's, Hartle-
pool:

> I was even as others are by nature a child of wrath and an heir of
> misery; I was going on in the broad way of destruction, careless and
> secure, and I am quite astonished to see the danger I was in; I
> tremble to behold the precipice over which I was ready to fall, when
> Jesus opened mine eyes and by the light of His Word and Spirit
> showed me my guilt and danger and put it into my heart to flee from
> the wrath to come. O what a merciful escape!

Once again we remark upon the independence of his awakening.
Although he had been a member of Christ Church, Oxford, at the
very time that the Holy Club was flourishing, he had no contacts
with the early Methodists. As in the case of so many others, it was
directly through the Scriptures of truth that Romaine was led to
accept Christ.

His conversion must probably be placed after the year 1748, for
it was then that he applied for the vacant lectureship of St.
Botolph's, Billingsgate, with a view to advancing his ecclesiastical

[1] *Evangelical Magazine*, 1795, p. 439.
[2] Ibid.
[3] Ryle, *op. cit.*, pp. 153-4; Overton, *op. cit.*, pp. 64-5.
[4] *Evangelical Magazine*, 1795, p. 440.
[5] Ibid.
[6] Ibid, p. 441.

career. In the following year he secured the afternoon lectureship of St. Dunstan's in the West and it was here that he first began to declare the doctrines of the Revival. In 1750 another opportunity offered when he was appointed as Assistant Morning Preacher at St. George's, Hanover Square, in the heart of the West End. Whenever he preached, huge crowds gathered and caused some embarrassment to the Churchwardens. It was for this reason that he was ultimately denied the use of St. George's in 1755 and in 1758 a similar attempt was made at St. Dunstan's. The Church-wardens refused to light or heat the building or even to open the doors a second before the hour of worship. Balleine's description is vivid and striking:

> Preacher and congregation had to wait in the street till the wooden giants on the tower had beaten out the hour of seven, and then grope their way cautiously to their seats. This was the only Evangelical service in any of the city churches, and very solemn and impressive it must have been, the crowded congregation sitting or standing in perfect darkness, while Romaine preached by the light of a taper which he held in his hand.[1]

St. Dunstan's became the focal point of Evangelicalism in London and Romaine was eventually recognized as the city's principal preacher. People even came in from the country on a dual errand —"to see Garrick act and hear Romaine preach."[2] Despite the fact that preferment tarried, Romaine could not think of relinquishing the Evangelical struggle. "Here my Master fixed me," he declared, "and here I must stay. I am alone in London, and while He keeps me there, I dare not move."[3] In the end he was inducted to the living of St. Andrew's, Blackfriars, which he held until his death.

Romaine was not altogether alone at this period. From 1750 Martin Madan was the Evangelical Chaplain to the Lock Hospital and preached regularly, first in the parlour and eventually in the adjoining Chapel which was opened in 1762. Madan was a brother of the Bishop of Peterborough and was called to the Bar in 1748. He was behaving as a typical man of the world when he was arrested by the hand of God in a quite unexpected manner. One evening he was disporting himself with some of his lively companions at a coffee house, when they begged him to go and hear John Wesley preach nearby in order that he might return to

[1] Balleine, *op. cit.*, p. 43.
[2] Ibid.
[3] T. Haweis, *Life of William Romaine*, pp. 82-3.

burlesque the sermon for their amusement. Just as Romaine
entered the chapel, Wesley announced his text, "Prepare to meet
thy God," with such solemnity that Madan was moved to listen,
in all seriousness, to a moving exhortation to repentance. He returned to the coffee house and was immediately asked "if he had
taken off the old Methodist?" "No, gentlemen," he answered
gravely, "but he has taken me off." From that moment Madan
severed himself from his former associates and prepared himself
for the ministry of the Church. He experienced some difficulty in
obtaining orders, but through the interest and perseverance of
Lady Huntingdon he was eventually successful. For thirty years
he acted as Chaplain to the Lock Hospital and ensured that its
Chapel remained a stronghold of London Evangelicalism.

Another valuable ally maintained a brave witness across the
Thames. Thomas Jones was appointed as Junior Chaplain of St.
Saviour's, Southwark, in 1753 and for some years he was the only
beneficed Evangelical in the entire London area. He endured many
trials and the bitterest opposition until his premature death in
1762. In 1750 Henry Venn left Cambridge and took a curacy at
St. Matthew's, Friday Street, but although he performed his
duties with fidelity, he could not be classed amongst the Evangelicals, for as yet the Lord had not opened his heart. It was during
his five years as curate of Clapham that he was brought to a satisfying knowledge of saving truth and before he left for Huddersfield in 1759 he was fearlessly proclaiming the Revival message
from London pulpits as often as six times a week.

When Henry Venn reached Yorkshire the Evangelical cause
had already been established in that county. The pioneer here was
William Grimshaw. He had once been a pleasure-loving parson.
Hunting, fishing and card playing were his preoccupations and he
considered his clerical duties completed when he had read prayers
twice and preached a borrowed sermon. All that could be said in
his favour was that "he refrained as much as possible from gross
swearing unless in suitable company, and, when he got drunk,
would take care to sleep it out before he came home."[1] In such a
condition he was altogether unable to help those who applied to
him in spiritual need. He told one such enquirer: "Put away these
gloomy thoughts; go into merry company; divert yourself; and
all will be well at last."[2] But from the year 1734 a change began to
come over this Todmorden curate. He gave up his pleasurable

[1] Middleton, *op. cit.*, Vol. IV, p. 398.
[2] Ryle, *op. cit.*, p. 111.

practices and started to pray four times a day—a habit which he maintained to his death. The passing of his young wife broke his heart and his thirst for God assumed a redoubled intensity. He clung even more firmly to the staff of prayer and the study of Scripture. He read for the first time with serious attention the books which had been given him at his ordination, Thomas Brook's *Precious Remedies Against Satan's Devices* and John Owen's *On Justification*. It was to this latter and his constant resort to the Word that he owed his conversion. The dawn came suddenly in 1742 when one Sunday morning his servant found him still on his knees at five a.m. During the day he fainted more than once, but nevertheless gave every spare moment to prayer. After his second fit he seemed to be in a state of rapture and his first words on re-gaining consciousness were, "I have had a glorious vision of the third heaven." So powerful was his sense of divine pardon and assurance that he prolonged the afternoon service from two until seven. Thus Grimshaw passed out of death into life without help from any human quarter and quite independently of the great movement then afoot in the land. His ministry took on a totally new aspect. "I was now willing," he confided to Venn later, "to renounce myself, every degree of fancied merit and ability, and embrace Christ as my all in all. O what light and comfort did I enjoy in my own soul and what a taste of the pardoning love of God!"[1] His preaching now became clear and profitable, according to Newton. The Bible was all renewed. He told someone that it was as though God had "drawn up his Bible to heaven, and sent him down another, it could hardly have been nearer to him."[2] His sole concern was to bring others to the light. "He was still a mighty huntsman," says Marcus Loane, "but the prey he stalked was the souls of men."[3]

The year 1742 was a crucial one for Grimshaw and for the Evangelical movement, for no sooner had he been converted than God transferred him to the appointed place of his future labours. In the month of May he was placed at Haworth to give it a fame prior to and more enduring than that which came to it through the Brontës. His preaching quickly filled the church. Sunday sports were soon abandoned for lack of supporters. Requests came in from surrounding villages and towns and soon Grimshaw was itinerating through much of West Yorkshire. He deserves the

---

[1] Wesley, *Journal*, Vol. IV, p. 484.
[2] G. G. Cragg, *Grimshaw of Haworth*, p. 15.
[3] M. L. Loane, *Cambridge and the Evangelical Succession*, p. 23.

title Apostle of the North bestowed in Reformation times on
Bernard Gilpin. His incursions into other parishes—a feature
which distinguishes him from the stricter Evangelicals—
aroused considerable opposition and complaints were registered
with the Archbishop of York, Matthew Hutton, who summoned
him to his palace. "How many communicants did you find on
coming to Haworth?" the Archbishop enquired. "Twelve, my
lord," replied Grimshaw. "How many have you now?" "In the
winter between three and four hundred, according to the weather.
In the summer sometimes nearer twelve hundred." "We can find
no fault with Mr. Grimshaw," decided the Archbishop, "seeing
that he is instrumental in bringing so many persons to the Lord's
Table." A further unfavourable report impelled the Archbishop
to visit Haworth for himself to discover whether there was any
substance in the complaints. He required Grimshaw to preach at
two hours' notice on a text that he himself selected. Grimshaw
thought that this was the end of his ministry, but he nevertheless
complied with the request of his diocesan. His prayers moved the
congregation to tears and his message stirred every heart. When
the service was ended, the Archbishop took him tenderly by the
hand and said with much emotion and in the hearing of all the
neighbouring incumbents who had gathered to rejoice over
Grimshaw's downfall, "I would to God that all the clergy in my
diocese were like this good man."

Henceforward Haworth was to be the Evangelical hub of Yorkshire. Grimshaw extended the bounds of his activity far beyond
the confines of his own parish. Eventually his circuit spread over
four counties—Yorkshire, Cheshire, Derbyshire and Lancashire.
In addition to his own parish duties he maintained two weekly
rounds for the remainder of his ministry. One of these he used to
call his lazy week because he only preached about fourteen times.
In what he regarded as his busy week he would often preach as
many as thirty times! He collaborated both with Whitefield and
the Wesleys when they visited the north. Through Lady Huntingdon he became friendly with Romaine. In 1757 Newton came to
Yorkshire for the first time and stayed with Grimshaw at Haworth.
"Had it been the will of God," he wrote, "methought I could
have renounced the world to have lived in these mountains with
such a minister!"[1] The arrival of Venn in 1759 brought great
joy to Grimshaw's heart, for he felt that now he had a colleague and successor. In 1763 Grimshaw was called home, but

[1] J. Bull, *John Newton, An Autobiography and Narrative*, p. 96.

the work that he had pioneered went on from strength to strength.

Thus the cause of Anglican Evangelicalism was fostered in various parts of the country. Although the leaders were separated from one another by long distances and had little means of communication with each other, they were nevertheless united by the same Spirit who inspired the whole Revival movement. As we remember once again the Evangelical fathers we are compelled to conclude that their collective achievement is to be explained only in terms of their submission to God.

CHAPTER X

THE MORAVIAN MISSION

OUR REVIEW OF THE MORAVIAN CONTRIBUTION TO THE eighteenth century Evangelical Awakening halted at the foundation of the Fetter Lane Society in 1742. We shall now trace the further progress of this sector of the Revival. In his Bampton Lectures on *Dissent in its Relation to the Church of England*, Prebendary G. H. Curteis picked out three distinct movements which combined in the general quickening. There was what he called the High Church, or Arminian mission, under the Wesleys. There was the Calvinistic mission, under Whitefield and Lady Huntingdon. But in pride of place he set the original Moravian mission, conducted latterly by Ingham and Cennick. It is to this that we must devote our attention.

We are dealing here with a history that is largely unchronicled and therefore generally unknown. This is a field of research still to be fully investigated. We can only hope to map out the terrain. It might be supposed that the departure of John Wesley would have weakened the Moravian cause. The reverse appears to have been the case. "From the day when Wesley left the Fetter Lane Society in July 1740," wrote J. E. Hutton, in an invaluable essay, "the influence of the Moravians in England began, not to decrease, but to increase. For the next fifteen years they were busily engaged, in various parts of the country, in vigorous evangelization."[1] This resilience and enterprise stemmed from what the Moravians themselves were accustomed to call "the spirit of service," and something of its astonishing quality can be gauged from the fact that of the seventy-two members of their first congregation in Britain, no less than sixty-five were subsequently engaged in full-time Christian work of one kind or another.

London was the earliest centre of operations. The meetings of the Fetter Lane Society were marked by unusual spiritual power. Visitors were deeply impressed and echoed the tribute paid to the

---

[1] *Historical Essays by Members of the Owens College, Manchester*, ed. T. F. Tout and J. Tait, p. 423.

Corinthian Church, "God is with you of a truth." Even though it was located in an inaccessible area, the chapel was filled to overflowing and the congregations spilled into the surrounding courtyard. Similar societies were inaugurated in various parts of the city. Meeting places multiplied. A second chapel was utilized in Moorfields and yet another attached to Lindsay House. The members of the London societies held themselves in readiness to respond to calls from every part of Britain, wherever the greatest need might be. Their organization was geared to the urgent task of evangelism. "The range of their activities was ever on the increase," according to Bishop Hassé. "A hundred letters were often written in one day (and that meant very much more than it does now); and these were mostly in answer to enquiries and appeals for spiritual help. Far into the night the leaders sat discussing the work, and planning how best to utilize the men and the means at their disposal for the spread of the kingdom of God. For that was the one great end in view, and it was never lost sight of. The edification of believers was desirable and necessary; but the salvation of the unsaved was better; and for this evangelism was required, and to evangelism they resolutely set themselves."[1]

This pressing concern for the redemption of souls was accompanied by an equally insistent urge to minister to the material needs of the distressed. The Moravian spirit, like the Methodist, was practical as well as evangelical. Prisoners in the London gaols were visited and supplied with much-needed comforts. Vagrants and social misfits were afforded poor relief. Meals were provided for the hungry underworld. In the working establishments employers of labour gathered their workers together and spoke to them about the gospel—a quite unheard of innovation. The early days of the Moravian mission were vital and venturesome indeed.

It has been pointed out that the members of the London societies considered themselves to be on constant call, ready to rise to any appeal for help throughout the length and breadth of Britain. One of the first of such requests came from Yorkshire. This, the largest of the counties, was destined to become one of the principal spheres of Moravian evangelism in Britain. This is all the more remarkable when the condition of this northern district is borne in mind. It was notorious for its neglect in the eighteenth century. The inhabitants were rough, depraved and addicted to the most cruel pastimes. Cock-fighting and bull-baiting were more popular here than anywhere else in the country. Nothing short of

[1] E. R. Hassé, *The Moravians*, pp. 54-5.

a miracle could move these uncouth, callous, pleasure-loving, sin-degraded Yorkshiremen. Such a miracle of grace God was preparing to perform, chiefly through the Moravians.

The evangelical apostle to Yorkshire was Benjamin Ingham, himself a native of Ossett. He began his notable work as early as 1737 and before long James Hutton could report to Zinzendorf that some thousand souls had been awakened and that the people were clamouring for a visit from one of the Moravian leaders in London to confirm them in their newly-found faith. Ingham, of course, had been a member of Wesley's Holy Club at Oxford and had accompanied the two brothers to Georgia as an ordained clergyman of the Church of England. Previous to this he had exercised what has been described as "a sort of ecclesiastical itinerancy"[1] in the London area, where his official capacity was that of a reader at Christ Church and St. Sepulchre's, Newgate. It is clear that Ingham was as much impressed as were the Wesleys by the Moravians he met aboard the *Simmonds* and again in Savannah. In his journal of the voyage Ingham described them as "a good, devout, peaceable, and heavenly-minded people" and added: "They are more like the Primitive Christians than any other church now in the world; for they retain both the faith, practice, and discipline delivered by the apostles."[2]

On his arrival from the colony, Ingham went back to the county of his birth and resumed the itinerant evangelism he had embarked upon in the metropolis. Whilst at the time he fully intended to return to Georgia and indeed busied himself with mastering the Indians' language, his missionary heart bled for the heathen around him at home. Whenever the occasion was afforded he preached in the pulpits of the Established Church and, in addition, was able to fulfil a ministry of personal counselling. He even tackled the local curate for the good of his soul. His name was Godly, which Ingham felt to be a trifle inappropriate! Fruit soon began to appear for, as Tyerman observed, "a man with a soul like his—burning with a zeal which would have led him gladly to sacrifice his life amongst the wild Indians of America—could scarcely fail to be an earnest successful evangelist in his own country."[3] His preaching caused a great sensation. After one sermon in Wakefield the whole congregation was in an uproar. Some said the devil was in him; others, that he was mad. Others

[1] Tyerman, *Oxford Methodists*, p. 61.
[2] Ibid., p. 68.
[3] Ibid., p. 86.

yet again dismissed his gospel preaching as a new and dangerous doctrine, for they had never heard it before. Nevertheless, he was enabled to speak with great authority and power and his message struck home to the hearts of many.

The event which captured Ingham for Moravianism and launched him on his mission in real earnest was his visit to Herrnhut in 1738 in company with John Wesley. He was received with the utmost cordiality—more so than Wesley—and was correspondingly more favourably impressed. His previous opinions were amply confirmed. A brief and passing note of his visit to Zinzendorf at Marienborn provides an inkling of his mood.

The worthy Count is occupied day and night in the work of the Lord; and, I must confess that the Lord is really among the Brethren. Yesterday a boy of eleven or twelve years of age was baptised; and such a movement of the Holy Spirit pervaded the whole assembly, as I have never seen at any baptism. I felt that my heart burned within me and I could not refrain from tears. I saw that others felt as I did, and the whole congregation was moved. The Brethren have shown me much affection; they have taken me to their conferences, and have not left me in ignorance concerning anything in their church. I am much pleased with my journey.[1]

The strength of Moravian influence amongst the Oxford Methodists can be measured by the fact that no fewer than seven of them—the Wesleys, Whitefield, Hall, Kinchin, Hutchins and Ingham—were present at the Fetter Lane love-feast on New Year's day 1739, which kindled the fire of evangelistic zeal and inaugurated the mission proper. From this Pentecostal occasion Ingham returned to Yorkshire and began his apostolic endeavours. We find him extending the radius of his preaching to include Leeds and Halifax. There were many seals to his ministry. Considerable numbers were converted. Religious societies were formed for mutual edification in the faith. As Tyerman rightly declared, "it was pre-eminently a day of divine visitation."[2] But opposition was soon aroused. The local clergy, so far from rejoicing at such signs of revival, proved jealous and hostile. At a congress held in Wakefield on 6th July, 1739, Ingham was prohibited from preaching in any of the churches within the Archdiocese of York. He was thus in the same position as Whitefield and Wesley at Bristol, and he proceeded to do what they did and resorted to extra-mural preaching as his only outlet. We hear of him addressing the populace on

[1] Ibid., p. 89.
[2] Ibid., p. 90.

village greens, in market places, at the street corners, in the open fields. Indoors he utilized barns, sheds, cottages and inns. Such was the divine blessing upon his consecrated labours that he could write in 1740: "There are now upwards of fifty societies, where the people meet for edification; and of two thousand hearers of the Gospel, I know at least three hundred in whose hearts the Spirit of God works powerfully; and one hundred who have found grace in the blood and atonement of Jesus."[1] Meanwhile, John Nelson, the Birstall stonemason, assisted him for a time.

By the year 1742 the work had reached such proportions, not only in Yorkshire but in Lancashire as well, that Ingham felt he must appeal for help. As Hutton put it, "he could not hold fifty societies in the hollow of his hand."[2] It was at this juncture that he was led to hand over his converts to Moravian supervision. He gathered them together—as many as could conveniently be called simultaneously—and set before them the simple question, "Will you have the Moravians to work among you?" The proposal was carried with acclamation and Ingham rode post-haste to London with a petition in his pocket, signed by twelve hundred. Without delay a pilgrim band of twenty-six was mustered, both men and women, and, headed by Spangenberg, embarked upon their long and arduous journey. Hence on 30th July, 1742, the transfer was made.[3]

On arrival in Yorkshire the Moravian contingent immediately secured suitable headquarters. It was a large building at Wyke, near Halifax, known as Smith House. Later they removed to Fulneck. They fanned out into the neighbourhood in an intensive evangelistic campaign and were warmly welcomed everywhere. Ingham's societies rejoiced in their new allegiance and, we learn, "flocked together to Smith House like hungry bees."[4] Soon preaching places were established at Mirfield, Pudsey, Great Horton, Holbeck, Adwalton and Gomersal, each with a settled minister. Before long they went farther afield and we hear of preaching in Leeds, Huddersfield, Sheffield, York and Hull. Spangenberg was the director and Töltschig later came to assist. Zinzendorf himself inspected the Yorkshire work in 1743. Throughout this period of expansion, however, there was no attempt at systematic church extension. The aim of the Moravians

---

[1] Ibid., p. 99.
[2] Hutton, *op. cit.*, p. 193.
[3] It would seem that Ingham was never actually a member of the *Unitas Fratrum;* cf. Towlson, *op. cit.*, p. 133 and n.
[4] *Historical Essays*, p. 425.

was evangelism pure and simple. They were out to make Christians rather than Brethren. After two years' work in Yorkshire, whilst the number meeting in societies had risen steeply, only sixty-two were actually affiliated to the *Unitas Fratrum*. The Moravian zeal to evangelize was matched by their equally notable reluctance to proselytize. No one was ever invited to become a Moravian and those who expressed a desire to join the community were subjected to the most deterring tests, including a probationary term of two years. Writing to Edward Gibson, Bishop of London, in 1744, James Hutton could readily defend his communion from any charge of interfering with the flocks of rightful shepherds. On the contrary, he affirmed that "they receive none into the Moravian Church but those who have actually left their respective religions, and will not, at any rate, be persuaded to return to them again; such they receive into their Church, if otherwise worthy, according to their ancient custom. . . . And in this manner have they dealt with the Established Church here; having never persuaded any one soul, but rather as much as possible kept back people from joining themselves to them."[1] From all this it may be surmised that any suggestion of schism was abhorrent to the Moravians. They desired to maintain cordial relations with the Church of England as an episcopal body of parallel status.

Despite their pacific intentions, the Moravians soon found that considerable opposition was aroused by their witness in Yorkshire and elsewhere. Not only did the Established Church continue to treat them as Dissenters, until the official act of recognition was passed in 1749, but the Dissenters suspected them of collusion with the Church. The man in the street scarcely knew what to make of them. Sometimes they were called Germans, sometimes Herrnhuters, sometimes Antinomians. They even inherited the Quaker designation of "the Quiet in the Land," though everywhere they seemed to occasion unrest. When riots broke out because of the famine, it was darkly hinted that the Moravians were to blame. The preachers were hauled before the courts of justice and falsely charged with every sort of improbable misdemeanour. As open-air witness proceeded until its proscription in 1744, the messengers of the gospel provided a standing target for rotten eggs and brickbats. Some fell victim to even more serious mass violence. When Ingham went to preach at Colne, along with Grimshaw of Haworth, he was attacked by an infuriated mob incited by the parish in-

[1] Benham, *op. cit.*, p. 162.

cumbent, the notorious George White. The Vicar demanded that
he sign a document undertaking not to offend again. Ingham tore
it to shreds. "Bring him out and we'll make him," howled the
multitude. So the Vicar made way for his incensed parishioners to
wreak what vengeance they wished upon the defenceless evangelists. Brandishing clubs "as thick as a man's leg" they made to fell
Ingham on the spot.[1] He and his colleagues were pelted with mud
and dirt: he himself was hit in the neck with a stone as big as a
man's fist. Eventually they were conducted to the Swan Inn, with
Ingham's coat-tails torn and trailing the ground and the crowd
jeering, "See, he has got wings!"

J. E. Hutton placed the period of increasing resistance to the
Moravians in the years 1742 to 1745 and found five major causes.
The first was their foreign association. The very fact that the
Brethren were of German origin was sufficient to elicit hatred and
fear. Then again their system of Church discipline proved too
strict and regimental for the average liberty-loving Englishmen.
The third cause was their quietistic method. They deliberately
avoided the sensational and placed great stress upon a calm
waiting for the Lord. But this laid them open to the uninformed
charge of cherishing secret and unhealthy doctrines and practices.
Another reason for unpopularity lay in their somewhat unusual
phraseology. Their teaching was not altogether new, but it was
couched in unfamiliar terms. The "Blood and Wounds Theology,"
as it has been disparagingly dubbed, in its desire to draw attention
to the centrality of the Cross was at times proclaimed in a rather
crude and sentimental manner, which provoked revulsion and encouraged misconceptions. Lastly Hutton listed the unsympathetic
attitude of John Wesley. His accusations of antinomianism—un-
grounded save in respect of isolated individuals—lent unfortunate
force to the rumour that the Moravians were opposed to the
ordinances of the Church and the good works which faith must
needs produce. The general hostility reflected itself not only in
the hindrances placed in the path of the Moravian evangelists, but
also in the paper warfare in which Sir John Thorold and Gilbert
Tennent took part, along with Wesley. This period of persecution
was followed from 1746 to 1750 by a trying phase within the community itself, aptly labelled "The Sifting Time." Its seat was not
in Britain but in Germany, and there at Herrnhaag, the sister-
establishment to Herrnhut. The extravagances were reported by
Andrew Frey, whose evidence, though unpalatable, was accepted

[1] Hutton, *op. cit.*, p. 195.

by Hutton and Spangenberg. These indiscretions and the publication of Frey's indictment had their effect on the witness in this country and did little to alleviate the sharpness of hostility.

Meanwhile, another Moravian apostle had appeared on the scene in the person of John Cennick. It was in December 1745 that he took the same step in Wiltshire as had Ingham in Yorkshire. The representatives of the societies he had formed signed an invitation to the Brethren to come and take them over. Earlier in the year Cennick himself had severed his association with the Methodists. He had explained that this transfer of allegiance implied no reflection upon his former friends. "Whosoever understands the nature of religious communions knows that by passing out of one into another, a man does not always reflect some disparagement or censure upon his former society in itself; he may only be convinced, and that maturely, that the other will suit better upon the whole for his individual."[1] Cennick came of Bohemian stock. His grandparents had left during the religious persecutions of the seventeenth century and had settled in Reading, where they attached themselves to the Baptist cause. Before long they found themselves once again on trial for their faith and eventually their wealth was sequestrated. Cennick's parents attended the parish church of St. Lawrence. John was the youngest of seven children and was born in 1718. Despite a rigorous upbringing, he rebelled in his early 'teens and ran wild. His tastes, habits and companions were decidedly worldly and he had to confess, "I had forgotten Jesus." His conversion was at the age of nineteen, after a period of prolonged conviction and quest. He has left an account of his spiritual pilgrimage in which nothing is conealed or excused. As he hurried down Cheapside in London, little thinking of holy things, he tells us that the hand of the Lord touched him. From that moment he struggled in vain to evade the conquering compulsions of the Spirit. His soul was brought down to the pit. In desperation he prayed for the release of death. But God had better things in store for him. He began to seek salvation by the way of discipline, but all in vain. Then at last the sun broke in upon his darkened spirit. It was at an ordinary church service that the great illumination occurred and through the application of the healing Word. On Sunday, 6th September, 1737, the Psalm for the day was the thirty-fourth: "Great are the troubles of the righteous, but the Lord delivereth him out of them all; and they that put their trust in Him shall not be destitute." No sooner had the singing

[1] Cennick's Journal, in *London Quarterly Review*, July 1955, p. 212.

ended than the burden was removed from his soul and he found a glad deliverance. "I was overwhelmed with joy," he testified, "and I believed there was mercy. . . . I rejoiced in God my Saviour."[1] He was enabled to pursue his calling as land surveyor in a new world. Life took on a fresh and worthwhile meaning. Somebody loaned him a copy of Whitefield's *Journal*. His imagination was fired by the stirring accounts it contained of multiplied conversions. Already the way was being opened for his entry into the same sphere of service. He earnestly prayed that one day he might be privileged to meet the author of the volume which had so inspired him. His prayer was registered, but he was disciplined by waiting two years before an interview became possible.

In the month of May 1739 Cennick heard that Whitefield was in London and "set out from Reading in the dusk of the evening, and walked all night."[2] Arriving early next morning, he sought an audience with Whitefield and was offered a position as master in the school that Wesley proposed to build at Kingswood. Cennick hastened on foot to Bristol to see the spot. Near the site a crowd had collected beside a sycamore tree to hear an itinerant preacher who had failed to appear. Cennick was urged to supply his place. He had grave misgivings. He had made no preparations. He had never preached before. But the sight of that outdoor company hungering for the Word of life constrained him, and, commending himself to God in prayer, he stepped forward and opened his mouth in faith. "The die was cast," says Kelynack. "His prayer was heard. His vocation assured."[3] "On the 14th day of June 1739 the burden of the Lord came upon me," Cennick himself reported, "and I began to open my mouth to testify of Jesus Christ. The Lord bore witness with my words, insomuch that many believed in that hour."[4] Early in the ensuing week John Wesley arrived and Cennick was enlisted as his first lay preacher.[5]

The association, however, was not to be of long duration. After some months in charge of New Room in Bristol, Cennick began to devote himself more exclusively to the task of evangelism. In July 1740 revival broke out under his ministry in Wiltshire and his preoccupation with this mission led to his parting from Wesley. He had first gone in the company of his friend Howell Harris, but it was as he struck out on his own that the blessing

[1] Ibid., p. 209.
[2] Ibid.
[3] Ibid.
[4] Hassé, *op. cit.*, p. 77.
[5] Cf. *Proceedings of the Wesley Historical Society*, Vol. XXX, p. 32.

fell. "I preached for the first time in the streets of Castle Coomb to a vast concourse of people," he recorded in his *Journal*; and again, "At the invitation of some persons from Chippenham I preached in the time of harvest to a prodigious multitude on Langley Common."[1] He passed through scores of villages and towns and found that even in the remotest corners of the county hundreds gathered at his coming. "A wonderful revival began," said Hassé, "all the more gladdening because here also, as in Yorkshire, gross spiritual darkness had hitherto prevailed; ignorance and super-stition, almost heathenish in its character, abounded; the Gospel was but rarely preached, so that its proclamation came to the people as something new and refreshing. Speedily it proved its divine power; it exercised everywhere its old attractive influence. Curiosity gave place to thought; indifference was changed to con-viction of sin. The dry bones were stirred, they came together 'an exceeding great army'; the Spirit of God entered into them, and behold! they lived."[2] Inevitable opposition followed and Cennick joined the noble army of those who rejoiced that they were counted worthy to suffer for His name.

On one occasion in Swindon, when he and Harris were preach-ing in the Grove, the disturbers of the peace started firing muskets in the midst of the message. When this failed to deter the intrepid evangelists, they hurled the mud and filth of the roadside at them until they were covered in it. Finally they filled the local fire-engine with ditchwater and turned it upon them. "But while they played upon Bro. Harris," Cennick reported triumphantly, "*I* spoke to the congregation; and when they turned their engine upon me, *he* preached; and thus we continued till they had spoiled the engine."[3]

Cennick deserves his title "the apostle of Wiltshire." For five years the Awakening continued and he organized his groups into a circuit. By this time Cennick was Whitefield's lieutenant at the newly-opened Tabernacle in London. It is thus not altogether surprising that J. E. Hutton should liken Cennick to his chief. "Like Whitefield he spoke in the open air; like Whitefield, he held his hearers spellbound by his magic eloquence, and preached the telling Gospel that God gave His Son to save the world. Although he was poor and had to go on foot, he generally managed to preach two or three times a day. The people gathered in thou-sands to hear him. He made himself known in every cottage, knelt

[1] Hassé, *op. cit.*, p. 79.
[2] Ibid.
[3] Ibid.

down to pray by the bedsides of the dying, and spoke comfort from above to the sorrowful. Wherever he went John Cennick was loved by all who understood him aright."[1] The work so expanded that he mobilized a team of assistants and superintended his circuit after the Methodist fashion. At Tytherton, not far from Chippenham, he bought a house and converted it into a place of worship. But after four years he found, like Ingham in Yorkshire, that his hands were too full. "We shall never be right," he told his flock, "till we have the Brethren amongst us." And so it came about that the Wiltshire societies were placed under the supervision of the Moravian body. In the meantime, Cennick himself had become a Moravian and from that date he fulfilled his vocation as an evangelist in connexion with that cause.

A fresh field of gospel enterprise was opening up to him. For Cennick was to be the pioneer of the Evangelical Revival in Ireland. "The Isle of saints," as it had been christened, scarcely approximated to its name in the eighteenth century. Jonathan Swift painted a grim picture of its plight. He spoke of "the miserable dress, and diet, and dwelling of the people; the general desolation of most parts of the kingdom; the old seats of the nobility and gentry all in ruins and no new ones in their stead: the families of farmers who pay great rents living in filth and nastiness upon buttermilk and potatoes, without a shoe or stocking to their feet, or a house so convenient as an English hogsty to receive them," and concluded that a stranger might be forgiven for thinking himself in Lapland or Iceland.[2] Ireland seemed unlikely soil for the gospel seed. "A corrupt aristocracy, a ferocious commonality, a distracted government, a divided people"—such was the verdict of Lord Hutchinson.[3] Yet it was in this unpropitious island that a mighty quickening was shortly to occur under the ministry of John Cennick.

The initial invitation came from Benjamin la Trobe, a young Baptist who had recently completed his studies in Glasgow. He became the leader of a Christian group in the city of Dublin, formed originally by an English soldier some time previously. Already la Trobe had gained a reputation in the Irish capital as "an Israelite indeed, in whom there was no guile." It was with a certain reluctance that Cennick responded to this appeal of a few friends who had heard him preach in London. "I had a strong

[1] Hutton, op. cit., p. 201.
[2] J. H. Plumb, England in the Eighteenth Century, p. 180.
[3] J. R. Green, A Short History of England, p. 789.

prejudice against the Irish people," he admitted.[1] Despite his trepidation, he discovered that an unexpected welcome awaited him and that the ground had been fully prepared. The very place of his first preaching—the Baptist Hall in Skinner's Alley—had been linked with a puzzling prediction. A godly pastor of bygone days had foretold the time when a stranger from across the water would stand where he stood and instead of the half-empty pews there would be such crowds that neither the building itself nor the adjacent burial ground would be able to contain them all. Within a very short time of Cennick's arrival in Dublin that prophecy was remarkably vindicated. Those who desired to hear him had to take their places long before the scheduled hour. The windows had to be removed so that those outside could hear and Cennick himself had to enter by one of them and literally clamber over the shoulders of the congregation to reach the pulpit. From the start, he testified, "the Lamb was with me," and many hundreds were swept into the kingdom.[2] "If you make any stay in this town," exclaimed a Roman priest, "you will make as many converts as St. Francis Xavier among the wild pagans."

Cennick became the best known, best loved and best hated man in Dublin. Even when he went through the streets on pastoral errands, he was regularly shadowed by a posse of inquisitive hangers on. When he returned each night to his lodgings he had to be escorted by an armed guard, for the malcontents would bombard him with missiles. During a single service we are told that "near two thousand stones were thrown against Brothers Cennick and la Trobe, of which, however, not one did hit them."[3] Nevertheless, so mightily did the work grow and prosper that in one short year the Skinner's Lane Society rocketed to a membership of five hundred and twenty.

In 1748 Cennick set out for the North. A Quaker named Dean from Ballymena, County Antrim, came to Dublin and heard Cennick preach. He was so impressed with what he heard that he despatched a letter immediately on his return pleading with Cennick to visit his town. The opening of that mission was sufficiently sensational. On the first evening in Ballymena the floor of the hall suddenly began to sink, for the supports were rotten and unaccustomed to such a strain. By a miracle no one was hurt and the people accepted it as a sign sent to confirm the Word. They

[1] Hutton, *op. cit.*, p. 203.
[2] Ibid.,
[3] Ibid.

were doubtless reminded, too, of the curious prophecy made by the Scottish Covenanter, Alexander Peden, when preaching at the nearby village of Ballybollon. Standing in the ruins of an ancient battlement he uplifted his voice and cried, "O Fort, I charge you in the name of the Lord, never let anyone preach here any more till a bonny wee lad shall come from England, and preach the pure gospel of our Lord Jesus Christ." Not long after his arrival in the North, knowing nothing of this incident, Cennick delivered one of his most powerful sermons on the very spot. For five years he traversed the roads of Ulster and his figure grew as familiar there as it had been in Dublin. He was known to the people as "*the* preacher." The crowds would begin to collect as soon as it was heard that he was riding towards a village. They would stand for hours in pouring rain or driving snow to listen to his message.

Gradually the prejudice against him was worn down by the sheer godliness of his bearing and the divine authority of his utterances. The surprising day dawned when Presbyterians invited him to become their minister, clerics of the Irish Church sought his counsel and even Roman priests praised him for what he had done in their parishes! When a disgruntled minority of clergymen complained to the Bishop of Down and Connor that Cennick was emptying their churches, he answered: "Preach what Cennick preaches; preach Christ crucified, and then the people will have no need to go to Cennick to hear the gospel." The same sympathetic Bishop assured Cennick that he should always have fair play in his diocese.

The year 1749 proved to be crucial for Cennick—perhaps more so than he realized at the time. The tide had turned in his favour. Hostility was subsiding. Revival was spreading from county to county. He had established his headquarters at Crebilly and soon he was to found the Irish Herrnhut at Gracehill. In September Cennick was ordained a deacon of the Moravian Church by Peter Böhler. In November his third hymnal was published in Ireland. Still the work continued to expand until at length in 1755 Cennick was compelled by ill-health to quit the painful field. He just managed to reach Fetter Lane before he died at the early age of thirty-six. No history of the eighteenth-century Awakening can be comprehensive which does not recognize the importance of John Cennick. He deserves to stand beside the better-known leaders of the Revival. As Towlson remarks, "John Cennick was *sui generis*, as much a master of his own craft as John Wesley was, and no doubt would have preached to salvation had there been no Wesley, Harris, Whitefield or Böhler."[1]

Although the most notable achievements of the Moravian mission were witnessed in the areas we have discussed—namely, Yorkshire, Wiltshire and Ireland—it must not be supposed that the remainder of Britain was untouched. There was scarcely a county which did not feel the impact. The south country is associated with the name of Heatley; Bedfordshire with Jacob Rogers and Francis Okely; Oxford with Abraham Louis Brandt; Northamptonshire with William Hunt; the Midlands with Ocker-hausen, Brockshaw and Simpson, with Ockbrook as the centre; and Lancashire and Cheshire with David Taylor. South Wales was missioned by John Gambold, another member of the Holy Club, who was eventually elevated to the Moravian episcopate. Scotland received the notable ministry of John Caldwell and the Moravian witness reached as far as Lerwick in the Shetland Isles. One of the severest critics of the Brethren, John Roche, writing in 1753, considered their strength to be more formidable than that of the Methodists. Certainly, as Hutton suggested, "the time seemed to be not far off when the Moravian Church would take her stand as one of the leading Churches in the United Kingdom."[2] But such, of course, was not their intention, and the consequence of their exceptional evangelistic effort lay in the contribution they made to the life of every Christian communion and, most of all, the Church of England.

[1] Towlson, *op. cit.*, p. 256.
[2] Hutton, *op. cit.*, p. 210.

CHAPTER XI

THE SPREAD OF METHODISM

ALTHOUGH IN THE EIGHTEENTH CENTURY THE NAME METHODIST was applied indiscriminately to all supporters of the Revival, it is more strictly accurate to confine it to those followers of John Wesley who eventually broke away from the Established Church and formed the Christian communion which bears that title today. It is with the growth of Wesleyan Methodism, as distinct from Anglican Evangelicalism or the Calvinistic wing of the Awakening that we are concerned in this chapter. Wesley himself was careful to describe his disciples, in their collective capacity, as "the people *called* Methodists."[1] "By adopting this style," according to F. J. Snell, "he tacitly protested against the term 'Methodist,' which had been forced upon him from without. At the same time he showed by the colourless and almost colloquial word 'people,' that he considered the Methodist connexion as neither Church nor sect. Wider, more universal than the Church of England, inasmuch as it included Dissenters, it was still not an adverse, but a friendly organisation."[2]

The real starting-point of Methodism lay, as we have seen, in the conversion of the Wesleys. It was from the warmed heart in Aldersgate Street that the inextinguishable blaze was rekindled. But from the constitutional aspect it could be argued that the significant date was the 1st rather than the 24th May, 1738. That was when Wesley and Böhler drew up the rules for the Fetter Lane Society. Indeed Wesley himself traced the genesis of Methodism to this Moravian source. Its "first rise", he said was at Oxford in 1729, when the name Methodist was minted and cast at the members of the Holy Club.[3] The second stage of development was in Georgia in 1736 when the Savannah society was formed. But the final and determinative step was taken in 1738 with the founding of the Fetter Lane Society. Although the Methodists

[1] Cf. *A Plain Account of the People Called Methodists* written in 1748: Wesley, *Works*, Vol. VIII, pp. 248-68.
[2] F. J. Snell, *Wesley and Methodism*, p. 206.
[3] Wesley, *Works*, Vol. VII, p. 421.

were to leave the fellowship that cradled them, it nevertheless remains true that the germinating seed was planted there.

From this insignificant beginning Methodism has expanded into a global Church. Wesley was a man of far horizons. He looked beyond the confines of his little group to the conversion of his native land. He looked beyond the confines of his native land to the winning of a world for Christ. The gospel that was for all must be taken to all, irrespective of colour or clime. Early in his ministry Wesley uttered his now celebrated manifesto: "I look upon all the world as my parish; thus far I mean, that in whatever part of it I am, I judge it meet, right and my bounden duty to declare unto all that are willing to hear the glad tidings of salvation."[1] He was faithful to the injunction of Lady Huntingdon: "Attempt nothing less than all mankind."[2] From the start, then, Methodism was, as Stevens described it, "a revival Church in its spirit and a missionary Church in its organisation."[3]

Consequent upon his conversion, Wesley responded to the divine call to preach the gospel to every creature. His aim was clearly etched in his mind. He had pinpointed his objective. He set out "to reform the nation, particularly the Church, and to spread Scriptural holiness over the land."[4] The initial and most crucial step towards this end was taken in April 1739 when he "submitted to be more vile" and took to field preaching.[5] The text of Wesley's first open-air sermon was striking and appropriate. It was from Isaiah 61 : 1, 2: "The Spirit of the Lord God is upon me; because the Lord hath anointed me to preach good tidings to the meek; he hath sent me to bind up the broken-hearted, to proclaim liberty to the captives, and the opening of the prison to them that are bound; to proclaim the acceptable year of the Lord." The place was "a little eminence in a ground adjoining to the city" of Bristol, at the farther end of St. Philip's plain and that spot where he first "proclaimed in the highways the glad tidings of salvation" marks a pivotal stage in the growth of Methodism.[6] It was only with the utmost reluctance that the donnish Wesley could be persuaded to undertake such a distasteful mission. He said, "I could scarce reconcile myself at first to this strange way of preaching in the fields; having been all my life, till

---

[1] Wesley, *Journal*, Vol. II, p. 218.
[2] *Methodist Magazine*, 1799, p. 99.
[3] A. Stevens, *The History of Methodism*, Vol. I, p. 14.
[4] Wesley, *Works*, Vol. VIII, p. 299.
[5] Wesley, *Journal*, Vol. II, p. 172.
[6] Ibid.

very lately, so tenacious of every point relating to decency and order, that I should have thought the saving of souls almost a sin if it had not been done in a church."[1] Through the decision of Wesley to obey God rather than men by trampling upon personal inclination the door was opened to untold blessing for thousands.

It was field preaching that made Wesley an itinerant and brought his message within earshot of the common people who heard him gladly. No longer dependent upon the offer of a pulpit, he was free to go wherever the Spirit led him and to preach in every place where he could gain an audience. He embarked upon his first evangelistic tour in 1742 and thereafter scarcely slackened his pace until his declining days. Already his work was established in London and Bristol. A third centre in the north was soon added at Newcastle and provided the apex of a triangle which described his movements throughout his ministry. Wherever he went, he left a little nucleus of converts formed into a society and these he would revisit and encourage when he returned to the same area. As the Word ran and prospered, however, the mark of genuine revival was revealed in the fact that converts were made even before his arrival and awaited his advent to greet him. "When Mr. Wesley first came to Leeds," said a member of the original class meeting there, "we took him into society; he did not take us in."[2] This was in 1743 and already we hear of new societies in Northumberland, Somerset, Wiltshire, Gloucestershire, Leicestershire, Warwickshire, Nottinghamshire and South Yorkshire, whilst the older societies flourished. By 1747 Wesley was crossing to Ireland and in 1751 he paid the first of his twenty-two visits to Scotland. In 1760 the work began in America. The world parish was beginning to take shape. The numerical increase of early Methodism is all the more astonishing when we remember that Wesley drastically purged his membership to keep it pure. The first year when statistics were kept was 1767 and over 25,000 Methodists were registered. By 1790 the figure had risen to 71,000. No wonder Wesley was constrained to exclaim, "What hath God wrought!"

The organization of Methodism was incidental to and a necessary development from the primary task of evangelism. It was not Wesley's immediate aim to found a denomination or even to form a distinctive society within the Church. But the needs of the situation demanded it unless he was to forfeit his gains. For him it was unsatisfactory to deprive newborn souls of after-care. "I am more and more convinced that the Devil himself desires nothing more than this, that the people of any place should be half-awakened, and then left to themselves to fall asleep again; therefore I determined, by the grace of God, not to strike one stroke in any place where I cannot follow the blow."[1] Experience had impressed this necessity upon him. In 1748 he had preached for more than a year in the county of Northumberland without forming societies. He discovered that his labour was virtually in vain, for "almost all the seed had fallen by the wayside."[2] George Whitefield, who lacked the aptitude for such a task, confessed in a moment of depression, that with all his success he had only been "weaving a rope of sand."[3] Wesley was determined to leave behind something more substantial. Hence the organization which bears the stamp of his genius upon it.

We must not, however, exaggerate the originality of John Wesley nor misunderstand the precise nature of his gifts. He was not so much an innovator as an adapter. He had the unique skill to suit the measure to the occasion. There were no blue-prints of his plans. He improvised his schemes as the need arose and the situation demanded. Interesting as it is to compare his methods with those of the first or sixteenth centuries, we shall make a grave mistake if we imagine him as a conscious imitator. He was led by the Spirit of God to devise the most suitable expedient to match the challenge of the hour. "How was he competent to form a religious polity so compact, and permanent?" enquired his Irish friend, Alexander Knox. "I can only express my firm conviction that he was totally incapable of *preconceiving* such a scheme. . . . That he had uncommon acuteness in fitting expedients to conjunctures is most certain: this, in fact, was his great talent."[4]

It is an almost ironical feature of Wesley's work that, having cast off the restraints of Anglican authority, he should have imposed a highly complex and strictly enforced discipline of his own. In its finally developed form Methodist polity is connexional. The Annual Conference gathers within itself representatives from the District Synods which in turn draw upon the circuits and local societies. Each of these is closely interrelated, or "connected." Some have thought this an entirely original contribution, but, as H. B. Workman showed, the real founders of connexionalism were the Cistercians and the Friars.[5]

[1] Wesley, *Journal*, Vol. III, p. 71.
[2] Stevens, *op. cit.*, Vol. I, p. 324.
[3] Cf. R. D. Urlin, *A Churchman's Life of Wesley*, p. 188.
[4] Cf. G. H. Curteis, *Dissent in its Relation to the Church of England*, p. 345n.
[5] *New History of Methodism*, Vol. I, p. 43.

The starting-point in the growth of Methodist organization was the fundamental Christian need for fellowship. This Wesley regarded as the most serious deficiency in the Established Church of his day. "Look east, west, north and south, name what parish you please, is Christian fellowship there? Rather, are not the bulk of the parishioners a mere rope of sand? What Christian connexion is there between them? What intercourse in spiritual things? What watching over each other's souls?"[1]

The basic unit was the society. This was broken down into classes and bands or collected into circuits and districts, but the earliest and most accurate description of the Methodist connexion is "the United Societies." Considerable controversy still surrounds the question as to which may claim to be the first Methodist society. In a very real sense the Fetter Lane Society founded in May 1738 might be regarded as such, but it must be remembered that it was much more a religious society on the lines of those described by Woodward than the Methodist societies were destined to be. Moreover, although the Fetter Lane Society was not actually designated as Moravian until 1742, its tendency was in that direction from the start. After Wesley had separated from Fetter Lane in 1740, it was evident that any claim from this quarter to represent the first Methodist society would be resisted. The Bristol society inaugurated in April 1739 has a stronger case to present. But since it was associated with Whitefield as well as with Wesley, and eventually separated after the outbreak of the Calvinistic controversy, it cannot now be described as the first Wesleyan Methodist society. It is for these reasons that the society gathered exclusively by Wesley and on his own terms at the end of 1739 at the Foundery in Moorfields, London, is usually regarded as the parent group of modern Methodism. It was so recognized by the Conference of 1749 and by John Wesley himself in the account he has left of its inception:

> In the latter end of 1739, eight or ten persons came to me in London, who appeared to be deeply convinced of sin and earnestly groaning for redemption. They desired (as did two or three more the next day) that I would spend some time with them in prayer, and advise them how to flee from the wrath to come, which they saw continually hanging over their heads. That we might have more time for this great work, I appointed a day when all might come together; which, from thenceforward, they did every week—viz. on Thursday, in the evening. To these and as many more as desired to join with them (for their number increased daily), I gave those

[1] Wesley, *Works*, Vol. VIII, pp. 251-2.

advices from time to time which I judged most needful for them; and we always concluded our meeting with prayer suited to our several necessities. This was the rise of the United Society, first in London, then in other places.[1]

The increase over the next few years was nothing short of phenomenal and indicates the power of the Revival. By June 1741 the figure stood at 900. By 1743 it had soared to 2,200 and eventually the Foundery became the parent of other societies, such as those at Greyhound Lane, Whitechapel, Long Lane, Southwark and Short's Gardens, Drury Lane.

Certain practices were taken over from the Fetter Lane Society. The bands were continued under their leaders, as under the rules of 1738. These met weekly in groups of no more than four or five for the purpose of sharing Christian experience and telling each other's faults "and that plain and home."[2] They were responsible for the expulsion of members. Their discussion was strictly secret: hence "in band" in Methodist parlance is the equivalent of *in camera*. It was to the bands that membership tickets were originally issued, no doubt in imitation of the *tesserae* of the primitive Church. Later the distribution of such tokens was transferred to the class meeting. This, the most distinctive of all Methodist groups, represents a practical development from the bands within the Foundery Society. Wesley endeavoured to acquaint himself with the members by writing their names on a roll, by meeting the bands regularly, and by house visitation. But he found the task too great and in April 1741 he had to enlist the aid of leaders. Then in March 1742 Captain Foy's financial proposal at Bristol that members should contribute a penny per week towards the funds, gave Wesley the clue to his pastoral dilemma. "This is the thing," he declared, "the very thing we have wanted all along. The leaders are the persons who may not only receive the contributions but also watch over the souls of their brethren." Thus originated the classes, which proved to be of such "unspeakable usefulness."[3] The appointment of class leaders as the under-shepherds of the flock was to prove one of the inspired innovations of the Methodist movement. "As soon as possible the same method was used in London and all other places," Wesley informs us. "Evil men were detected and reproved. They were borne with for a season. If they forsook their sins, we received them gladly; if they obstinately persisted therein, it was openly declared that they were not

[1] Ibid., p. 269.
[2] Ibid., p. 272.
[3] Wesley, *Letters*, Vol. II, p. 296.

of us. The rest mourned and prayed for them, and yet rejoiced that as far as in us lay the scandal was rolled away from the society."[1] This method spread with the spread of Methodism. A new ministry of the laity had come into being and what Dr. R. W. Dale called "a great and remarkable Church institution"; "perhaps one of the most striking and original of all the fruits of the Revival."[2]

In February 1743 Wesley co-ordinated all his societies throughout the country by drawing up a comprehensive set of regulations. The title is instructive—"The Nature, Design, and General Rules of the United Societies in London, Bristol, King's-wood and Newcastle-upon-Tyne." "The Methodists under Wesley were one people," wrote George Eayrs, "a connexion, united for the same purpose and subject to the same discipline."[3] The Rules are in seven sections, but in fact they comprise only three obligations, expressed in the simplest possible terms. (1) Do no harm. (2) Do good. (3) Attend the ordinances of God. "There is nothing so amazing in this document as its omissions," says Dr. Rattenbury. "Not one word is said about evangelical experience as a necessary qualification for membership in the society; it is assumed that it will be absent with some; the form of godliness was all that was essential, along with the resolution to seek the power. It was a Society not for the converted only, but for the seeker. . . . But what is more amazing is that there was no intellectual or doctrinal test whatever. Anyone could belong to a Methodist society, whatever his theological convictions, so long as he proved himself a sincere seeker after God by doing good, abstaining from harm, and acknowledging the social character of religion by using the means of grace. While these practices, of course, implied certain beliefs, it was the practice that was demanded, not the creed. The Methodist tenets were, and are, ethical and social."[4] Dr. Rattenbury goes on to show that this is best brought out in Wesley's tract, *The Character of a Methodist*.

> The distinguishing marks of a Methodist are not his opinions of any sort. Whoever imagines a Methodist is a man of such or such an opinion is grossly ignorant of the whole affair: he mistakes the truth totally. We believe indeed that "all Scripture is given by inspiration of God"; and herein we are distinguished from Jews, Turks and infidels. We believe the written Word of God to be the only and sufficient rule both of Christian faith and practice; and herein we are

[1] Ibid., pp. 296-7.
[2] R. W. Dale, *The Evangelical Revival, and Other Sermons*, p. 31.
[3] *New History of Methodism*, Vol. I, p. 285.
[4] Rattenbury, *Wesley's Legacy to the World*, pp. 113-14.

fundamentally distinguished from those of the Romish Church. We believe Christ to be the eternal, supreme God; and herein we are distinguished from the Socinians and Arians. But as to all opinions which do not strike at the root of Christianity, we think and let think. . . . You ask me, Who is a Methodist according to your own account? I answer—A Methodist is one who has "the love of God shed abroad in his heart by the Holy Ghost given" unto him; one who "loves the Lord his God with all his heart, with all his soul, with all his mind, and with all his strength". . . . And while he exercises his love to God by praying without ceasing, rejoicing evermore, and in everything giving thanks, this commandment is written in his heart, "That he who loveth God, love his brother also".[1]

There is a subtlety about the Rules which some have mistaken for inconsistency. Is not this a counsel of perfection and therefore of despair? How can the man who merely desires to be saved but has not yet actually entered into the experience of salvation, ever hope to fulfil these conditions, however simple they may appear to be? Is it possible to display this form without the power? From his own religious experience Wesley knew well enough the futility of work-righteousness. His Rules were devised at once to test the saved and to challenge the unsaved. They fulfilled the double function of the law. He was not blind to the peril of such an apparently liberal charter, yet he never saw any need to alter it and even as late as 1788 he could rejoice in its uniqueness.

The Foundery Society represents Methodism in microcosm. The Rules of the United Societies were simply an extension of this localized polity. Within the space of a few brief years there emerged all the main features of Methodism as it was to be. Not only was the condition of membership laid down and bands and classes formed, but the Love Feast, the Watchnight and the Covenant service were transplanted from their Moravian background. Lay preaching was regularized at the Foundery when first Maxfield and then Richards and Westell were commissioned. By 1744 the number had risen to forty. In that same year the first Methodist Conference was also held at the Foundery and the organization of Methodism was virtually complete. Within five years the shape of things to come had been determined. And through it all, Wesley could declare: "I have one point in view— to promote, so far as I am able, vital, practical religion, and by the grace of God to beget, preserve and increase the life of God in the soul of man."[2]

[1] Wesley, *Works*, Vol. VIII, pp. 340-3.
[2] Wesley, *Letters*, Vol. III, p. 192.

So much, then for Methodism in a nutshell at the Foundery. We must next take a glance at the broader scene of Wesley's mission to Britain. The entire country was divided into circuits, or preacher's rounds, as they were called. John Bennett's Round, for instance, laid the foundation of Methodism in Cheshire. Here is his own description: "My circuit is one hundred and fifty-two miles in two weeks, during which time I preach publicly thirty-four times, besides meeting the societies and visiting the sick."[1] The first printed list in 1746 conveys some idea of the extensiveness of the circuits.

1. LONDON (which includes Surrey, Kent, Essex, Brentford, Egham, Windsor, Wycombe).
2. BRISTOL (which includes Somersetshire, Portland, Wiltshire, Oxfordshire, Gloucestershire).
3. CORNWALL.
4. EVESHAM (which includes Shrewsbury, Leominster, Hereford, and from Stroud to Wednesbury).
5. YORKSHIRE (which includes Cheshire, Lancashire, Derbyshire, Nottingham, Rutlandshire, Lincolnshire).
6. NEWCASTLE.
7. WALES.

The circuits were supervised by superintendents. These were the more experienced of Wesley's preachers, or Assistants. It was their duty "in the absence of the Minister, to feed and guide, to teach and govern the flock,"[2] and to lead the other preachers in the circuit. From 1748 onwards the societies within a circuit met quarterly to discuss its temporal and spiritual affairs.

 The itinerants moved around all the circuits as Wesley decided. Some of them were lay preachers. Some were in holy orders. Some were known as half-itinerants, devoting part of their time to this work. They were virtually travelling evangelists. The qualifications laid down for their appointment sufficiently indicate their character:

1. Do they know in whom they have believed? Have they the love of God in their hearts? Do they desire and seek nothing but God? ...
2. Have they gifts (as well as grace) for the work? ...
3. Have they success? Do they not only so speak as generally either to convince or affect the hearts, but have any received remission of their sins by their preaching? a clear and lasting sense of the love of God?[3]

For these the Twelve Rules of a Helper were drawn up.

[1] *New History of Methodism*, Vol. I, p. 298.
[2] Ibid., pp. 298-9.
[3] Wesley, *Works*, Vol. VIII, pp. 324-5.

Wesley strongly insisted on the need for regular pulpit change. "I know were I to preach one whole year in one place, I should preach both my congregation and myself asleep. Nor can I believe it was ever the will of the Lord that any congregation should have one teacher only. We have found, by long and constant experience, that a frequent change of teachers is best. This preacher has one talent, that another. No one whom I ever yet knew has all the talents which are needful for beginning, continuing and perfecting the work of grace in one whole congregation."[1] Indeed, Wesley went so far as to assert that it was positively harmful for both preacher and people if he stayed in one place for more than six or eight weeks. "Neither can he find matter for preaching every morning and evening; nor will the people come to hear him. Hence he grows cold by lying in bed and so do the people. Whereas if he never stays more than a fortnight together in one place, he may find matter enough, and the people will gladly hear him."[2] The reference to morning preaching touches on another of Wesley's insistences. John Eliot, the apostle of the Red Indians, used to say to students, "Look to it that ye be morning birds!" and Wesley made the selfsame recommendation, as an aid to health, as well as for its spiritual value. He himself preached regularly at five a.m. and urged his itinerants to do the same. "Morning preaching," he claimed, "that is the glory of the Methodists. Whenever the morning preaching is given up, the glory is departed from us."[3]

In his eighty-second year Wesley indulged in reminiscence:

I was now considering how strangely the grain of mustard seed, planted about fifty years ago, has grown up. It has spread through all Great Britain and Ireland: the Isle of Wight and the Isle of Man; then to America from the Leeward Islands, through the whole continent, into Canada and Newfoundland. And the societies, in all these parts, walk by one rule, knowing religion is holy tempers, and striving to worship God, not in forms only, but likewise in spirit and in truth.[4]

The blessed effects of this phenomenal spread are no less notable. Wesley depicted them in his sermon at the foundation of City Road Chapel:

Multitudes have been thoroughly convinced of sin; and, shortly after, so filled with joy and love, that whether they were in the body, or out of the body, they could hardly tell; and, in the power of this

[1] Wesley, *Letters*, Vol. II, p. 195.
[2] Ibid.
[3] Ibid., Vol. VIII, p. 177.
[4] Wesley, *Journal*, Vol. VII, p. 59.

love, they have trampled under foot whatever the world counts either terrible or desirable, having evidenced, in the severest trials, an invariable and tender good-will to mankind, and all the fruits of holiness. Now, so deep a repentance, so strong a faith, so fervent love, and so unblemished holiness, wrought in so many persons in so short a time, the world has not seen for many ages.[1]

It was Wesley's vision of a world parish which ultimately led to the spread of Methodism beyond the boundaries of the Established Church. It is not without significance that the drastic step of ordination was taken in answer to the pressing challenge of the evangelistic opportunity in America. But the probability of separation was present from the very start. Indeed, it clearly appears in the letter to James Hervey in which Wesley embraced the whole world as his parish. "Permit me to speak plainly," he said, in reply to an appeal to catholic principles. "If by catholic principles you mean any other than Scriptural, they weigh nothing with me. I allow no other rule, whether of faith or practice, than the Holy Scriptures; but, on Scriptural principles, I do not think it hard to justify whatever I do. God in Scripture commands me, according to my power, to instruct the ignorant, reform the wicked, confirm the virtuous. Man forbids me to do this in another's parish; that is, in effect, to do it at all; seeing I have now no parish of my own, nor probably ever shall."[2] That was written so soon as March 1739 and it reflects Wesley's undeviating position. It was on this precise issue of ecclesiastical order that the Methodists were eventually to part company from the Church of England. They were not ejected. Canon Overton was quite justified in rebutting such a charge. Indeed, as the years passed, the tensity of the situation was somewhat eased. In his old age Wesley commented quizzically, "Somehow I have become an honourable man!" But whilst the Methodists were never officially excommunicated, their distinctive work was hampered at almost every stage. Pulpits were closed to their ordained preachers and the clergy were often to the fore in rallying opposition. The attitude of officialdom was more remote and less violent, but at no time was it actively sympathetic and helpful. "Considered in retrospect," wrote Henry Carter, "it is astonishing that this nation-wide revival of spiritual religion, extending throughout half a century under the preaching and teaching of the Wesleys and a few brother clergy, evoked no considered episcopal effort to aid or guide it, or to retain the immense

[1] Wesley, *Works*, Vol. VII, p. 426.
[2] Wesley, *Letters*, Vol. I, pp. 285-6.

body of converts organically within the ministrations of the Anglican Church."[1] It was, in fact, only the personal effort of the Wesleys which held the people called Methodists to the Establishment. But from the first the tendency of the large majority lay in the direction of nonconformity.

It is apparent from the Minutes of the first Conference held in 1744 that even at such an early date the question of secession was being canvassed. Indeed the question was directly put: "Do we separate from the Church?" "We conceive not," was the recorded reply. "We hold communion therewith for conscience' sake, by constant attending both the Word preached and the sacraments administered therein."[2] The conscience of Wesley was evidently imposed upon his followers, who were unlikely to have displayed such scrupulosity of their own accord. The answer to a further query is even more significant:

Do you not entail a schism on the Church, i.e. is it not probable that your hearers after your death will be scattered into all sects and parties? or that they will form themselves into a distinct sect?

(1) We are persuaded the body of our hearers will, even after our death, remain in the Church unless they be thrust out. (2) We believe notwithstanding either that they will be thrust out, or that they will leaven the whole Church. (3) We do, and will do, all we can to prevent those consequences which are supposed likely to happen after our death. (4) But we cannot with good conscience neglect the present opportunity of saving souls while we live, for fear of consequences which may possibly or probably happen after we are dead.[3]

In thus remaining faithful to his own maxim, "Church or no Church, we must save souls," Wesley, despite his personal loyalty to the Church of England, enunciated the principle which almost inevitably led to separation.

Three years later, the Conference, whilst reaffirming its adherence to the Establishment, declared that it was aware of no Scriptural justification for a national Church or for the divine right of episcopacy. It was agreed that no single, determinative plan of Church government is discoverable in the Word of God and that there was no thought of uniformity until the time of Constantine. When Wesley later read Edward Stillingfleet's *Irenicum*, he only found his own views confirmed. "I think he has unanswerably proved that neither Christ nor His Apostles pre-

---

[1] H. Carter, *The Methodist Heritage*, p. 152.
[2] J. S. Simon, *John Wesley and the Methodist Societies*, p. 212.
[3] Ibid., p. 213.

scribed any particular form of Church government, and that the divine right of episcopacy was never heard of in the Primitive Church."[1] He had already been convinced by Lord Peter King's *Account of the Primitive Church*, read in 1746, and made this comment in his *Journal*: "In spite of the vehement prejudice of my education, I was ready to believe that this was a fair and impartial draught; but, if so, it would follow that Bishops and presbyters are (essentially) of one order, and that originally every Christian congregation was a church independent on all others."[2]

The theoretical disruption had already taken place in Wesley's mind. There was no strong inclination within the societies to cling to the Church. It is not therefore surprising that at various points in its development Methodism allowed itself to be drawn further and yet further from Anglicanism. We cannot concentrate the separation on the single issue of Wesley's ordinations. A number of prior factors had already determined the course of Methodism virtually beyond recall. The employment of un-ordained preachers; the planned invasion of parishes under the itinerant system; the setting up of a connexional organization as distinct from the Anglican constitution; the erection of rooms and preaching places; and from 1760 the administration of Holy Communion on such unconsecrated premises—all these contributed to the ultimate secession and drove a wedge between Methodists and Evangelicals within the Revival movement. "The grand breach," Wesley wrote in 1761, "is now between the regular and irregular clergy."[3]

The year 1784 was to provide the culmination of this process of disengagement. On 2nd September Wesley ordained Thomas Coke as superintendent of the work in America, with Richard Whatcoat and Thomas Vasey as assistants. The Rubicon was crossed. When Charles Wesley heard of what had happened he recalled the epigrammatic comment of Lord Chief Justice Mansfield that "ordination is separation." and this seemed to sum up the significance of the step. That the theological conclusions which John had reached thirty years ago prompted his action now is evident from his defence before Charles. "I firmly believe I am a Scriptural *episkopos* as much as any man in England or in Europe; for the uninterrupted succession I know to be a fable, which no man ever did or can prove."[4] In the same year the Deed of Declara-

---

[1] Wesley, *Letters*, Vol. III, p. 182.
[2] Wesley, *Journal*, Vol. III, p. 232.
[3] Wesley, *Letters*, Vol. IV, p. 143.
[4] Ibid., Vol. VII, p. 284.

tion supplied Methodism with legal status as an independent, corporate and continuing body, and in 1787 the licensing of the preaching places under the Toleration Act conceded the point that the Methodists were in fact Dissenters. After Wesley's death, the Plan of Pacification in 1795 completed the secession.

Thus the spread of Methodism carried Wesley's followers not only beyond the shores of England but also beyond the shores of the Church of England. It would seem that the freedom of the Spirit made such an expansion inevitable. There is a sense in which the Methodists did not leave the Anglican fold, for they never really belonged to it. In this conclusion we find both High Churchman and Evangelical Methodist at one as, with Dr. Simon, we compare the statements of Canon Overton and Dr. J. H. Rigg. "It is a purely modern notion that the Wesleyan movement ever was—or ever was intended to be, except by Wesley—a Church movement,"[1] said the one. "Methodism, therefore, as an organization was altogether outside the Church of England during Wesley's own lifetime,"[2] said the other. Nevertheless, it was this "peculiar people" who were unmistakably blessed and used of God in furthering His purposes and it is in its contribution to the Evangelical Revival as a whole that Methodism finds at once its vindication and its *raison d'être*.

[1] J. H. Overton and F. Relton, *The History of the English Church from the Accession of George I to the end of the Eighteenth Century*, p. 75.
[2] J. H. Rigg, *Is Modern Methodism Wesleyan Methodism?*, p. 6.

CHAPTER XII

THE CALVINISTIC WING

W E HAVE ALREADY NOTED THE WAY IN WHICH PREBENDARY Curteis distinguished three separate though similar agencies engaged in the promotion of revival in the eighteenth century. There was the Moravian mission which we have now examined. There was what he called the High Church or Arminian mission under the Wesleys. This, too, we have outlined, though we have described it as Methodist or Wesleyan rather than associating it with the Laudian reform. But there was also the Calvinistic mission, under Whitefield and Lady Huntingdon. This will occupy our next two chapters, for it represents an outgrowth from Methodism in the same fashion in which Methodism was an outgrowth from Moravianism. To his list Curteis might have added the Evangelical mission, although this was the least organized of all.

The theological affiliation of each of these strands, whilst true to the Reformation tradition, reflected varying aspects of that rootage. The Moravians, of course, were largely Lutheran. The Methodists were classed as Arminian, although this categorization needs to be re-examined. The Anglicans were mostly moderate Calvinists, although again this is a designation not to be accepted uncritically. There did grow up, however, within the framework of the Revival movement a party associated with the names of George Whitefield and the Countess of Huntingdon, and yet distinct from the regular Church Evangelicals, which assumed a more emphatically Calvinistic position. It is to the emergence of this group that we are now to devote attention.

In a sense it is one of the saddening features of the Revival, for it represents a rupture of the original unity. One of the recognizable traits of genuine revival lies in the realization of oneness which prevails amongst Christian brethren irrespective of their denominational or doctrinal attachment. "Names, and sects, and parties fall" and the Holy Spirit effects a truly ecumenical integration. "It is gloriously impossible for those who are reconciled to

God in Christ Jesus," wrote John Bonar in a glowing passage, "to be permanently unreconciled to one another, and a time of revival, bringing out all the great realities in which they are at one, and sinking all the minor points on which they are divided, has a blessed tendency to unite their hearts, and so gradually to unite their hand in the work of the Lord."[1] It is significant that during the years of visitation in the eighteenth century, when the power of the Spirit descended upon the quiet in the land, the clash of party strife was stilled. It was only as something of the first fine careless rapture disappeared and the more prosaic tasks involved in continuous evangelism were undertaken that divisions began to make themselves unfortunately evident.

Yet it must not be imagined that the Calvinistic controversy, which not only caused a rift in the Methodist movement, but more widely affected the Revival as a whole, was guilty of creating mountains out of molehills. It was not a dispute over unessential trivialities. As Ronald Knox reminds us, "the point at issue was not—as it was between the Dominicans and the Jesuits—one of abstract theology, it was a burning question that touched the very heart of the Revival's message."[2] Nor was it confined exclusively to the mysterious issue of predestination and election. The debate included all the five points of the Quinquarticular controversy of the previous century, which revolved round the Remonstrance against which the Dutch Arminians protested. Is election conditional upon the foreknowledge of God or it is absolute and predetermined by the inflexible decrees of the Almighty? Is the atonement universal in that it was effected for all, irrespective of whether its benefits are appropriated by all, or is redemption limited to the elect? Is the fall of man such that he is still susceptible to the operation of prevenient grace and capable of responding to the divine overture, or is it so complete that man is altogether unable to exercise saving faith? Is the grace of God not only indispensable but also irresistible and indefectible, so that the elect are assured of final perseverance? Is the righteousness of Christ imputed or imparted to the believer, or both? These are some of the issues involved.

The heart of it, however, concerns the age-old controversy as to whether the absolute sovereignty of God's purpose is compatible with the freedom of man's will. This dilemma has provided the subject of continuing dispute in the Church of the West since the

[1] *Lectures on the Revival of Religion, by Ministers of the Church of Scotland*, p. 19.
[2] Knox, *op. cit.*, p. 495.

time of Augustine. It was raised again at the Reformation and it is
not altogether surprising that in a season of evangelical renascence
it should recur, for it is an issue which seems acute only to those
who are seeking to interest their fellowmen in salvation. Since the
terms Calvinist and Arminian were bandied about as freely in the
eighteenth century as they tend to be today, it is wise to be aware
of their precise connotation. There is a danger lest they should be
employed unthinkingly as smear words in the dogmatic contest.
Wesley pleaded that each party should refrain from using these
titles in a derogatory manner. The term Calvinism should be
strictly confined to the teaching of John Calvin himself, as, along
with Luther and the rest of the reformers, he denied free will after
the Fall, and added his own distinctive emphasis upon the in-
amissibility of grace, the certitude of eternal salvation for the
elect and the stringency of predestination in respect both of the
regenerate and the reprobate. Similarly the term Arminianism
should be reserved for the teaching of Jacobus Arminius (Jakob
Harmensen) of Leyden in his insistence that the divine sovereignty
was compatible with real freedom in man and that the atonement
was universal in its scope though not necessarily in its effect.
These same terms, Calvinist and Arminian, are not to be applied
indiscriminately to all the self-accredited followers of these men
unless they stand in an undeviating succession.

With these provisos in mind, let us return to the eighteenth
century and the doctrinal logomachy between Wesley and Whitefield. 1740 was a fateful year in the history of the Revival. It saw
the separation of Methodists from Moravians, and it also marked
the beginning of the further disruption of Methodism itself into
two wings, Arminian and Calvinistic. A month before the Fetter
Lane secession, a leading member of the London society, named
Acourt, complained that he had been refused admission by Charles
Wesley on the ground that he differed from the Wesleys in opinion.
When John later enquired what the particular opinion was,
Acourt replied, "That of election. I hold that a certain number are
elected from eternity, and these must and shall be saved, and the
rest of mankind must and shall be damned." He added, moreover,
that many of the society thought as he did. This Wesley did not
attempt to deny or denounce. In such matters of opinion he was
prepared to advocate a policy of peaceful coexistence. Charles had
only ordered Acourt's dismissal because the latter wished to make
a dispute of the issue. John therefore begged Acourt not to insist
upon his Calvinistic views. "Nay, but I will dispute about it,"

he replied doggedly. "Why, then," enquired Wesley, "would you come among us, whom you know to be of another mind?" "Because you are all wrong, and I am resolved to set you all right." "I fear," returned Wesley, "your coming to us with this view would neither profit you nor us." "Then," retorted Acourt, "I will go and tell all the world that you and your brother are false prophets. And I tell you in one fortnight you will all be in confusion." This, then, was the issue which would not be concealed and which ultimately led to the breach between Wesley and Whitefield.

Prior to Whitefield's first visit to America, he and the Wesleys had worked together with the utmost goodwill and harmony. No serious doctrinal disparity appeared. But in New England Whitefield came into contact with a number of Calvinistic ministers who introduced him to the writings of the great Puritan divines. These he read with avidity and heartily embraced their teaching.[1] No doubt his convictions were confirmed by consultation with Jonathan Edwards, but already he had declared his allegiance and had begun to preach election and predestination. He candidly confessed that he had never seen a single line of Calvin, but that he accepted the "Calvinistical scheme" because he considered it to be the most Scriptural.[2] "Alas," he admitted to Wesley, "I never read anything Calvin wrote; my doctrines I had from Christ and His apostles: I was taught them of God."[3] Certainly by the summer of 1739 Whitefield was setting forth these truths in his sermons. "Man is nothing," he declared, "he hath a free will to go to hell, but none to go to heaven, till God worketh in him to will and to do."[4] Man could no more contribute to his own salvation than he could "turn the world upside down" or "measure the moon for a suit of clothes."[5] This stress upon man's total inability to save himself seemed to demand as its only logical consequence that salvation is reserved for the chosen few.

Hence it occasions no surprise that later in the same year Whitefield confessed that the doctrines of "election, and free justification in Christ Jesus" were increasingly pressed upon his heart.[6] In his great sermon on "The Seed of the Woman and the Seed of the Serpent" he took Archbishop Tillotson to task for treating

---

[1] Southey, *op. cit.*, p. 225n.
[2] Whitefield, *Works*, Vol. I, p. 442.
[3] Ibid., p. 205.
[4] Ibid., p. 495.
[5] Whitefield, *Eighteen Sermons*, pp. 6-7.
[6] Whitefield, *Works*, Vol. I, p. 79.

Genesis 3 : 15 as a second covenant with Adam, "made, as the first was, of some mercies to be afforded by God, and some duties to be performed by us."[1]

> This is exceedingly false divinity [argued Whitefield], for these words are not spoken to Adam: they are directed only to the serpent. Adam and Eve stood by as criminals, and God could not treat with them, because they had broken His covenant. And it is so far from being a covenant wherein "some mercies are to be afforded by God, and some duties to be performed by us", that here is not a word looking that way; it is only a declaration of the free gift of salvation through Jesus Christ our Lord. . . . God, therefore, to secure the second covenant from being broken, puts it into the hands of the second Adam, the Lord from heaven. . . . The truth is this: God, as a reward of Christ's sufferings, promised to give the elect faith and repentance, in order to bring them to eternal life: and both these, and everything else necessary for their everlasting happiness, are infallibly secured to them in this promise.

"This is a consistent Scripture scheme," he concluded; "without holding this, we must run into one of these two bad extremes; I mean, Antinomianism on the one hand, or Arminianism on the other: from both which may the good Lord deliver us."[2]

If Whitefield's views had crystallized by 1739, those of Wesley had been formulated even so far back as 1725 when he had corresponded with his mother on this very subject.

> What, then, shall I say of predestination? [he had enquired]. An everlasting purpose of God to deliver some from damnation does, I suppose, exclude all from that deliverance who are not chosen. And if it is inevitably decreed from eternity that such a determinate part of mankind should be saved, and none beside them, a vast majority of the world were only born to eternal death, without so much as a possibility of avoiding it. How is this consistent with either divine justice or mercy? Is it merciful to ordain a creature to everlasting misery? Is it just to punish man for crimes which he could not but commit? How is man, if necessarily determined to one way of acting, a free agent? To lie under a physical or a moral necessity is entirely repugnant to human liberty. But that God should be the author of sin and injustice (which must, I think, be the consequence of maintaining this opinion) is a contradiction to the clearest ideas we have of the divine nature and perfections.[3]

It is evident that Wesley's acute logical mind was probing the mystery, but that he had not yet made that necessary submission of reason to the World of God which would lead him to a more

---

[1] *Select Sermons*, p. 93.
[2] Ibid., pp. 93-4.
[3] Wesley, *Letters*, Vol. I, pp. 22-3.

Scriptural approach to this controverted topic. In this respect his mother's reply is instructive, for it obviously played no small part in leading him to his ultimate position. She began by saying that the subject is beyond the wit of man to fathom and that such enquiries tend to confound rather than inform the understanding. She firmly rejected the rigid Calvinist view on the ground that it directly charges God with responsibility for sin. Then she proceeded to enlarge upon her own version.

> I verily believe that God, from eternity, has elected some to eternal life; but then I humbly conceive that this election is founded on His foreknowledge, according to Romans 8 : 29, 30. Whom, in His eternal prescience, God saw would make a right use of their powers, and accept of offered mercy, He did predestinate and adopt for His children. And that they may be conformed to the image of His only Son, He calls them to Himself, through the preaching of the Gospel, and internally, by His Holy Spirit; which call they obeying, repenting of their sins and believing in the Lord Jesus, He justifies them, absolves them from the guilt of all their sins, and acknowledges them as just and righteous persons, through the merits and mediation of Jesus Christ. And having thus justified them, He receives them to glory—heaven. This is the sum of what I believe concerning predestination, which I think is agreeable to the analogy of faith; since it does in no wise derogate from the glory of God's free grace, nor impair the liberty of man. Nor can it with more reason be supposed that the prescience of God is the cause that so many finally perish, than that one knowing the sun will rise tomorrow is the cause of its rising.[1]

Incidentally, as Dr. W. R. Cannon reminds us, these views, so typical of the English Arminian school, were also expressed by Samuel Wesley. "God made man upright," he wrote, "and a free agent. God's prescience presides over man's free agency, but doth not overrule it by saving man whether he will or no, or by damning him undeservingly."[2] These, substantially, were the inherited views of John Wesley at the outbreak of the Calvinistic controversy in 1740. There is no evidence that his evangelical conversion radically altered his convictions on this subject.

It seems that Wesley and Whitefield had entered into a gentleman's agreement to refrain from pressing their differences. Before Whitefield left on his second voyage to America he heard that Wesley was thinking of publishing a sermon on predestination, and he twice begged him to abandon the idea. Wesley wrote to him opposing the Calvinist doctrine of election and insisting upon

[1] Tyerman, *Wesley*, Vol. I, p. 40.
[2] W. R. Cannon, *The Theology of John Wesley*, pp. 45-6.

the possibility of entire sanctification. This brought an earnest response from Whitefield in Savannah:

> For once hearken to a child who is willing to wash your feet. I beseech you, by the mercies of God in Christ Jesus our Lord, if you would have my love confirmed towards you, write no more to me about misrepresentations wherein we differ. To the best of my knowledge, at present, no sin has *dominion* over me; yet I feel the strugglings of indwelling sin day by day. I can, therefore, by no means come unto your interpretation of the passage mentioned in your letter, and as explained in your preface to Mr. Halyburton. If possible, I am ten thousand times more convinced of the doctrine of election, and the final perseverance of those that are truly in Christ, than when I saw you last. You think otherwise. Why then should we dispute, when there is no probability of convincing? Will it not, in the end, destroy brotherly love, and insensibly take from us that cordial union and sweetness of soul, which I pray God may always subsist between us? How glad would the enemies of the Lord be to see us divided! How many would rejoice, should I join and make a party against you! How would the cause of our common Master suffer by our raising disputes about particular points of doctrines! Honoured sir, let us offer salvation freely to all by the blood of Jesus; and whatever light God has communicated to us, let us freely communicate to others.[1]

This plea was reiterated in a further letter:

> The more I examine the writings of the most experienced men, and experiences of the most established Christians, the more I differ from your notion about not committing sin, and your denying the doctrines of election and final perseverance of the saints. I dread coming to England, unless you are resolved to oppose these truths with less warmth than when I was there last. I dread your coming over to America, because the work of God is carried on here (and that in a most glorious manner) by doctrines quite opposite to those you hold.[2]

Wesley's reply seems curt, not to say cryptic. No doubt he felt that he was doing a great work and could not descend into controversy.

> My dear Brother, I thank you for yours of May 24th. The case is quite plain. There are bigots for predestination and against it. God is sending a message to those on either side. But neither will receive it, unless from one who is of their own opinion. Therefore, for a time, you are suffered to be of one opinion, and I of another. But when His time is come, God will do what man cannot, make us both of one mind. Then persecution will flame out, and it will be seen whether we count our lives dear unto ourselves, so that we may finish our course with joy.[3]

[1] Whitefield, *Works*, Vol. I, p. 156.
[2] Ibid., p. 182.   [3] Wesley, *Letters*, Vol. I, p. 351.

Yet despite Whitefield's impassioned appeals and Wesley's apparent readiness to hold his polemical horses in the interests of evangelical unity, a step had already been taken which, when made public, precipitated a crisis that one suspects was virtually unavoidable. Wesley gave an account of the matter in a letter to James Hutton in May 1739. He indicated that he was in some considerable doubt as to how he ought to proceed. Not only Whitefield but the members of the London Society and William Chapman of Bath had unanimously urged him to enter into no dispute. And this was his own inclination, too, until he received a long anonymous letter accusing him of "resisting and perverting the truth as it is in Christ Jesus by preaching against the decree of predestination."[1] Wesley maintained that as yet he had done no such thing, but that he now began to wonder whether he ought not to speak out on this matter and declare the whole counsel of God, as he saw it. As was his custom in a dilemma, he had recourse to sortilege. The lot directed him both to preach and print.[2] On the following Sunday we learn from the *Journal* that he "declared the free grace of God to about four thousand people,"[3] from Romans 8 : 32. This was the famous sermon which, as Piette put it, constituted a declaration of war on the eternal decrees.[4]

It was not, however, the preaching of it that raised the storm: it was its publication in the following year, hot on the heels of Whitefield's persistent pleas to avoid controversy. It appeared as a twenty-four page booklet with Charles Wesley's "Hymn of Universal Redemption" appended. Southey called it "the most able and eloquent of all his discourses; a triumphant specimen of impassioned argument."[5] Lord Liverpool believed that portions of it were unsurpassed either in ancient or modern oratory. Quite apart from its merits as a piece of sustained and animated persuasion, measured by the consequences which ensued it must be reckoned as one of Wesley's most significant utterances. Space does not permit any lengthy review of it. From the start Wesley made it clear that this was a question of unshakeable personal belief.

Nothing but the strongest conviction, not only that what is here advanced is "the truth as it is in Jesus", but also that I am indis-

---

[1] *Messenger*, 1877, p. 99.
[2] This seems to have been on Thursday 26 May 1739. Cf note in Diary: "12 appealed to God concerning Predestination" (Wesley, *Journal*, Vol. II, p. 184n.).
[3] Ibid., p. 185.
[4] Piette, *op. cit.*, p. 362.
[5] Southey, *op. cit.*, p. 486.

pensably obliged to declare this truth to all the world, could have induced me openly to oppose the sentiments of those whom I esteem for their work's sake; at whose feet may I be found in the day of the Lord Jesus.

"How freely does God love the world?" he enquired from his text as he came to grips with his theme, and laid down this fundamental principle: "The grace or love of God, whence cometh our salvation, is free in all and free for all."[1] It was the latter affirmation which led him to weigh in the balances and find wanting the various shades of predestinarian belief.

> Call it therefore by whatever name you please, "election, preterition, predestination, or reprobation," it comes in the end to the same thing. The sense of all is plainly this—by virtue of an eternal, unchangeable, irresistible decree of God, one part of mankind are infallibly saved, and the rest infallibly damned; it being impossible that any of the former should be damned, or that any of the latter should be saved.[2]

Wesley then proceeded to list his eight objections to the doctrine. He summed up the matter thus.

> This is the blasphemy clearly contained in the horrible decree of predestination. And here I fix my foot. On this I join issue with every asserter of it. You represent God as worse than the devil. But you say, you will prove it from Scripture. Hold! What will you prove by Scripture? That God is worse than the devil?. . . But it cannot be. Whatever that Scripture proves, it can never prove this; whatever its true meaning be, this cannot be its true meaning. Do you ask, "What is its true meaning then?" If I say, "I know not," you have gained nothing; for there are many Scriptures, the true sense of which neither you nor I shall know till death is swallowed up in victory. But this I know, better it were to say it had no sense at all, than to say it had such a sense as this.[3]

The publication of this forthright sermon set the Arminian cat amongst the Calvinistic pigeons.[4] Soon a controversy of major magnitude was raging. Angry and embittered responses were soon elicited. At first Whitefield resolved not to be embroiled in this doctrinal battle, but eventually he succumbed to pressure from his friends on both sides of the Atlantic and addressed "A Letter to the Rev. Mr. Wesley: in reply to his sermon entitled Free Grace." In a note scribbled on board the *Minerva* as he sailed for

---

[1] Wesley, *Works*, Vol. VII, p. 373.
[2] Ibid., pp. 375-6.
[3] Ibid., p. 383.
[4] The sermon was preached and published in 1739, not in 1740 as wrongly stated in the *Works*, Vol. VII, p. 373. Cf. Wesley, *Journal*, Vol. II, p. 421n.

home Whitefield told Ralph Erskine that he had endeavoured to answer "dear Mr. Wesley's sermon ... in the spirit of meekness."[1] Meanwhile, he wrote a personal letter to John and Charles explaining his action:

> My dear, dear Brethren, Why did you throw out the bone of contention? Why did you print that sermon against predestination? Why did you, in particular, my dear Brother Charles, affix your hymn and join in putting out your late hymn book?[2] How can you say you will not dispute with me about election, and yet print such hymns, and your brother send his sermon against election to Mr. Garden, and others in America? Do you not think, my dear brethren, I must be as much concerned for truth, or what I think truth, as you?[3]

Then he told them that he had published a reply and ended:

> If it occasion a strangeness between us, it is not my fault. There is nothing in my answer exciting to it, that I know of. O my dear brethren, my heart almost bleeds within me! Methinks I could be willing to tarry here on the waters forever, rather than come to England to oppose you.[4]

Although the spirit of this and other letters is, as Tyerman concedes, admirable, it is quite obvious that Whitefield had not been moved a single inch from his attachment to the Calvinist interpretation of election and predestination.[5] He may not have been able to match Wesley's incisive logic, but he took an unambiguous stand, as he supposed, on the Word of God. This he charged Wesley with failing to do. Referring to Wesley's use of the lot to decide whether or not to preach free grace, he said:

> I have often questioned, as I do now, whether, in so doing, you did not tempt the Lord. A due exercise of religious prudence, without the lot, would have directed you in that matter. Besides, I never heard that you enquired of God whether or not election was a gospel doctrine. But, I fear, taking it for granted it was not, you only enquired whether you should be silent, or preach and print against it.[6]

Whitefield contended as vigorously for free grace as Wesley did, but by it he meant, "free because not free to all; but free, because God may withhold or give it to whom and when He pleases."[7]

---

[1] Tyerman, *Whitefield*, Vol. I, p. 462.
[2] In 1740 had appeared *Hymns and Sacred Poems* including certain stanzas on universal redemption and a preface by John Wesley expounding the doctrine of Christian perfection.
[3] Tyerman, *Whitefield*, Vol. I, p. 465.
[4] Ibid.
[5] Ibid., p. 471.
[6] Ibid., p. 469.
[7] Ibid., p. 471.

No doubt the over-zealous advisers of the leading protagonists must bear much of the responsibility for intensifying the unfortunate dispute. Certainly neither Wesley nor Whitefield wished to create a schism within the Revival movement over the issue. Such divergences as existed between them in matters of doctrine are reconciled in the totality of Scriptural truth and it ought to have been possible for both vewpoints to be amicably contained within the one body of believers. But this was not to be. As in the case of Wesley's sermon, so in that of Whitefield's letter, it was injudicious publication which made reconciliation more difficult. When Whitefield showed the manuscript to Charles Wesley, the latter handed back the sheets with the wise advice, "Put up thy sword into its scabbard!" The letter, however, was printed without Whitefield's knowledge or permission and a large number of copies were distributed at the Foundery by his misguided supporters. John Wesley took one into the pulpit with him and after his sermon related the facts of the case. Then he told them, "I will do just what I believe Mr. Whitefield would do if he were here himself." He then tore the pages into shreds and everyone else in the congregation followed suit. In a couple of minutes the scene resembled an indoor snowstorm. But though Wesley's was a gesture of conciliation in its refusal to believe that Whitefield would wittingly have publicized his letter, the wholesale tearing up of the pamphlet was misinterpreted as a declaration of war. "On that day," says Piette, "there took place the irreparable scission in the work of the revival."[1]

Later, in March 1741, Wesley went to see Whitefield and in that critical interview the two evangelists agreed to go their separate ways. Whitefield told Wesley that they preached two different gospels and that therefore he could no longer unite with him in the work. Moreover, he felt compelled to preach against the Methodist doctrines wherever he went. So came "the parting of friends" which Knox describes so sympathetically and with such discernment.[2] "Here was the first breach," commented Wesley sadly, "which warm men persuaded Mr. Whitefield to make merely for a difference of opinion. Those, indeed, who believed universal redemption had no desire at all to separate; but those who held particular redemption would not hear of any accommodation, being determined to have no fellowship with men that were 'in such dangerous errors.' So there were now two sorts of Methodists, so

[1] Piette, *op. cit.*, p. 365.
[2] Knox, *op. cit.*, pp. 483-512.

called: those for particular, and those for general, redemption."[1]
The coolness between Whitefield and Wesley was not of long
duration. Once they had agreed to differ they allowed no animosity
to mar their relationship. Within the space of eighteen months
Whitefield wrote with his customary breadth of spirit, "Let controversy die. . . It has died with me long ago."[2] When Wesley preached
in the new church built for Whitefield at Plymouth he said, "Thus it
behoveth us all to trample on bigotry and party zeal" and again,
recording a visit from his friend, he added: "Disputings are now
no more; we love one another."[3] And so until Whitefield's death
in 1770 the truce was observed, even if at times it was a little un-
easy. But then the controversy flared up again with redoubled
intensity. That, however, is not our province at the moment. It is
with the consequences of the breach in 1741 that we are occupied.

A new wing was added to the Revival. Henceforward not only
were Methodists distinguished from Anglican Evangelicals, but the
Methodists themselves were sundered into two camps—Arminian
after Wesley and Calvinist after Whitefield. Wesley and Whitefield
had separate congregations and separate meeting places. But the
breach was not hostile. It was recognized that they both sought
the furtherance of God's gracious work, even though for theological reasons they felt unable to be identified. There was continual intercouse between the two parties. Whitefield often
preached for Wesley and scrupulously avoided commending predestination or disparaging perfection. Wesley was welcomed at
Whitefield's tabernacles and also preached in the Countess of
Huntingdon's chapels from 1768 onwards. It does not seem that
the progress of the Awakening was seriously hindered and both
leaders continued to see abundant fruit for their labours. But one
cannot help feeling with Knox that, despite the external indications of amity, the division went deeper than was permitted to
appear, and the fact that the rupture became final in 1771 bears out
his contention that "the inevitable separation was only staved off
by the immense respect which the rival controversialists had for
one another." It was, he adds, "against their own better judge-
ment" that "they persisted in trying to persuade themselves that
their differences were of minor importance. Never were theologians so resolved to make a molehill out of a mountain."[4]

It is pleasant, however, to conclude this chapter with further

[1] Wesley, *Works*, Vol. VIII, p. 349.
[2] Whitefield, *Works*, Vol. I, p. 448.
[3] Wesley, *Journal*, Vol. IV, pp. 79 and 139-40.
[4] Knox, *op. cit.*, p. 496.

instances of the genuine Christian affection which, amidst all the
noise of party strife, yet bound these men of God together. Whitefield's attitude to Wesley is perhaps best reflected in his reply to the
enquiry of a censorious Calvinist who asked whether he thought
they might see John Wesley in heaven. "I fear not," replied Whitefield; "he will be so near the throne, and we shall be at such a
distance, that we shall hardly get a sight of him." It was Wesley
who preached Whitefield's funeral sermon and singled out the
capacity for friendship as the most remarkable trait in his character. "Should we not mention, that he had a heart susceptible of
the most generous and tender *friendship*? I have frequently thought
that this, of all others, was the distinguishing part of his character.
How few have we known of so kind a temper, of such large and
flowing affections! Was it not principally by this that the hearts of
others were so strangely drawn and knit to him? Can anything
but love beget love?"[1] Charles Wesley did well to rejoice, as he
looked upon these two comrades in arms, that "friends at first"
were "friends again at last."[2]

[1] Tyerman, *Whitefield*, Vol. II, pp. 616-17.
[2] C. Wesley, *Poetical Works*, Vol. VI, p. 63.

CHAPTER XIII

THE COUNTESS AND HER CONNEXION

THE INITIAL OUTBREAK OF THE CALVINISTIC CONTROVERSY IN 1740 led to the separation of Whitefield from Wesley and the formation of two distinct parties within the Methodist movement. Even though amicable relations were speedily re-established, the seeds of a more permanent schism had been sown. It is not therefore to be wondered at that when Whitefield died in 1770 the whole unhappy conflict should be renewed. "Over Whitefield's ashes the fire of the great Calvinistic controversy was rekindled," wrote Fitchett, "and burned more fiercely even than at first; perhaps for the reason that this time there was a woman in it!"[1] The woman involved was a remarkable one by any standards and it is high time that in our survey of the Revival we should introduce ourselves to her. Not for nothing was Selina, Countess of Huntingdon, known as the "Queen of the Methodists."

The Awakening boasted both a Count—Zinzendorf—and a Countess, and the influence of the latter was by no means secondary. Lady Huntingdon was, in fact, the patroness of the Revival. Her wealth and power were placed unreservedly and even sacrificially at the disposal of the spiritual leaders of the movement. It was she who protected Evangelical preachers when driven from their pulpits and found them a place in her chapels or drawing-rooms. It was she who opened the door for the proclamation of the gospel amongst the upper classes. It was she who assumed the organizational control of the Calvinistic Methodists, for Whitefield made no real attempt to co-ordinate his evangelistic conquests. It was she, too, who appears as the rallying-point for left-wing Evangelicalism within the Church of England, at least until her secession in 1781.

Her focal position, however, is only now being realized by historians of the period. Knox singles her out as the pivotal figure of the entire group. It would be a capital mistake, he says, to suppose that Wesley, however valuable his contribution to the genius

[1] Fitchett, *op. cit.*, p. 378.

of the Revival may have been, was in any sense the leader of the whole, for he was at issue with the rest on a crucial point of theology. Nor was Whitefield the general of the movement, for it was not his *métier* to be the captain of any cause. There is one single figure, he concludes, which, without dominating the entire picture, interprets and unifies it—that of Lady Huntingdon.[1] More recently still, Elliott-Binns has recognized to the full the prominent and determinative place in the Revival occupied by the Countess. He finds it to be all the more astonishing in view of her sex.

> The wind bloweth where it listeth, and the Spirit of God chooses for its instruments and agents some who in the eyes of men might seem to be the most unlikely subjects. This is perhaps especially marked in the choice of a woman. In the fourteenth century Caterina Berincasa, the daughter of a poor dyer, can be transformed into St. Catherine of Siena, the adviser and reprover of popes; and in the century which followed, a peasant girl from the countryside of Domrémy is raised up to become, as St. Joan of Arc, the saviour of her country. By recalling such examples of the Spirit's working we shall find the career of Lady Huntingdon less inexplicable than otherwise it might seem. That one of the most active and influential leaders of the revival should have been a woman, and a woman of quality, was something that mere human foresight could never have anticipated, for women in the eighteenth century were expected to keep in the background and to submit to the guidance and control of their fathers and husbands.[2]

Horace Walpole christened Lady Huntingdon the St. Teresa of the Methodists and the comparison is apt.[3] Like the Carmelite reformer, the Countess was a woman of strong personality, considerable discernment and outstanding organizational ability.[4]

Selina Shirley was born in 1707, the second daughter of Washington, Earl Ferrers, and in 1728 she married the ninth Earl of Huntingdon. From early childhood she seems to have been of a serious disposition. At the age of nine she was deeply affected at the sight of a funeral procession, which she followed to the grave. "There the first impression of deep seriousness concerning an eternal world took possession of her heart," recorded Seymour, "and with many tears she earnestly implored God, on the spot, that whenever He should be pleased to take her away, He would

---

[1] Knox, *op. cit.*, pp. 483-4.
[2] Elliott-Binns, *Early Evangelicals*, pp. 134-5.
[3] *The Letters of Horace Walpole*, ed. P. Toynbee, Vol. IV, p. 382.
[4] Lady Huntingdon has been unfortunate in her biographers. A worthy account of this mother in Israel has yet to be published. The jumbled and undocumented chronicle of A. C. H. Seymour is still the major source of information.

deliver her from all her fears, and give her a happy departure. She often, afterwards, visited that grave, and always preserved a lively sense of the affecting scene she had there witnessed."[1] After her marriage we are given a glimpse of her as the Lady Bountiful of Donnington Park, presenting to the world the appearance of piety, and yet still a stranger to saving grace.

> She aspired after rectitude, and was anxious to possess every moral perfection—she counted much upon the dignity of human nature, and was anxious to act in a manner becoming her exalted ideas of that dignity. And here her Ladyship outstripped the multitude in an uncommon degree: she was rigidly just in her dealings, and inflexibly true to her word; she was a strict observer of her several duties in every relation of life; her sentiments were liberal, and her charity profuse; she was prudent in her conduct, and courteous in her deportment; she was a diligent enquirer after truth, and a strenuous advocate for virtue; she was frequent in her sacred meditations, and was a regular attendant at public worship. Possessed of so many moral accomplishments while she was admired by the world, it is no wonder that she should cast a look of self-complacency upon her character, and consider herself, with respect to her attainments in virtue, abundantly superior to the common herd of mankind. But while the Countess was taken up in congratulating herself upon her own fancied eminence in piety, she was an absolute stranger to that inward and universal change of heart, wrought by the gracious operations of the Spirit of God, by which new principles are established in the mind, new inclinations are imparted, and new objects pursued.[2]

It was through the witness of her sister-in-law, Lady Margaret Hastings, that Lady Huntingdon was brought to an evangelical conversion. The transformation of Lady Margaret's life became apparent to all and she was immediately eager to testify to her family about Christ. Next to her own soul, the salvation of her relatives was her chief concern. One by one she exhorted them to accept God's provision of redemption in the Lord Jesus. Talking one day with Lady Huntingdon she happened to say that since she had known and believed in Christ for salvation, she had been as happy as an angel. Now Lady Huntingdon could bear no such testimony. For all her external piety, she knew nothing of the joy and peace of believing. She began to examine herself to discover why she lacked such blessed assurance and at the same time she intensified the austerity of self-discipline in order to secure the conviction she desired. But the more she strove the more she

[1] A. C. H. Seymour, *The Life and Times of Selina, Countess of Huntingdon*, Vol. I, p. 8.
[2] Ibid., pp. 10-11.

realized that even her cherished righteousness was but as filthy rags. Soon afterwards a prostrating illness brought her almost to the verge of the tomb and reminded her of her childhood vows. She was led to cast herself solely on Christ, renouncing every other hope. From her sick bed she lifted to heaven the importunate prayer of repentance and faith, and immediately she was at her desired haven.

Now the day began to dawn, Jesus the Sun of Righteousness arose, and burst in meridian splendour on her benighted soul. The scales fell from her eyes, and opened a passage for the light of life which sprang in, and death and darkness fled before it. Viewing herself as a brand plucked from the burning, she could not but stand astonished at the mighty power of that grace which saved her from eternal destruction just when she stood upon its very brink, and raised her from the gates of hell to the confines of heaven; and the depths from which she was raised, made the heights which she reached only the more amazing; she felt the rock beneath her, and from that secure position looked with astonishment downward, to that horrible pit from which she was so mercifully delivered—and upwards, in ecstasy, to that glory to which she should be raised. The "sorrow of the world, which worketh death" was now exchanged for that godly sorrow which worketh repentance unto life; and "joy unspeakable and full of glory" succeeded that bitterness that comes of the conviction of sin; she enjoyed, already, a delightful foretaste of heaven. Her disorder from that moment took a favourable turn; she was restored to perfect health, and, what was better, to newness of life. She determined thenceforward to present herself to God, as a living sacrifice, holy and acceptable, which she was now convinced was her reasonable service.[1]

The exact date of Lady Huntingdon's conversion is not preserved, but it must have occurred sometime in 1738, for from then onwards she joined the Fetter Lane Society, as did her husband, though he did not share all her views. She became the friend and supporter of the Wesleys and accompanied John to the fatal Love Feast in 1740 when he withdrew from the Moravian fellowship. Lady Huntingdon was also instrumental in persuading Charles that such a step was justified. Although she abetted the secession of the Methodists from the Moravians because she disapproved Molther's doctrine of "stillness", she did not condemn the Brethren outright. "Many good souls are among them," she told Philip Doddridge, "and, by and by, the Lord will separate them from the chaff."[2] She sent her Christian salutations to Count Zinzendorf when he was visiting England in 1748 and hoped she

[1] Ibid., p. 15.
[2] Ibid., p. 102.

might have an opportunity "to speak a word in the spirit of love and meekness, but with plainness, to him, on many points he established as fixed, on which, in some particulars, the Scripture is silent; and in many others, it is absolutely contrary to most of their avowed opinions."[1] No doubt the occasion arose when Zinzendorf and his entourage spent a few days at Donnington Park. The fact that Lady Margaret Hastings had married Benjamin Ingham and that the Molther episode had faded into near oblivion smoothed the path for closer co-operation between the Countess and the Moravians as the years went by. David Taylor, who became one of their foremost evangelists, had been a member of her household staff.

If Lady Huntingdon's first association was with the Wesleys it was to George Whitefield that she was more permanently attached. She had heard him preach in London as early as 1736 and he may have had some indirect influence on her conversion. Certainly before his third visit to America in 1744 she had become personally acquainted with him. In one of his letters from Boston he referred to her Ladyship's kindness and his joy at hearing that she remained steadfast in the faith. Again from Bethesda in 1746 he expressed his pleasure to Howell Harris that the Countess had been visiting his Tabernacle. "She shines brighter and brighter every day; and will yet I trust be spared for a nursing mother to Israel. This revives me, after the miserable divisions that have taken place amongst my English friends. I trust the storm is now blown over, and that the little flock will enjoy a calm. Her Ladyship's example and conduct in this trying affair will.be productive of much good."[2] As a friend of the Wesleys and of Whitefield, of Anglican Evangelicals like Romaine and Grimshaw and of Dissenters like Watts and Doddridge, the Countess was in a strategic position to bridge some of the widening gaps in the Revival movement. And this she succeeded in doing for some considerable time. But her increasing predilection for extreme Calvinist opinions also foreshadowed the day when she would be responsible for the final severance of the Whitefieldite group from the Wesleyan. It is said that her correspondence with Harris and others of the Welsh clergy won her over to the Calvinistic wing.

It was on the death of her husband in 1746 that Lady Huntingdon began to throw herself into the work of the Revival. She did not hesitate to associate herself with the despised leaders of a des-

[1] Ibid.
[2] Ibid., p. 88.

pised cause. She sacrificed her position, her talent, her time and her fortune to further the interests of the Kingdom. She is reputed to have spent over £100,000 for this purpose and to have sold much of her jewellery and valuables. Her zeal was intense and impelling. "Oh, that I might be more and more useful to the souls of my fellow-creatures," she wrote. "I want to be every moment all life, all zeal, all activity for God, and ever on the stretch for closer communion with Him."[1] It was in pursuit of these earnest aspirations that she embarked upon what Knox has called "her deliberate effort to Christianise the *beau monde*."[2] Like William Wilberforce at the close of the century, she felt she had been entrusted with a special commission to win the aristocracy for Christ. Whilst the Methodists made their appeal principally to the working classes, she used her social status to secure an entrance for the gospel amongst the ranks of the élite. She generously opened her house in Park Street, London, and converted her spacious drawing-room into a preaching place. "Paul preached privately to those that were of reputation" and so by courtesy of the Countess did Whitefield and Romaine, Shirley and Venn and many more. It was a remarkable sight that met their eyes. No wonder Whitefield confessed, "I went home, never more surprised at any incident in my life."[3] The list of hearers so sedulously compiled by Seymour reads like a Court Circular. It is not to be wondered at that not all were equally enamoured with what they heard: the astonishing thing is that they were ever there at all. It would, of course, be a pious exaggeration to suggest that all were irresistibly drawn by the compulsion of the Spirit. To hear the unusual preachers in Lady Huntingdon's select mansion was, for a time, a recognized feature of London's social round. As Horace Walpole wrote to a friend in 1749: "Methodism is more fashionable than anything but brag; the women play very deep at both—as deep, it is much suspected, as the Roman matrons did at the mysteries of Bona Dea. If gracious Anne were alive she would make an admirable defendress of the new faith, and would build fifty more churches for female proselytes."[4] Some, no doubt, like the eccentric Lady Townsend, flitted from place to place sipping honey from a variety of spiritual flowers. She was ostensibly an orthodox Anglican, yet frequented the Countess's drawing-room to hear Whitefield. But then George Selwyn, the wit, caught her crossing

[1] L. Tyerman, *Wesley's Designated Successor*, p. 151.
[2] Knox, *op. cit.*, p. 486.
[3] J. Gillies, *Memoirs of Whitefield*, pp. 174-5.
[4] Walpole, *Correspondence*, ed. G. S. Lewis, Vol. IX, p. 74.

herself before a Roman altar. "She certainly means to go armed
with every viaticum," commented Walpole, to whom Selwyn
told the tale, "the Church of England in one hand, Methodism in
the other, and the Host in her mouth!"[1]

Whitefield had the moral courage to tackle this unpredictable
peeress and his words assume a new significance when we understand their bearing.

> It is a true and living faith in the Son of God that can alone bring
> present peace, and lay a solid foundation for future and eternal com-
> fort. I cannot wish your Ladyship anything greater, anything more
> noble, than a large share of this precious faith. When, like Noah's
> dove, we have been wandering about in a fruitless search for happi-
> ness, and have found no rest for the sole of our feet, the glorious
> Redeemer is ready to reach out His hand and receive us into His ark.
> This hand, honoured madam, He is reaching out to you. May you be
> constrained to give your heart entirely to Him, and thereby enter
> that rest which remains for the happy, though despised, people of
> God.[2]

Others were patently offended, like Lady Suffolk, mistress of
George III. Whitefield was quite unaware of her presence and
preached a searching sermon which implied a damaging condemnation of her character. She was so enraged that there and then she
accused Lady Huntingdon of plotting the whole thing and grew
so abusive that eventually she had to be pacified by the rest of the
guests and constrained to apologize. Or there was the Duchess of
Buckingham, who having been persuaded to attend, despatched
a curt note to the Countess to the effect that she found the Methodist doctrine "most repulsive and strongly tinctured with impertinence and disrespect towards their superiors, in perpetually endeavouring to level all ranks, and do away with all distinctions. It
is monstrous to be told that you have a heart as sinful as the common wretches that crawl on the earth. This is highly offensive and
insulting; and I cannot but wonder that her Ladyship should
relish any sentiments so much at variance with high rank and good
breeding."[3] Amongst those who seem to have been impressed,
though not convinced, may be listed such well-known names as
Bolingbroke, Chesterfield, David Hume and Bubb Dodington.

Some genuine converts there were, however, and amongst
them the Earl of Dartmouth was to prove the most significant.
He became a leading patron of Evangelicalism, advocating its

[1] Ibid., Vol. X, p. 216.
[2] Tyerman, *Whitefield*, Vol. II, pp. 211-12.
[3] Seymour, *op. cit.*, Vol. I, p. 27.

cause at Court and using his considerable influence to obtain livings for Evangelical clergy. He is the subject of Cowper's lines:

> We boast some rich ones, whom the gospel sways,
> And one who wears a coronet and prays.[1]

He was not alone. The Earls of Buchan and Bath, together with such honourable ladies as Lady Fanny Shirley and Lady Hotham, represent further conquests for the cause.

As yet another means of advancing the work of Revival, Lady Huntingdon began to appoint a series of Chaplains. It was quite customary for members of the nobility to keep domestic clergy to conduct their family devotions and preach in their private chapels. Often an impoverished curate was relieved to find shelter in such a protective office, even though his status was little higher than that of a servant. But the Countess saw in this practice a further opportunity to propagate the Gospel to advantage. The only Chaplain of hers who appears to have fulfilled the more familiar household duties was George Baddelley, Rector of Markfield. The remainder preached under her patronage to congregations she had gathered to hear the Word of God, either in her private apartments, or eventually in the chapels which she herself erected. She supposed, perhaps somewhat naïvely, that as a peeress of the realm she had an unassailable legal right to use her Chaplains in this manner. At a later stage, she was to discover the misapprehension under which she had been labouring, and this led to her secession from the Church of England.

As Knox remarks, these Chaplains were not the domestic nonentities we might be tempted to imagine.[2] Some of the leading figures of the Revival wore the Countess's scarf. Probably the first of them was William Romaine, whom we have already encountered as a pioneer of London Evangelicalism. Whitefield we know was appointed in 1748 and swiftly rose to be Lady Huntingdon's faithful lieutenant. His approach to her is at times somewhat overwhelming in its servility and offends our more egalitarian tastes, but, as Overton reminds us, in those days a Countess *was* a Countess, and far more deference was paid to rank then than now.[3] Walter Shirley, Joseph Townsend, Martin Madan, Thomas Haweis, Cradock Glascott and, later, William Jesse, all acted in this capacity.[4] In none of these can we discover any undue obse-

---

[1] W. Cowper, *Poems*, "Truth", Vol. I, p. 92.
[2] Knox, *op. cit.*, p. 487.   [3] Overton, *op. cit.*, p. 41
[4] Venn was a close ally, but never a Chaplain: cf. J. Venn, *Annals of a Clerical Family*, p. 94.

quiousness. It is clear that the Chaplains were glad to work with her rather than under her, for all were united in common subservience to Christ. Most independent of all was John Berridge, Vicar of Everton in Cambridgeshire, one of the Evangelical eccentrics, yet nevertheless a faithful and valuable protagonist for the truth. Knox thinks that he is the only one of the galaxy who wrote to his patroness with no hint of approaching her on all fours.[1] This is a little unjust to the rest, but there is certainly no minutest suspicion of flattery in Berridge's correspondence with the Countess. His buffoonery offended Southey and Newman, who failed to recognize him as one of the "characters" of the Awakening and to judge him in that light. Here he is replying to a somewhat peremptory summons from Lady Huntingdon to supply her chapel at Brighton. "You threaten me, madam, like a pope, not like a mother in Israel, when you declare roundly that God will scourge me if I do not come: but I know your Ladyship's meaning, and this menace was not despised. It made me slow in resolving. . . . Whilst I was looking towards the sea, partly drawn thither with the hope of doing good, and partly driven by your Vatican Bull, I found nothing but thorns in my way."[2] On another and similar occasion Berridge descended to more questionable taste when he told the Countess that his instructions "must come from the Lamb, not from the Lamb's wife, though she is a tight woman."[3]

The first of Lady Huntingdon's proprietary chapels was opened at Brighton in 1760, followed in 1761 by Oathill, in 1765 by Bath and Tottenham, and in 1769 by Tunbridge Wells. By 1773 we hear of work in Wiltshire, Sussex, Kent, Lincolnshire, Worcestershire and even in Wales and Ireland. Her concern for the Emerald Isle was particularly acute. "Poor wicked Ireland, I trust shall yet have a gospel day. I can't yet see how or when—but it must be; and till I find that opportunity, my eye is only waiting darkly for its accomplishment."[4] In addition to the Chaplains we meet the names of itinerant preachers like Hawksworth, Peckwell, and White. By now the work was being supplied with students trained at the College the Countess had opened in Wales in 1768. The need to provide preachers for the expanding witness prompted her to this step. She had always displayed an interest in clerical education. She subscribed to the evangelical seminary established by Dissenting ministers in London, and also to Dr. Doddridge's

[1] Knox, *op. cit.*, p. 488.
[2] Seymour, *op. cit.*, Vol. I, p. 324.
[3] Abbey and Overton, *op. cit.*, p. 351.
[4] Seymour, *op. cit.*, Vol. II, p. 169.

academy in Northampton. As her preaching places multiplied she was unable to fill the pulpits with ministers of the Church of England and therefore resolved to found a College to train men at her own expense. In 1754 Howell Harris had started a religious community at Trevecka and it was from him that Lady Huntingdon rented an ancient building that had originally been part of a castle in Henry II's reign. It was formally opened as a College by Whitefield on the Countess's sixty-second birthday. It was destined to provide a steady stream of preachers to supply not only Lady Huntingdon's chapels but many Dissenting meeting places as well.[1] Indeed, in the very nature of the case this was unavoidable. The rules permitted students to proceed to any ministry they desired. But, as Overton shows, the type of training received at Trevecka was much more likely to feed Dissent than the Establishment.[2] Berridge recognized this and wrote to the Countess: "However nasty or rickety the Dissenters may appear to you, God hath His remnant among them; therefore lift not up your hand against them for the Lord's sake or yet for consistency's sake, because your students are as real Dissenting preachers as any in the land, unless gown and band can make a clergyman. The Bishops look on your students as the worst kind of Dissenters; and manifest this by refusing that ordination to your preachers which would be readily granted to other teachers among the Dissenters."[3]

For a time the followers of Wesley shared this enterprise. John Wesley, writing to his brother on the eve of the opening, calls it "our college."[4] The first Principal, Joseph Easterbrook, was a Wesleyan: so was Joseph Benson, one of the tutors. Fletcher was one of the visiting lecturers and took an active part in the administration. Such co-operation, however, was brought to a swift and unfortunate close by the renewal of the Calvinistic controversy. Later, Wesley was to speak disparagingly of "a school set up at Trevecka" and its students who, "as they disclaimed all connection with the Methodists, so they disclaimed the Church also; nay, they spoke of it upon all occasions with exquisite bitterness and contempt."[5] This was remote from the Countess's original intention, for she still regarded her chapels as contained within the Church of England and was scrupulous to ensure that the liturgy was regularly employed in worship.

[1] A lengthy list of Trevecka students who entered the ministry is given in Seymour, *op. cit.*, Vol. II, pp. 112-13. Only a fraction took orders in the Church of England.

[2] Abbey and Overton, *op. cit.*, p. 354.   [3] Ibid.

[4] Wesley, *Letters*, Vol. V, p. 88.   [5] Wesley, *Works*, Vol. VII, p. 429.

Before considering the relationship of Lady Huntingdon's societies to the Anglican Church and her ultimate separation from the Establishment, we must revert to the recrudescence of the unhappy Calvinistic dispute. After its initial outburst had caused the cleavage between Whitefield and Wesley, a rather precarious truce had been patched up. At the death of Whitefield the controversy blazed out again. On this occasion it was Lady Huntingdon who assumed the mantle of Whitefield and took a stand against the Arminian tendencies of Wesley. It was all the more unfortunate in that the Countess had taken the lead in seeking a reconciliation between these two parties within Methodism. She had invited the Wesleys to preach in her chapels and in Whitefield's Tabernacles. And the Wesleyans, as we have seen, were more than adequately represented at Trevecka. But this gesture fell short of its objective and seems rather to have precipitated the gathering storm. One wonders whether the issue was not more temperamental than theological. As Knox delicately puts it, "Wesley found in Lady Huntingdon's attitude traces of an autocratic manner which he altogether failed to detect in himself."[1] "Trevecka is much more to Lady Huntingdon than Kingswood is to me," he told Benson. "*I* mixes with everything. It is *my* College, *my* masters, *my* students. I do not speak so of this school."[2] At the same time Wesley censured the innocent Fletcher for associating with "the genteel Methodists" and "those who denied the doctrine of general redemption."[3] The Countess deplored this reprimand administered to one who sought "to maintain peace and unity in the household of God."[4] At the same time Wesley was disturbed by the spread of Antinomianism and was persuaded that this was due to an unwarranted leaning towards Calvinism. Hence at the Conference of 1770 a series of propositions was drawn up in which the representatives indicated their disagreement with the more extreme assertions of the Calvinistic creed. Lady Huntingdon refused to countenance such a repudiation from members of her College staff and required that they should either retract or resign. When Benson refused to rescind his subscription to the Wesleyan manifesto, he was dismissed. Fletcher thereupon withdrew his association with the College. Lady Huntingdon then published a circular inviting all who agreed with her to assemble in Bristol in 1771 to demand that the Conference should revoke its heresies and to

---

[1] Knox, *op. cit.*, p. 500
[2] Wesley, *Letters*, Vol. V, p. 166.
[3] Ibid.
[4] Seymour, *op. cit.*, Vol. II, p. 235.

sign a formal protest against them. However, on the eve of the Conference, she apologized to John Wesley for this intervention. "As Christians we wish to retract what more deliberate consideration might have prevented, as we would as little wish to defend even truth itself presumptuously, as we would submit servilely to deny it."[1] In the event, less than a dozen objectors presented themselves at the Conference. They were received by Wesley with the utmost courtesy and fifty-three of his preachers appended their signatures to a document which Walter Shirley himself had prepared, making it clear that the 1770 Minutes were in no way intended to favour justification by works. On his part, Shirley signed a public acknowledgement to the effect that he had misunderstood the meaning of the resolutions. Unhappily, the matter did not end there. A further battle of words ensued when Wesley permitted the publication of Fletcher's defence of the Minutes entitled *Checks to Antinomianism*. There was launched what Fitchett with justification describes as "the most lively and exasperated tempest of theological controversy that ever broke on English literature."[2] It was as exasperating as it was exasperated. Toplady responded to Fletcher with *A Treatise upon Absolute Predestination*. Wesley submitted a brief synopsis of it which reached this climax:

> The sum of all is this: One in twenty, suppose, of mankind are elected; nineteen in twenty are reprobated. The elect shall be saved, do what they will; the reprobate shall be damned, do what they can. Reader, believe this or be damned. Witness my hand—A.T.[3]

Toplady thereupon addressed Wesley as *An Old Fox Tarred and Feathered* and even castigated the mild and earnest Fletcher by saying that in the few pages he had perused "the serious passages were dulness double-condensed and the lighter passages impudence double-distilled." Fortunately this hurricane subsided as unexpectedly as it arose, but its permanent effect lay in the irreconcilable demarcation of Wesleyan and Calvinistic Methodists. The followers of Whitefield and Lady Huntingdon were drawn off more decisively than ever before into a camp of their own.

Further events were to result in the separation of Lady Huntingdon and her societies from the Church of England as well as from the Wesleyans. This was far from her real desire or intention.

[1] Ibid., p. 341.
[2] Fitchett, *op. cit.*, p. 384.
[3] Wesley, *Works*, Vol. X, p. 370.

From the start she had regarded her witness as lying within the context of the Established Church. Until the founding of Trevecka only ordained clergymen officiated at her chapels. Whilst she had friends amongst the Dissenters with whom she co-operated, she could not condone schism. When the members of her chapel at Reading were dissatisfied with the appointment of a minister a move was made by some to organize the polity on an independent basis. The Countess strongly objected to any such proposal and roundly accused the malcontents of wanting to see the congregation "reduced to a mere Dissenting church."[1] "You ask of what Church we profess ourselves?" replied Thomas Haweis to a correspondent. "We desire to be esteemed as members of Christ's Catholic and Apostolic Church, and essentially one with the Church of England, of which we regard ourselves as living members. The doctrines we subscribe—for we require subscription, and, what is better, they are always truly preached by us—are those of the Church of England in the literal and grammatical sense. Nor is the liturgy of the Church of England performed more decently in any Church."[2]

Nevertheless the pressure of events conspired to compel a secession. It began with a plan to extend the work in London. In 1774 a large building in Spa Fields, Clerkenwell, formerly used as a place of amusement, was advertised for sale. It was a spacious circular auditorium named and built after the Pantheon in Rome. The Countess considered the possibility of purchase but reluctantly abandoned the idea on the ground of excessive expense. Almost immediately a syndicate of Christian men stepped in and bought it. They opened it as Northampton Chapel and appointed Herbert Jones and William Taylor as ministers. Large congregations were attracted and the news of this reached the ears of the Vicar, William Sellon, who protested at this unwarranted intrusion into his parish. He claimed the right to preach whenever he wished and to nominate any other officiating clergy. A lawsuit followed in the Consistorial Court and Jones and Taylor were restrained from preaching in the chapel, which had to be closed. This afforded Lady Huntingdon a second opportunity to secure the building. She lost no time in appropriating it and in March 1779 Spa Fields Chapel was opened with Thomas Haweis and Cradock Glascott as Chaplains. Oblivious of the judicial decision which had ousted Jones and Taylor, she innocently imagined that

[1] Seymour, op. cit., Vol. II, p. 404.
[2] Overton, op. cit., pp. 185-6.

she was entitled to employ her own Chaplains as she desired on her own premises. She was speedily to be disillusioned. Not surprisingly, Sellon repeated his complaints. Haweis and Glascott were cited to the Consistorial Court in May 1780 and the case went against them as before. They were inhibited from preaching in the chapel and severely reprimanded by the judge. Thomas Wills and William Taylor, who had filled the pulpit in the interim, were similarly prosecuted. This legal decision naturally jeopardized the status of all the Countess's chapels. The Spa Fields crisis brought the whole matter to a head. It became urgently necessary for Lady Huntingdon to define her position. The issue is clearly stated by Overton and Relton. "If her chapels were still to be regarded as belonging to the Church, then the laws of the Church must be obeyed. If not and they were to be sheltered under the Toleration Act, they must be registered as Dissenting places of worship."[1] In 1781 the Countess of Huntingdon's chapels ceased to be societies within the Established Church and became a sect. This secession was ratified when the first ordinations were held in 1783. A consequence was that to a man the Countess's Chaplains withdrew from her service, for, as Beilby Porteus, later Bishop of London, observed, it was impossible for a clergyman "to divide himself between sectarianism and the Establishment, between the Church of England and the Church of Lady Huntingdon."[2]

Thus Lady Huntingdon found herself compelled to become a Dissenter and at the same time forfeited the support of her Anglican Chaplains. She felt that a certain injustice attended her position. "I am to be cast out of the Church now, only for what I have been doing these forty years—speaking and living for Jesus Christ! And if the days of my captivity are now to be accomplished, those that turn me out, and so set me at liberty may soon feel what it is, by sore distress themselves, for those hard services they have caused me."[3] But she found occasion to praise God even under this trial. "Blessed be the Lord, I have not one care relative to this event, but to be found exactly faithful to God and man through all. You will smile and rejoice with me in all I may suffer for our dear Immanuel's sake! I have asked none to go with me—and none that do not come willingly to the help of the Lord, and by faith in the Son of God lay all at His feet—any other would do me no good, and He only knows these."[4] Thus there came into

---

[1] Overton and Relton, *op. cit.*, p. 88.
[2] R. Hodgson, *The Life of Beilby Porteus*, p. 268.
[3] Seymour, *op. cit.*, Vol. II, p. 315.
[4] Ibid.

being what were quaintly described as "the societies in the secession patronized by Lady Huntingdon" and later as "the Countess
of Huntingdon's Connexion."[1]

Before her death the Countess was evidently concerned to ensure the perpetuation of her cause. She herself had superintended
the entire work, retaining the sole power of appointing and re-
moving ministers and of selecting managers to supervise the
secular affairs of her chapels. Now she was placed in a similar
position to John Wesley when in 1784 he constituted the Legal
Hundred in order to conserve his organization. In 1790 a number
of ministers and laymen formed themselves into an Association,
at her Ladyship's invitation, to devise some means of maintaining
the oversight of her Connexion. It was entitled a "Plan of an
Association for Uniting and Perpetuating the Connection of the
Right Honourable the Countess-Dowager of Huntingdon."[2] The
Connexion was to be sub-divided into twenty-three districts, each
with its own Committee, responsible through the London Acting
Association to the General Association at its annual meeting.
Each district was to send a minister and two laymen as repre-
sentatives to the yearly conference. A special delegated power was
to be vested in the London Acting Association. Arrangements
were also proposed for raising a fund to support the Association.
However, because of objections raised by Lady Anne Erskine,
Haweis and others, the plan was ultimately abandoned. Both
Seymour and New regret that it was not carried into effect.[3] The
latter contended that had the trustees and ministers been compelled to adhere to a constitutional order, the Countess of Huntingdon's Connexion would by his time (1857) have occupied a
conspicuous position amongst the religious denominations of
England. "The auspicious moment, however, passed, and the
golden opportunity has never yet returned."[4] As it was, the
Countess's will devised "all her chapels, houses and furniture
therein, and all the residue of her estates and effects, to Thomas
Haweis and Janetta Payne, his wife, Lady Anne Erskine, and John
Lloyd,"[5] and directed that on the death of any one of them, the
survivors should appoint one other person to fill the vacancy, so
that there should always be four trustees. On Lady Huntingdon's

[1] Ibid., p. 490. Latourette, *op. cit.*, p. 1029 seems to confuse the Countess of
Huntingdon's Connexion with the Calvinistic Methodists.
[2] Seymour, *op. cit.*, Vol II, pp. 483-6.
[3] Ibid., p. 488: A. H. New, *The Coronet and the Cross*, p. 358.
[4] New, *op. cit.*, p. 358.
[5] Seymour, *op. cit.*, Vol. II, p. 490.

death in 1791 the superintendency of her chapels devolved upon Lady Anne, together with the financial administration, whilst Haweis undertook the pulpit supply.

The Countess of Huntingdon must be regarded as an outstanding leader of the Evangelical Revival. Not for nothing did Horace Walpole dub her "the patriarchess of the Methodists."[1] She was a remarkable woman judged by any criterion. Despite her natural imperiousness, she was prepared to sacrifice herself and her possessions for a despised and unpopular cause. As Newman said of her, "She devoted herself, her name, her means, her time, her thoughts to the cause of Christ. She did not spend her money on herself; she did not allow the homage paid to her rank to remain with herself; she passed these on, and offered them up to Him from whom her gifts came. She acted as one ought to act who considered this life a pilgrimage, not a home—like some holy nun, or professed ascetic, who had neither hopes nor fears of anything but what was divine and unseen."[2]

---

[1] Walpole, *Correspondence*, Vol. XI, p. 296.
[2] J. H. Newman, *Essays Critical and Historical*, Vol. I, pp. 388-9.

CHAPTER XIV

THE EXPANSION OF EVANGELICALISM

IT WAS THE CONSIDERED OPINION OF DEAN INGE THAT THE secession of the Methodists from the Church of England constituted a blow comparable to that inflicted on the Papacy by the loss of Northern Europe.[1] That is a characteristically shrewd comment. Yet just as the Roman Church sought to repair its loss through the Counter-Reformation, so in the Church of England the movement of Anglican Evangelicalism provided the possibility of renewal from within. In the period when the Wesleyans were preparing to depart, the impact of the Evangelical party was markedly increasing until by the close of the century it appeared to be the strongest sector of the Church.

There have been diversities of estimate concerning the precise numerical representation of Evangelicalism within the Establishment, but it can hardly be denied that, assessed in terms of influence, this viewpoint prevailed over any other by the end of the eighteenth century. Before the advent of the Oxford movement, High Church principles commanded a declining assent. Bishop Blomfield is reported as saying that after William Law's letters to the Bishop of Bangor, no writer asserted the Apostolical Succession until the rise of Tractarianism. On the other hand, Broad Church principles had fallen into discredit since the failure of Archdeacon Blackburne and others to relax the obligation of subscription to the Articles. The dominant party, so far as high position went, appears to have represented no very distinctive conviction at all. The Evangelicals, on the other hand, had a clearly defined objective and a coherent doctrinal system to expound. In the popular mind they stood for sincerity and zeal within the Church. "In short," concludes Canon Overton, "it would be no exaggeration to say that, morally and spiritually, though by no means intellectually, the dominant religious power, both inside and outside the Church of England at the close of the eighteenth century, was that which had been evoked by the Evangelical

[1] W. R. Inge, *Outspoken Essays*, Vol. I, p. 108.

Revival."[1] This is not to suggest, of course, that the Evangelical party had seized the reins of official authority. Far from it. No Evangelical had as yet been elevated to the episcopate or held any major position within the ecclesiastical hierarchy. Considerable opposition was still encountered. But, measured in terms of growing influence, it may rightly be said that the Evangelicals seemed most likely to repair the damage and fill the gap caused by the Methodist separation.

A noticeable change of attitude is to be seen amongst second-generation Evangelicals. It focuses upon the vexed question of itinerant evangelism. Although many of the Evangelical pioneers were prepared to overstep the boundaries of their own parishes in the interests of the gospel, their successors were inclined to be more scrupulous in this regard. They were ready to admit that the exigencies of the evangelistic situation in the first flush of the Revival might have excused such irregularities, but they were not anxious to perpetuate these practices. Just as few of the Evangelical leaders were to any great degree indebted to Methodism for their own awakening or for their methods of disseminating the truth, so they grew increasingly suspicious of the way in which the wider movement was developing and gradually withdrew from its ministrations. The impressive strength of Anglican Evangelicalism at the turn of the century was mainly due to this fidelity to Church principles and practice. Indeed Edwin Sidney could assert that he wrote his life of Samuel Walker expressly "to prove that the spirit of wisdom and zeal which now animates such numbers of the ministers of our Establishment, is the fruit, not of the ardour of the *irregulars* of the last century, but of the gradual influence of that example which was set by Mr. Walker and his contemporary *regulars*."[2]

It was in this second phase that Anglican Evangelicalism was largely purged of its inconsistencies and assumed the uniform mould which became definitive. In the earlier period there were many border-line cases: men who had a foot in both camps. Fletcher of Madeley and Perronet of Shoreham were more Methodist than Evangelical; Romaine, Grimshaw, and Berridge were more Evangelical than Methodist; and yet all were itinerant and irregulars. But as the century wore on and the need for consolidation grew more apparent, the emphasis upon regularity was more marked. The "pure" Evangelical, as distinct from the

---

[1] Overton, *op. cit.*, p. 161.
[2] Elliott-Binns, *Early Evangelicals*, p. 169.

Methodist, or irregular, was essentially a Churchman. His attachment to the new movement did not detract from his belief that the Establishment was the framework within which evangelism could be most effectively prosecuted. He clung to the traditional standards of the Church, doctrinal, homiletical and liturgical—the Articles, Homilies and Prayer Book. He recognized that the parochial system was basic to the whole constitution of Anglicanism and that submission to episcopal authority and jurisdiction was the linchpin of the Church's discipline. He therefore disapproved of itinerant preaching and avoided what has been described as "the organized intrusion of Wesley into other parishes."[1] To him an itinerant ministry, however justifiable it might appear in an emergency, plainly involved an act of ecclesiastical insubordination. Whereas the Methodist looked upon all the world as his parish, the Evangelical restricted himself to his appointed cure. Wesley's preference for an itinerant ministry as over against the pastoral and parochial did not command the assent of Evangelicals. Newton took a more generous position than most in recognizing the place of itinerancy even if he regarded it as inferior.[2] The Evangelical, moreover, could by no means countenance the employment of unordained evangelists. He would agree with Thomas Adam that "lay preaching is a manifest irregularity, and would not be endured in any Christian society."[3] He also objected to the erection of preaching places, which, as events were to prove, led to separation.

It was men of this more restrained outlook who carried on the witness of Anglican Evangelicalism in the second generation. It is to them that we owe the continued expansion of the Revival within the Church of England. The work was still devoid of any deliberate organization or a conscious attempt at co-ordination. Believing that the parochial and diocesan system was sufficient, the Evangelicals were careful to avoid setting up any further machinery. In the remainder of this chapter we can do no more than glance at some of the chief areas of progress.

We begin with London. Already Romaine and Madan had established themselves. Venn left Clapham in 1759. Bateman died in 1761 and Jones in 1762. Haweis removed to Aldwincle in 1764. In 1767 Henry Foster was appointed curate to Romaine and later assumed some strategic lectureships. In 1769 Roger Bentley, who

---

[1] H. M. Larner in *Dictionary of English Church History*, p. 216.
[2] J. Newton, *Cardiphonia*, p. 359.
[3] Sidney, *op. cit.*, p. 224.

had been curate to Richard Conyers at Helmsley, was presented by
John Thornton to the vicarage of St. Giles', Camberwell. In 1773
Charles de Coetlogon came to assist Madan at the Lock Chapel.
Thus name by name the succession was built up. The most significant reinforcement, however, was in 1779 when John Newton
moved from Olney to the united cure of St. Mary Woolnoth and
St. Mary Woolwich Haw. Once again John Thornton was the
patron, and we see the emergence of a policy which was to reach
its fruition under the guidance of Charles Simeon. Newton announced his decision to his friend William Bull, an Independent minister, in a typically whimsical way. "My race at Olney is
nearly finished. I am about to form a connection for life with one
Mary Woolnoth, a reputed London saint in Lombard Street."[1]
Opponents of Evangelicalism disputed the presentation and Newton wrote again to Bull: "Molly Woolnoth and I are not yet
married. I told you someone forbade the banns, and the prohibi-
tion is not yet taken off."[2] However, the difficulties were overcome and Newton preached his first sermon on 19th December.
"I stand here," he declared, "as a pattern of the longsuffering of
God, and, having obtained mercy myself, I have encouragement
from my own case to hope that the strongest prejudices may be
softened by the power of His grace."[3] This converted slave-
trader exercised as remarkable a ministry in London as he had
done in Buckinghamshire. Already his fame had preceded him
and the publication in 1781 of *Cardiphonia*—"a volume of pure
apostolical and evangelical truth," according to Alexander Whyte[4]
—following upon his previous compositions, brought so many
strangers to the church that the parishioners complained that they
could not reach their pews. St. Mary Woolnoth was situated in a
prosperous area, close to the Royal Exchange and the Bank of
England. The Lord Mayor sometimes worshipped there and
altogether it was regarded as one of the most important of the city
churches. For twenty-eight years Newton delivered the evangelical message from this strategic pulpit and did perhaps more
than any other to commend the cause. Round his figure there
gathered a group of second-generation Evangelicals who were to
kindle their torches from his flame. John Venn, Daniel Wilson,
Henry Martyn, Charles Simeon, William Wilberforce all owed
much to Newton.

[1] B. Martin, *John Newton*, p. 271.   [2] Ibid.
[3] J. Newton, *Works*, Vol. II, p. 135.
[4] Newton, *Cardiphonia*, Preface to 1911 Edition, p. 5.

In the same year that saw the arrival of Newton, Watts Wilkinson began his sixty-one years' service as afternoon lecturer at St. Mary Aldermary and later also became Chaplain of Aske's Hospital, Hoxton. In 1780 William Bromley Cadogan, who combined the living of St. Giles', Reading, and St. Luke's, Chelsea, was converted to evangelical views, largely through the influence of William Talbot's widow, whom he spoke of "not only as the best friend I ever had in my life, but as a mother to me in love, in every good office and in continual prayers for my person and ministry."[1] However, Cadogan's ministry was necessarily divided and, as the work at Reading prospered, he increasingly left St. Luke's in the care of his curate, Erasmus Middleton. In 1780 also Richard Cecil joined the London group when he was appointed to the proprietary chapel of St. John in Bedford Row. Ill health had compelled him to leave his curacy at Lewes and to take up residence in Islington. He accepted a number of invitations to preach in London pulpits and this paved the way for his acceptance not only of the chapel but several lectureships as well. Overton selected Cecil as "perhaps the most cultured and refined of all the Evangelical leaders."[2] He was destined to wield a weighty influence, although uncertain health prevented him from doing as much as he would have wished. In 1785 Basil Woodd took over Bentinck Chapel and John Eyre, later prominent in the founding of the London Missionary Society, came to the Ram's Chapel at Homerton. Thus the Evangelical representation in London was substantially implemented.

Most of the London Evangelicals were members of the Eclectic Society which, in fact, was the main means of keeping these scattered units in touch with each other. Founded in 1783 by Newton, Cecil and Foster, with a layman, Eli Bates, it met fortnightly in the vestry of St. John's, Bedford Row. Evangelicals within travelling distance of the city also joined as did at least two Dissenting ministers. The Eclectic Society came to be recognized as a clerical counterpart of the Clapham Sect and fostered some of the greatest movements to emerge from the Church of England at this period, including the Church Missionary Society. Matters of moment relative to the Evangelical witness as a whole were frequently referred to it for consideration.

It is only possible to mention one or two areas throughout the remainder of the country where the Evangelical work was strong-

<hr/>

[1] W. B. Cadogan, *Discourses*, p. 32.
[2] Abbey and Overton, *op. cit.*, p. 388.

est and to meet in passing some of the outstanding leaders of this expansion. John Berridge has been named already in connexion with Lady Huntingdon, and he is the central figure in East Anglia. He cannot fail to catch the eye. "Of all the evangelists of the eighteenth century," wrote Bishop Ryle, "this good man was undeniably the most quaint and eccentric."[1] He was indeed an unusual character, but, though some have been offended by his oddities, there can be no questioning his earnestness and the way in which his ministry was owned by God. Even his friend John Thornton could grow a little impatient with him. "I remember," he wrote, "you once jocularly informed me you were born with a fool's cap on; pray, my dear sir, is it not high time it was pulled off?" To which Berridge replied: "A very proper question; and my answer is this—a fool's cap is not put off so readily as a night cap; one cleaves to the head, the other to the heart."[2] The transforming power of God's grace did not remove Berridge's whimsicalities at his conversion: it rather baptized them into a new spirit and employed them as an extraordinary means of drawing many into the kingdom. He was presented to the living of Everton in 1755 whilst still a stranger to the evangelical experience. His preaching was unfruitful and his own soul dry and unsatisfied. He confessed afterwards that his own view of salvation was like "a solar system without the sun."[3] Little wonder his congregation was unblest! He said that an angel might preach such doctrine till his wings dropped off without doing the slightest good. Eventually he was driven to his knees to search his heart and ask what he lacked. He began to call upon the Lord with great intensity. "Lord, if I am right, keep me so; if I am not right, make me so. Lead me to the knowledge of the truth as it is in Jesus."[4] For ten days he was kept in suspense and soul travail, but then God graciously granted his request. Let him recount the story in his own words:

> As I was sitting in my house one morning and musing upon a text of Scripture, the following words were darted into my mind with wonderful power, and seemed indeed like a voice from heaven, viz. "Cease from thine own works." Before I heard these words my mind was in a very unusual calm; but as soon as I heard them, my soul was in a tempest directly, and the tears flowed from my eyes like a torrent. The scales fell from my eyes immediately, and I now clearly saw the rock I had been splitting on for near thirty years.[5]

[1] Ryle, *op. cit.*, p. 216.
[2] J. Berridge, *Works*, ed. R. Whittingham, pp. 526-7.
[3] Loane, *Cambridge and the Evangelical Succession*, p. 70.
[4] Berridge, *Works*, p. 350.   [5] Ibid., pp. 350-1.

The rock to which he referred was that which he himself described so aptly as "the mixed covenant" of man's own invention, "consisting *partly* of works and *partly* of grace."[1] Christ, he confessed, had only been thrown in as a makeweight. But he discovered that "Christ will either be a whole Saviour or none at all. And if you think you have any good service of your own to recommend you to God, you are certainly without any interest in Christ; be ye ever so sober, serious, just and devout, you are still under the curse of God, as I was, and know it not, provided you have allowed reliance on your own works, and think they are doing something for you, and Christ to do the rest."[2] One of the first things Berridge did when the illumination came was to thumb through his Concordance to trace the Scriptural occurrences of "faith" and "believe" and he was astonished to find that they filled many columns. Thus it came about that at the age of forty-one, this Fellow of Clare Hall, Cambridge, intellectual and wit, was made a new creature in Christ Jesus and became in Wesley's words "one of the most simple as well as one of the most sensible men of all whom it pleased God to employ in reviving Primitive Christianity."[3]

The whole tenor of Berridge's preaching changed. Instead of salvation by self-effort he proclaimed justification by faith alone. The effect was immediate and sensational. "As soon as ever I preached Jesus Christ, and faith in His blood, then believers were added to the Church continually; then people flocked from all parts to hear the glorious sound of the Gospel, some coming six miles, others eight, and others ten, and that constantly."[4] His messages were couched in homely terms which country folk could understand for, as has been said, few preachers in the Church of England have better known how to get in touch with the ploughboy mind. Within two years of Berridge's conversion revival broke out in his parish in an unmistakable manner. On Sunday, 20th May, 1759, there were amazing scenes, painted by an eyewitness and transcribed in Wesley's *Journal*. At the morning service several fainted and cried out under conviction. In the afternoon the church was again crowded.

The windows being filled within and without, and even the outside of the pulpit to the very top; so that Mr. B. seemed almost

[1] Ibid., pp. 208-9.
[2] Ibid., p. 355.
[3] Wesley, *Letters*, Vol. IV, p. 58.
[4] Berridge, *Works*, p. 357.

stifled by their breath. The text was, "Having a form of godliness, but denying the power thereof." When the power of religion began to be spoken of, the presence of God really filled the place. And while poor sinners felt the sentence of death in their souls, what sounds of distress did I hear! The greatest number of them who cried or fell were men; but some women, and several children, felt the power of the same almighty Spirit, and seemed just sinking into hell. . . . Great numbers wept without any noise; others fell down as dead; some sinking in silence, some with extreme noise and violent agitation.[1]

After the service the seekers all squeezed into the vicarage where Berridge gave them a word of exhortation.

And now did I see such a sight as I do not expect again on this side eternity. The faces of . . . all the believers present did really shine; and such a beauty, such a look of extreme happiness, and at the same time of Divine love and simplicity did I never see in human faces until now.[2]

It was this manifest work of grace which led to Berridge's itinerations, as he began to preach beyond his parish in farm-houses and barns. He and William Hicks, Vicar of Wrestlingham, who had hitherto been hostile, went together into Hertfordshire. Their circuit extended into Huntingdonshire and to within a mile of Cambridge. This irregularity brought Berridge into serious conflict with the Bishop of Peterborough, who summoned him to appear before him to account for his conduct. Impressed by his sincerity, he took up a kindlier attitude on meeting Berridge, and assured him that he was his friend, but that Church rules must be obeyed. Berridge found himself on the episcopal carpet more than once. On one occasion he was reproved for preaching at all hours of the day and on all days of the week. "My lord," he replied, "I preach only at two times." And when the Bishop enquired, "And which are they, Mr. Berridge?" he quickly responded, "In season and out of season, my lord." He remained the apostle of Cam and Fen until his death in 1793. His work was of incalculable value and paved the way for Simeon. Although he contributed so notably to the expansion of Evangelicalism, Berridge himself must be regarded as typical of the pioneering period rather than of the more settled phase of consolidation.

The Midlands of England rejoiced in a favourable share of Evangelical ministry. Abraham Maddox, once curate to James Hervey, was a prominent name here, first at Kettering and then at

[1] Wesley, *Journal*, Vol. IV, p. 318.
[2] Ibid., p. 320.

Creaton, where he was succeeded by Thomas Jones, a convert of Daniel Rowland. For more than fifty years Thomas Haweis was Rector of Aldwincle and, of course, Newton had been at Olney since 1763. He was followed by Thomas Scott, whose commentary became a standard of reference and devotion amongst Evangelicals. In 1774 Thomas Robinson began his forty years' ministry in Leicester. Of him Robert Hall, a fellow townsman, wrote, "The revolution which Baxter accomplished at Kidderminster Robinson effected at Leicester."[1] From 1766 to 1793 Thomas Clarke, perhaps the most learned of all the Evangelicals, was Rector of Chesham Bois in Buckinghamshire. Romaine called him the "walking synopsis" and Henry Venn declared, "I will always take Clarke's opinion until Solomon rises from the dead."

We have seen that William Grimshaw pioneered the Evangelical witness in Yorkshire. Others, however, were early associated with the work in the north of England. Of these, Thomas Adam of Winteringham was one of the first. He was presented to his living as early as 1725. As yet he had no real spiritual experience. Indeed, at the time of his ordination he referred to himself as "a youth of levity and frolic" and that he took orders "more for the sake of worldly advantage than anything else."[2] In 1736 a reading of Law's *Serious Call* affected him deeply. He could not overlook the disparity between his own life and the ideal offered by Law. For the space of some years he remained in uncertainty. Sometimes he trembled and wept whilst conducting worship and could not manage to preach. He was delivered from this Slough of Despond as, like Luther in the tower room at Wittenberg, he sat before the open page of Romans and drew life from the Word of God. Adam was now a man with a message for his people. James Hervey wrote to a friend about "the amazing reformation amongst the people in his neighbourhood and of the large congregations he drew, not only from his own parish but from round about."[3] However, the visible results of Adam's ministry were comparatively few and at his death Henry Venn commented on the "exceeding small success" which attended his thirty years of Gospel preaching.[4] He nevertheless wielded a wide and weighty influence in Evangelical circles and was resorted to as a kind of oracle by many who came from all parts of the country to seek his advice. He entered into a prolonged correspondence with Samuel Walker

---

[1] Balleine, *op. cit.*, pp. 95-6.
[2] Elliott-Binns, *Early Evangelicals*, p. 159.
[3] Ibid.
[4] J. Venn, *The Life of Henry Venn*, p. 387.

who later travelled from Truro to see him. Elliott-Binns compares him to John Keble in his adherence to his parish and avoidance of preferment.[1] The pertinent aphorisms contained in his *Thoughts on Religion* indicate his sagacity and insight. Amongst the most quotable are: "Hell is truth seen too late"; "I see the devil's hook, and yet cannot help nibbling at his bait"; and "It is much easier to join oneself to a sect than to God."[2]

The arrival of Henry Venn in Huddersfield in 1759 marks a milestone in the progress of northern Evangelicalism. Grimshaw died in 1763 and Venn was destined to be his successor in leadership. Venn became Vicar of Huddersfield at the age of thirty-five and gave the best years of his life to the town. He is inaccurately designated "the first evangelist of the modern slum" for the Industrial Revolution had not yet laid its grimy hand upon the pleasant countryside. Although it was a centre of wool manufacture the weaving was still done in the homes of the people. But the inhabitants were a rough and untutored race. Two years prior to Venn's coming, John Wesley had left his impressions. "A wilder people I never saw in England. The men, women and children filled the street as we rode along and appeared just ready to devour us."[3] And again in 1759: "I preached near Huddersfield to the wildest congregation I have seen in Yorkshire." But he added, "yet they were restrained by an unseen hand, and I believe some felt the sharpness of His Word."[4] Strangely enough, Venn met Wesley as he travelled up to Yorkshire when by chance they put up at the same inn on the Great North Road, and doubtless these unfavourable reports would be passed on. Venn was to learn for himself that his flock were uncouth indeed and yet not deaf to the call of the Saviour. Soon he was attracting such congregations that the church was inadequate to accommodate them and he had to go out into the open. "Few parish ministers in English history," says Bishop Loane, "have so moved and shaken town and county by the simple art of preaching."[5] His twelve years of ministry witnessed a remarkable transformation in the life of the parish. He turned the world upside down and the church inside out, so it has been said. As Michael Hennell has reminded us afresh, Venn's real success lay in the changed lives of many who came to hear him.[6] These included a prosperous woollen manufacturer, Thomas Atkins, and the distinguished surgeon,

[1] Elliott-Binns, *Early Evangelicals*, p. 161.
[2] Ibid., p. 402.   [3] Wesley, *Journal*, Vol. IV, p. 21.
[4] Ibid., p. 33.   [5] Loane, *Cambridge and the Evangelical Succession*, p. 134.
[6] M. Hennell, *John Venn and the Clapham Sect*, p. 23.

William Hey. No less than twenty-two men entered holy orders during his stay. It was the need for providing funds to train such candidates which led to the foundation of the Elland Society in 1767. Venn's contribution to Evangelicalism in the north can hardly be overestimated.

Other names are too numerous to mention. There was William Richardson at York and Joseph Milner at Hull. There was Richard Conyers at Helmsley and James Stillingfleet at Hotham. There was John Crosse at Bradford and Miles Atkinson at Leeds. Nor was the northern work confined to Yorkshire. Although the Methodists made the greater headway in Lancashire, Cornelius Bayley was a prominent Evangelical leader in Manchester and by the end of the century Robert Housman had started his ministry in Lancaster.

In the south-west of England the centre of gravity seems to have shifted from Cornwall to Devon. Despite the influence of Samuel Walker and the clergy in his Club, Methodism made great inroads into the duchy. Devon enjoyed its first taste of revival preaching when Hervey went there as curate in Bideford in 1743. Nearby was Thomas Bliss, a convert of Haweis, and son of a future Astronomer Royal, who held the livings of Ashford and Yarnscombe. Augustus Montagu Toplady came to Broadhembury in 1768, although ill health compelled him to leave in 1775. Cradock Glascott was Vicar of Hatherleigh from 1781.

Bristol has been correctly called the cradle of Methodism, but it was not untouched by Anglican Evangelicalism. The first centre was St. Werburgh's where Richard Symes was the incumbent. Walker wrote to him in 1755, "I greatly rejoice that God has introduced into your large city the purity of gospel doctrines by your means in a regular way."[1] Here James Rouquet was curate from 1768 to 1776. The son of Huguenot refugees, he had fallen under the spell of Whitefield. Charles Wesley came upon him at St. John's College, Oxford, and testified that he was not "ashamed to confess Christ before men."[2] For a time he acted as master at Kingswood school. He relinquished a substantial living at West Harptree to come to Bristol and some of his best work was done as Chaplain to St. Peter's Hospital and the city gaol. His radical views caused no small offence, but he was beloved of the poor who flocked out of the slums to attend his funeral when he died at forty-six. Another centre was St. George's, Kingswood, where

[1] *Christian Guardian*, 1804, p. 274.
[2] C. Wesley, *Journal*, Vol. II, p. 15.

Richard Hart laboured for almost half a century from 1759 onwards. Sir James Stonehouse abandoned his medical practice and his Deist scepticism to undertake the lectureship of All Saints. William Tandey was curate in charge of St. Mary-le-Port, where Whitefield had first preached, and Joseph Easterbrook, who had taught for a time at Trevecka, was at the Temple Church. Bristol was also the home of the wealthy sugar refiner, James Ireland, who has been called the John Thornton of the West because of his services to the Evangelical cause. It was by his help that the Bristol Clerical Society was formed, which fulfilled a similar function to that at Elland in enabling young men to secure a place in the Universities. It was in the same city that Hannah More was brought up and near which she settled in 1780 to pursue her evangelical work amongst the neglected people in the Mendips.

No survey of expanding Evangelicalism would be complete without a reference to the Universities. Oxford had been the first to respond to the Revival and in the earlier days it was customary for young Evangelicals to enter there. Joseph Jane was instituted as Vicar of St. Mary Magdalene and his church soon became the evangelical focus of the town. Jane's father had been Rector of Truro before St. John Elliot, the absentee incumbent for whom Samuel Walker acted as Curate. The younger Jane does not appear to have met Walker until 1755, but he was in complete sympathy with his views. In his volume on *The Evangelicals at Oxford*—a mine of information—J. S. Reynolds compiles an impressive list of Oxford men of this period who played a prominent part in the Revival.[1] In the summer of 1755 Whitefield, who had recently returned from America, could report: "Many in Oxford are awakened to the knowledge of the truth" and again: "Many students at Oxford are earnestly learning Christ."[2] At the same time Lady Huntingdon wrote to James Stillingfleet "I am really rejoiced that so many at the Universities are determined to be on the Lord's side" and mentioned undergraduate prayer meetings as being common.[3] The preaching of William Romaine no doubt furthered the quickening work until he was forbidden the University pulpit. But soon a helper was to be raised up to stand beside Jane. Thomas Haweis, a protégé of Walker, had come up to Oxford at Jane's expense. He matriculated from Christ Church in December 1755 and early in 1757 he was responsible for inaugur-

[1] J. S. Reynolds, *The Evangelicals at Oxford*, pp. 10-11, 22-3.
[2] Gillies, *Memoirs of Whitefield*, p. 188.
[3] Seymour, *op. cit.*, Vol. I, p. 226.

ating what Tyerman does not hesitate to term a second Holy Club.[1] Haweis gathered together those who, like himself, were preparing themselves for the ministry of the Church and who felt the need for Christian fellowship. They met regularly to read the Greek Testament, discuss theology, share their experience of Christ and unite in prayer. Amongst the number were Thomas Biddulph, later Vicar of Padstow; Matthew Powley, who figured amongst the leading Yorkshire Evangelicals; David Pugh, Rector of Newport, Pembrokeshire; Thomas Wills, one of Lady Hunting-don's preachers; and in all probability Cradock Glascott. William Jesse may have been a member, too, and perhaps Richard Hill, on occasion, for he attended Haweis's ministry as Curate to Jane at St. Mary Magdelene.

Haweis assisted Jane from the autumn of 1757 until his service was terminated by the intervention of the Bishop in 1762. His forthright Evangelical preaching drew large crowds, aroused considerable opposition and proved richly fruitful. Haweis looked upon this period as "amongst the most useful days of my labours, from the number of young men who went forth to preach the everlasting gospel in the land."[2] Early in 1761 Samuel Walker visited Oxford and recorded with pleasure that "he met a group of promising young men preparing for orders, for whom he was at pains to draw up some instructions."[3]

On the departure of Haweis in 1762 and Jane in 1763, James Stillingfleet became the leader of Oxford Evangelicalism. What must have been a continuation of Haweis's club met in the house of a Mrs. Durbridge, the widow of one of Whitefield's converts. As Reynolds points out, whilst Stillingfleet himself was in con-trol, all went well. His appointment to the incumbency of Coy-church, Glamorgan, in 1767 left the Evangelical group without a head. John Hallward, of Worcester College, did what he could to keep it together, but it would seem that a certain irregularity may now have crept in which eventually led to the St. Edmund Hall expulsions of 1768. Not that the extreme steps taken at that time against the six Evangelical undergraduates were in any measure justified, but the fact, for example, that the meetings of the society were no longer confined to members of the University and that some were preaching without a licence, gave a handle to the critics. The prejudice against these zealous, if unwisely guided,

[1] Tyerman, *Whitefield*, Vol. II, p. 375: cf. *Proceedings of Wesley Historical Society*, Vol. XXIX, pp. 73-5.
[2] T. Haweis, MS. Autobiography, p. 76.
[3] *Christian Observer*, 1877, p. 159.

young men was so evident as to be almost ridiculous. Even the
President of Magdalene, George Horne, observed that "if these
six gentlemen were expelled for having too much religion, it
would be very proper to enquire into the conduct of some who
had too little."[1]

It has been too easily assumed that the expulsions of 1768
brought the Evangelical witness at Oxford to a halt.[2] But, as
Reynolds has shown, although the situation was inevitably made
more difficult, a continuing stand was made for the truths of the
Revival which paved the way for the flourishing years at the close
of the century, when, by what Canon Ollard called "the irony of
fate," St. Edmund Hall became the headquarters of Evangelicalism in Oxford.[3] The Vice-Principal, Isaac Crouch, was destined to
prove the Simeon of Oxford and, as Reynolds expresses it, "the
real nursing-father of evangelicalism" there.[4]

At about the same time the Evangelical cause in Cambridge
entered upon a similar phase of expansion and good success, with
Magdalene as its centre. But before that, in 1764, when he came up
to St. John's, Rowland Hill had collected a club very like that
started by Haweis at Oxford. They searched the Scriptures together, joined in prayer, visited the prison and preached in town
and country. Amongst the members were David Simpson, who
afterwards laboured at Macclesfield; Thomas Pentycross, Rector
of St. Mary's, Wallingford, whom Horace Walpole found "very
sensible, rational and learned;"[5] and Charles de Coetlogon, who
went to help Madan at the Lock Chapel. When Henry Venn came
to Yelling in 1771, Cambridge Evangelicals gained a friend and
supporter. His influence was immeasurable and smoothed the path
for the happier circumstances which were soon to obtain. The
factor which brought Magdalene so much to the fore as an Evangelical centre was the arrival within a short space of time of three
most able and ardent young men—Samuel Hey, William Farish
and Henry Jowett. Hey belonged to an Evangelical family in
Leeds and his brother, William, a physician and Fellow of the
Royal Society, was the friend and adviser of Wilberforce. Samuel
became Rector of Steeple Aston in Wiltshire. Farish, a Senior
Wrangler, was appointed Professor of Chemistry in 1784 and com-

[1] E. Sidney, *The Life of Rowland Hill*, p. 41.
[2] Cf. Balleine, *op. cit.*, pp. 99-100; Elliott-Binns, *Evangelical Movement*, p. 37;
Smyth, *op. cit.*, p. 215.
[3] S. L. Ollard, *The Six Students of St. Edmund Hall*, p. 47.
[4] Reynolds, *op. cit.*, p. 59.
[5] H. Walpole, *Correspondence*, Vol. XII, p. 208.

bined the duties of his chair with the living of St. Giles. Jowett—
not to be confused with his brother Joseph of Trinity Hall and
Professor of Civil Law, who was also sympathetic to the Revival
—was a Fellow and tutor. It was this trio who won the confidence
of the Elland Society and were entrusted with the training of
Evangelical candidates for orders from the north.

After Isaac Milner became President of Queens' in 1788 the
balance veered towards that College. Milner—brother to Joseph of
Hull, the Church historian of the Revival—was a most remarkable
man by any standards. So far did he outstrip his rivals for the
Senior Wranglership that the examiners added *incomparabilis* after
his name. He was "the clerical Dr. Johnson"[1] and many of his
shrewd observations have been recorded. In 1791 he was preferred to the Deanery of Carlisle, whilst retaining his Presidency.
This was the man who, as Elliott-Binns says, "did so much to lay
the foundations of Evangelicalism in Cambridge."[2]

As the Evangelical cause prospered in the University, so the
influence spread to the pulpits of the town. Wesley reports a visit
to Charles Simeon in 1784 when he received "the pleasing information that there are three parish churches in Cambridge wherein
true Scriptural religion is preached, and several young gentlemen
who are happy partakers of it."[3] These would be Holy Trinity,
where Simeon himself exercised his significant ministry; St.
Edward's, where Christopher Atkinson—brother to Miles of
Leeds—was Curate; and St. Sepulchre's, where Henry Coulthurst
was the incumbent before going to Halifax.[4] These three pulpits
maintained the Evangelical witness in Cambridge in the latter
part of the century. The contribution of Simeon was by far the
most important. He was Vicar of Holy Trinity for fifty-four years
and represents the living link between the age of the Revival and
the consolidation of Anglican Evangelicalism. But, since he
properly belongs to the transitional period following the Revival,
we must content ourselves with leaving his as the last and greatest
of all the names we have considered in the story of the Awakening
within the established Church. Let us therefore conclude with the
measured and not at all exaggerated tribute of Canon Smyth. "I
doubt whether the genius of that man as an ecclesiastical states-
man has ever received sufficient recognition. He seems to me to

[1] Carpenter, *op. cit.*, p. 226.
[2] Elliott-Binns, *Early Evangelicals*, p. 363.
[3] Wesley, *Journal*, Vol. VII, pp. 39-40.
[4] H. C. G. Moule, *Charles Simeon*, p. 102, has St. Giles' as the third, but Farish was
not then instituted.

rank with Samuel Wilberforce, Bishop of Oxford—the Re-modeller of the Episcopate, as Burgon calls him—as one of the founding fathers, or Remodellers of the Church of England in the nineteenth century."[1]

[1] Smyth, *op. cit.*, p. 6.

POSTLUDE

CHAPTER XV

THE MESSAGE OF THE REVIVAL

THE GROWTH OF THE EVANGELICAL REVIVAL WAS SO START-ling and its effects so widespread that the investigator turns to examine the doctrines that were preached in the expectation that they will provide a major clue to explain the phenomenal advance of the movement. He supposes that there was something novel in the message itself or in its presentation to account for the remarkable results that ensued. Such a quest is foredoomed to failure, for there is in fact nothing new in the preaching of the Revival and little that is unusual in its delivery. Indeed, a perusal of the sermons of Wesley or Whitefield or Edwards makes us wonder why these utterances proved so exceptionally effective. This is not to disparage the merits of such preachers: it is to suggest that their message was neither new nor newly expressed. By and large it was the same gospel as had been proclaimed by faithful men in every generation. It was a simple, earnest, unequivocal declaration of God's whole counsel.

There was nothing subtle or abstruse in its interpretation of the perennial theme. Like John Wesley, the preachers of the Revival as a body aimed at offering "plain truth for plain people."[1] It is noteworthy that the message of the Evangelical Awakening of the eighteenth century is enshrined almost entirely in homiletic and devotional literature. Few volumes of systematic theology or original contributions to philosophical learning flowed from the pens of Evangelical leaders. Their interest was practical rather than speculative. They were more concerned with reaching the masses with the Word of life than with entering the lists against the rationalist opponents of the faith. This they were content to leave to the evidence-writers of the period who, as Overton points out, not only prepared the way for the Revival by beating down the enemies of Christianity on all sides but also kept them under control.[2] But invaluable as was this intellectual defence of

---

[1] *The Standard Sermons of John Wesley*, ed. E. H. Sugden, Vol. I, p. 30.
[2] Overton, *op. cit.*, p. 122.

the faith, it was not the primary concern of the Revival and the leaders of the movement displayed a singular concentration of purpose as they unswervingly kept to their brief.

It is for this reason that the common assumption that the Evangelical Revival lacks theological significance requires reconsideration. Its representatives can hardly be faulted for failing to accomplish what they never intended to achieve. Moreover, theology may be fashioned in experience and evangelistic action as well as in the seclusion of the study, and from this angle the contribution of the Revival may prove weightier than is generally admitted. Criticism is levelled at two principal targets. It is said that the Evangelical message lacks originality either in content or expression. "It is useless to look to the evangelical movement, in any of its forms," wrote Professor A. V. G. Allen, "for any theologian who directly advanced the progress of Christian thought."[1] It is furthermore claimed that the Evangelical message lacks balance and wholeness. "The Evangelical Movement," affirmed Canon Liddon, "partly in virtue of its very intensity, was, in respect of its advocacy of religious truth, an imperfect and one-sided movement. It laid stress only on such doctrines of Divine Revelation as appeared to its promoters to be calculated to produce a converting or sanctifying effect upon the souls of men. Its interpretation of the New Testament—little as its leaders ever suspected this—was guided by a traditional assumption as arbitrary and as groundless as any tradition which it ever denounced. The real sources of its 'Gospel' were limited to a few chapters of St. Paul's Epistles . . . understood in a manner which left much else in Holy Scripture out of account; and thus the Old Testament history, and even the life of our Lord Jesus Christ, as recorded by the Evangelists, were thrown comparatively into the background. The needs and salvation of the believer, rather than the whole revealed Will in Whom we believe, was the governing consideration. As a consequence, those entire departments of the Christian revelation which deal with the corporate union of Christians with Christ in His Church and with the Sacraments, which by His appointment are the channels of His grace to the end of time, were not so much forgotten as unrecognised."[2] Charges like these have led contemporary historians to contrast the Evangelical message with what is described as our own "much more adequate theology."[3]

[1] A. V. G. Allen, *The Continuity of Christian Thought*, p. 377.
[2] H. P. Liddon, *The Life of E. B. Pusey*, Vol. I, pp. 255-6.
[3] Elliott-Binns, *Early Evangelicals*, p. 16.

The time has clearly arrived when a reassessment of the doctrinal foundation of the eighteenth-century Awakening is called for. It is one thing to observe that the prophets of the movement made no attempt to meet the onslaught of philosophical scepticism: it is quite another to suggest that the theological undergirding of their preaching was unsure. Indeed, even on the first count the Evangelicals were not altogether ineffectual. They succeeded in refuting Deism in an indirect manner. As Canon Smyth remarks, a purely intellectual triumph is always something of a Pyrrhic victory and no sooner was rationalistic Deism driven from the field than it returned in the form of Unitarian heterodoxy. "The Church is indeed bound to defend her faith," he continues, "but she can never afford to be content with defending it on the intellectual plane. The Evangelical Revival was conspicuously unintellectual. That was, indeed, its limitation. It was, no doubt, incapable of fighting the Socinians with their own weapons. But it turned the Socinian flank by its appeal to the hearts and consciences of men."[1] It is with the theological presuppositions of the Revival message that we must now concern ourselves. In a certain sense it is undeniable, of course, that there was a noticeable absence of originality, for it was the aim of the Evangelical preachers to recall their hearers to the old neglected truths of ths gospel. Their preoccupation was with the fidelity of their sermons to the Word of God rather than with the progress of Christian thought—which in itself is a more recent concept. Indeed, so long had the vital doctrines of the faith lain buried under the felicitoue ineffectualities of much Latitudinarian rhetoric that they now appeared as some new thing. Edmund Gibson, in a pastoral letter to the diocese of London, had occasion to warn his flock against the enthusiasm of the Methodists. He vigorously protested against Whitefield's claim to "propagate a new Gospel, as unknown to the generality of ministers and people, in a Christian country."[2] But in his "Answer to the Bishop" Whitefield held that it was sadly true that though he preached the old gospel of salvation by grace it was nevertheless totally new to his hearers since they had been misled by an irresponsible or unregenerate clergy. But the Evangelical leaders would by no means affirm that their doctrines were novel. On the contrary, they gloried in their antiquity. Nor would they regard them as the monopoly of a party. Their plea was that what they proclaimed was the core of Christian truth in every

[1] Smyth, *op. cit.*, p. 106.
[2] Whitefield, *Works*, Vol. IV, p. 15.

faithful generation. But to this central corpus of received belief they added their own peculiar stresses, largely in response to the demands of the living situation with which they were confronted. Thus Elliott-Binns is justified in saying that what differentiates them is not a distinctive essence but a distinctive emphasis.[1] It is this which at times gives the appearance of imbalance.

Another phrase of Elliott-Binns also aptly delineates their position. The Evangelicals, he says, were not only orthodox in doctrine, but enthusiastically orthodox.[2] They were aware that orthodoxy is not enough. It may be barren and unfruitful unless it is charged with the sap of life. "Orthodoxy, I say, or right opinion," declared Wesley, "is but a slender part of religion at best, and sometimes no part at all. I mean, if a man be a child of God, holy in heart and life, his right opinions are but the smallest part of his religion: if a man be a child of the devil, his right opinions are no part of religion, they cannot be; for he that does the works of the devil has no religion at all."[3] It was this recognition that truth is to be tested by love, that the practical and experiential outcome of belief counts for more than mere soundness of view, which marked the Evangelical approach to doctrine.

It is clear that the message of the Revival carried with it an irresistible authority. It could not have produced the effects it did had it been otherwise. "All religion, historically speaking, has depended and must depend for the masses of mankind upon authority," wrote Leslie Stephen. "A creed built on elaborate syllogisms is a creed with 'perhaps' in it, and no such creed can command men's emotions."[4] Where lay the authoritative source of the Revival message? There can be no question that for the preachers themselves it lay in the Word of God. Their power derived, they would have said, from their wielding of the Spirit's sword. The orthodox divines of the day had withstood the assaults of the Deistic writers as they sought to undermine the authority of Scripture by elevating reason above revelation, so that the mind of man is permitted to sit in judgment on the truth of God. Tindal's *Christianity as Old as Creation*, which appeared in 1730, represents the climax of such rationalistic speculation and no less than one hundred and fifty replies were evoked. But even in their hour of triumph the defenders of the faith succumbed to the methods of their Deistic opponents and "conceived of revela-

---

[1] Elliott-Binns, *Evangelical Movement*, p. 98.
[2] Ibid., p. 91.
[3] Wesley, *Letters*, Vol. III, p. 183.
[4] L. Stephen, *The History of English Thought in the Eighteenth Century*, Vol. I, p. 175.

tion as a limited number of moral dicta, extra to those already known by natural religion, and against the excesses of the enthusiasts they regarded it as a body of communicated truths demanding an unquestioning assent."[1] "The result of such views," continues Dr. H. D. McDonald, "of revealed religion, was to make the preaching of the period lacking in life and warmth. It was coldly apologetic and fiercely polemical. Religion was a matter of debate, the attainment of right notions. Thus in the pulpit, as Dr. Johnson informs us, 'the apostles were tried once a week on the charge of committing forgery.' It was all wonderfully impressive, but weakly ineffective: there was a certain evidence of learning, but little evidence of life."[2] It is no marvel, then, that the impassioned, convinced and convincing utterances of the Revival messengers should elicit the response they did. The note of authority returned to the pulpit: an authority springing from the Word and finding its corroboration in the heart of man.

In their attitude to the Holy Scriptures the Evangelical preachers traced their pedigree through the Puritans and the Reformers to the primitive Church and the Bible itself. They took their stand unambiguously on the Sixth Article of the Church of England: "Holy Scripture containeth all things necessary to salvation: so that whatsoever is not read therein, nor may be proved thereby, is not to be required by any man, that it should be believed thereby as an Article of the Faith, or be thought requisite or necessary to salvation." From the greatest to the least the instruments of the eighteenth-century Revival were unanimous in their conception and treatment of God's Word. They adopted what has been described as the reverential approach to the Bible and sought only to be faithful ambassadors who refused to go beyond their brief. For them the written Word of God was the final and indisputable authority because of its divine inspiration and unique character. Here is George Whitefield appealing to a hypothetical agnostic in a sermon on the Holy Spirit:

> If thou canst prove, thou unbeliever, that the book, which we call the Bible, does not contain the lively oracles of God; if thou canst shew, that holy men of old did not write this book, as they were inwardly moved by the Holy Ghost, then we must give up the doctrine . . . ; but unless thou canst do this, we must insist upon it . . . if for no other, yet for this one reason, because that God, who cannot lie, has told us so.[3]

[1] H. D. McDonald, *Ideas of Revelation*, p. 149.
[2] Ibid.
[3] G. Whitefield, *The Indwelling of the Spirit*, p. 12.

Here is John Wesley providing what he called a short, clear, strong argument on the same theme:

> The Bible must be the invention of either good men or angels, bad men or devils, or of God. (1) It could not be the invention of good men or angels, for they neither would nor could make a book, and tell lies all the time they were writing it, saying, "Thus saith the Lord," when it was their own invention. (2) It could not be the invention of bad men or devils, for they would not make a book which commands all duty, forbids all sin, and condemns their souls to hell to all eternity. (3) Therefore I draw this conclusion that the Bible must be given by divine inspiration.[1]

Elsewhere he declared that he allowed no other rule of faith or practice than the Holy Scripture and affirmed with evident emphasis his belief in the Bible as the Word of God. "According to the light we have, we cannot but believe the Scripture is of God; and, while we believe this, we dare not turn aside from it, to the right hand or to the left."[2] Here is Thomas Haweis, the Anglican Evangelical, asserting that "all Scripture is of divine authority" and "therefore on God's testimony to be received with faith,"[3] and adding that it is "perfectly pure from all falsehood and corrupt intention" and "the unadulterated fountain of truth."[4]

This was the presupposition of revival preaching, as it has been in every age. In all the voluminous sermonic literature of the eighteenth-century Awakening no single exception can be found. As Bishop Ryle reminded readers of his time:

> ... the spiritual reformers of the last century taught constantly *the sufficiency and supremacy of the Holy Scripture*. The Bible, whole and unmutilated, was their sole rule of faith and practice. They accepted all its statements without question or dispute. They knew nothing of any part of Scripture being uninspired. They never allowed that man has any "verifying faculty" within him by which Scripture statements may be weighed, rejected or received. They never flinched from asserting that there can be no error in the Word of God; and that when we cannot understand or reconcile some parts of its contents, the fault is in the interpreter and not in the text. In all their preaching they were eminently men of one book. To that book they were content to pin their faith, and by it to stand or fall.[5]

The Bible-based ministry of the revivalists inevitably produced preaching of an unashamedly doctrinal nature. It involved a re-

---

[1] Wesley, *Works*, Vol. XI, pp. 478-9.
[2] Ibid., Vol. VIII, p. 6: cf. Wesley, *Letters*, Vol. I, p. 285.
[3] T. Haweis, *The Evangelical Expositor*, Vol. III, p. 597.
[4] Ibid., Vol. I, pp. 3, 298.
[5] Ryle, *op. cit.*, p. 26.

turn to the forgotten truths of the evangelical faith of which regeneration was the first and most significant. In a very real sense
the new birth represents the fundamental teaching and experience
of the Awakening. Whitefield, Wesley and all the preachers of the
Revival proclaimed it incessantly. It was the particular preoccupation of the first-named. "There was scarcely one sermon," claimed
Joseph Smith in delivering his funeral oration, "in which Mr.
Whitefield did not insist upon the necessity of the new birth.
With passionate vehemency and earnest repetition he cried again
and again: 'Except a man be born again, he cannot see the kingdom of God'." Whether he addressed the colliers of Kingswood
or the intelligentsia of London in the Countess of Huntingdon's
drawing-room, George Whitefield chose the same subject. And
even when he wrote to Benjamin Franklin, one of the foremost
scientific investigators of his day who had recently expounded the
phenomenon of the Leyden jar, he could not keep away from his
magnificent obsession. "I find that you grow more and more
famous in the learned world. As you have made a pretty considerable progress in the mysteries of electricity, I would now
humbly recommend to your diligent unprejudiced pursuit and
study the mystery of the new birth."[1] On one occasion somebody
asked him: "Mr. Whitefield, why do you preach so often on 'Ye
must be born again'?" "Because," replied the great evangelist,
fixing his questioner with a solemn gaze, " 'ye *must* be born
again'."

Wesley was equally insistent upon the need for regeneration,
but in his famous sermon on "The New Birth" he rightly related
it to the work of justification.

> If any doctrines within the whole compass of Christianity may
> properly be termed fundamental, they are doubtless these two, the
> doctrine of justification, and that of the new birth; the former relat-
> ing to that great work which God does *for us* in forgiving our sins;
> the latter to the great work which God does *in us* in renewing our
> fallen nature. In order of *time* neither of these is before the other; in a
> moment we are justified by the grace of God, through the redemp-
> tion that is in Jesus, we are also "born of the Spirit," but in order of
> *thinking*, as it is termed, justification precedes the New Birth. We
> first conceive His wrath to be turned away, and then His Spirit to
> work in our hearts.[2]

As has already been seen, the turning-point in Wesley's spiritual

[1] Whitefield, *Works*, Vol. II, p. 440.
[2] Wesley, *Sermons*, Vol. II, pp. 226-7.

career came when he accepted salvation by faith alone and hence-forward the preaching of this Reformation principle led to the fruitful consequences described in previous chapters. A major section of Professor George Croft Cell's volume, *The Rediscovery of John Wesley*, considers "the increment of power in Wesley's preaching, due to his rediscovery and adoption in 1738 of the Luther-Calvin idea of the sovereign saving significance of a God-given faith in Christ as the clue and key to the objective signifi-cance and historical importance of his conversion experience."[1]

The stress laid by the Revival message on justification and re-generation presupposes a serious doctrine of sin. The *quam longissime* in the original Latin of the Ninth Article—*quia fit ut ab originali iustitia quam longissime distet*—was dwelt upon as the fallen state of man was described. All mankind was involved in the fall of Adam since he was the federal head of the human race. Consequently every man is now "very far gone from original righteousness" and no unbeliever can excuse himself before God.

> I affirm that we all stand in need of being justified, on account of the sin of our natures [stated Whitefield], for we are all chargeable with original sin, or the sin of our first parents. Which, though . . . denied by a self-justifying infidel . . . can never be denied by anyone who believes that St. Paul's letters were written by divine inspiration; where we are told that "in Adam all died"; that is, Adam's sin was imputed to all; . . . "that we are all . . . by nature the children of wrath". And . . . that "death came upon all, . . . even upon those (that is, little children), who had not sinned after the similitude of Adam's transgression." . . . So that what has been said in this point seems to be excellently summed up in that article of our church, where she declares "Original sin . . . is the fault and corruption of every man."[2]

Yet this insistence on total depravity is not divorced from the good news of salvation in Jesus Christ. It is vitally linked with it and thus redeemed from despair.

Regeneration not only assumes a realistic doctrine of sin: it anticipates a lofty presentation of holiness. It was a marked feature of the Revival, most especially in the Methodist sector, that the full possibilities of life in the Spirit were portrayed. The Catechism taught that the peculiar office of the Holy Spirit lay in "sanctifying the elect people of God." It was by plainly proclaim-ing that such sanctification is the will of God for every believer and that God Himself has made available the resources which

---

[1] Cell, *op. cit.*, p. 165.
[2] Whitefield, *Works*, Vol. VI, pp. 217-18.

alone can enable him to attain it that the evangelists ensured that their converts would not easily lapse. Indeed, this necessary and Scriptural teaching is the only safeguard against spiritual mortality.

Although the central message of the Revival had to do with the individual and his salvation, it must not therefore be supposed that the communal aspect of Christianity was allowed to fall into the background. The Church and its ordinances are continually the subject of exhortation. In an age of indifference and sometimes of open contempt the Evangelical Revival helped to reinstate the dignity and sincerity of Christian worship. A new reverence and earnestness marked the conduct of services and the standard of Church music and especially of congregational singing was raised immeasurably. Much was done to restore the Holy Communion to its rightful place in the life of the Church. It had been observed with little frequency and often with little solemnity. But as the effects of the Revival began to be felt the sacrament was administered with greater regularity and attended by increasing numbers. Evangelical preachers were at pains to instruct their flock in this regard. Romaine wrote *The Scriptural Doctrine of the Lord's Supper briefly stated*. Walker carefully explained the nature and purpose of the rite to his communicants at Truro. Grimshaw laid especial stress upon its importance at Haworth and in his *Letter to a Christian Society* in 1754 urged the members to make every Communion a feast day. The Wesleys were constantly pressing their followers to attend their parish churches in order to participate and the incumbents were sometimes embarrassed by the numbers who presented themselves.

Although there was an astonishingly large measure of unanimity in the declaration of the evangelical message in the eighteenth century, it must not therefore be assumed that there was agreement at all points. This was clearly not the case. It might well be argued that in essentials there was unity and that the controverted themes were not of the essence of the faith. But whilst this conclusion might satisfy the dispassionate onlooker who views the scene from the calm vantage point of the twentieth century, it would not have seemed so to most of the contending parties. The most disruptive variation lay between the Calvinist and Arminian interpretations of the Christian gospel and on neither side would the protagonists have regarded their differences as merely circumferential. Nevertheless it must be recognized that both parties remained undeviatingly loyal to the great central emphases of the

Revival which we have already examined and were altogether at one in their submission to Scripture as the sole standard of faith and practice. Moreover, both Calvinist and Arminian preaching was honoured equally in the blessing of the hungry multitudes and where the seal of divine approval rests we can only conclude that the truth has indeed been set forth.

Recent surveys are showing that the gulf between these versions of the one gospel is not perhaps as wide as has been imagined. The Minutes of the second Wesleyan Conference assert that the true gospel "lies very near," "within a hair's breadth," "comes to the very edge of Calvinism."[1] And, as Dr. Cell makes clear, this refers not to the basic doctrine of sin and salvation which Wesley fully shared with the Calvinists, but to the single disputed item of predestination. But this matter was the subject of less than one in a hundred of Wesley's discourses, as he himself claimed.[2] The vast majority were concerned with the fundamentals of the evangelical faith which he held and expounded in harmony with his Calvinistic brethren. It must not be thought that the peculiar fire and force of the Revival message was derived either from Whitefield's ultra-Calvinistic insistences or from Wesley's Arminian correctives. Its true source lay in what they both held in common of the reformed and primitive faith.

> There need be no doubt whatsoever [says Cell] that the principle of power and the supreme resource in the preaching alike of Whitefield and the Wesleys by which, all agree, a religious revolution was begun in England, was the Luther-Calvin idea of the sovereign saving significance of a God-given faith in Christ as a perfect revelation of God and a complete atonement for sin. It is often, perhaps commonly, supposed that the theological differences between Whitefield and the Wesleys were profound while their doctrinal agreements were superficial, at any rate far less important. But they certainly did not think so and Wesley roundly denounced that view as close to absurdity. Wesley is on record, not once but often and always, that the peculiar energy of the Wesleyan Revival came out of the unity of the Protestant faith, the very heart of it, and not out of its divergences.[3]

Whatever may have been the extravagances of some of the later disputants, those who were most actively engaged in the work of the Revival, especially in its earlier stages, were least anxious to sharpen the edge of controversy. Here is James Hervey, himself a convinced Calvinist, confessing:

[1] Wesley, *Works*, Vol. VIII, pp. 284-5.
[2] Wesley, *Letters*, Vol. IV, p. 297.
[3] Cell, *op. cit.*, p. 247.

As for points of doubtful disputation,—those especially which relate to particular or universal redemption,—I profess myself attached neither to the one nor the other. I neither think of them myself nor preach of them to others. If they happen to be started in conversation I always endeavour to divert the discourse to some more edifying topic. I have often observed them to breed animosity and division, but never knew them to be productive of love and unanimity. I have further remarked that, in forming their sentiments on these doctrines, persons may be diametrically opposite, and yet be high in the favour of God, and eminently owned by Him in their ministry. Therefore I rest satisfied with this general and indisputable truth, that, the Judge of all the earth will assuredly do right; and whosoever cometh to Him, under the gracious character of a Saviour, will in no wise be cast out.[1]

Here is Henry Venn, another of the Calvinist school, though of the moderate wing, enjoying a quiet smile over the fact that he had "always been too much on the side of free grace for many Arminians, too much on the side of experimental religion for many Calvinists" and providing this testimony within eighteen months of his death:

> The whole Word of God is equally acceptable to me; not less those parts which are the fortress of Arminians, Perfectionists and Antinomians, than others; so that I am and have been for thirty-five years in the happy state of not being tempted to wrest any Scripture or pervert it in order to make it favour my own tenets.[2]

Here is John Wesley, the Arminian, acknowledging that he had come to know many believers in predestination whose "real Christian experience" could not be denied, and adding that this fact stared him in the face, and was clear proof that predestination

> Is only an opinion, not subversive of the very foundations of Christian experience, but compatible with a love to Christ and a genuine work of grace. Yea, many hold it at whose feet I desire to be found in the day of the Lord Jesus.[3]

Here is Charles Simeon summing up the issue:

> The author is no friend of systemizers in theology. He has endeavoured to obtain from the scriptures alone his view of religion; and to them it is his wish to adhere, with scrupulous fidelity; never wresting any portion of the Word of God to favour a particular opinion, but giving to every part of it that sense, which it seems to him to have been designed by its great Author to convey. He has no doubt but that there is a system in the Holy Scriptures (for truth cannot be inconsistent with itself); but he is persuaded that neither

---

[1] *Arminian Magazine*, 1778, p. 34.
[2] J. and H. Venn, *op. cit.*, pp. 208, 532.
[3] Wesley, *Letters*, Vol. IV, p. 298.

Calvinists nor Arminians are in *exclusive* possession of that system. He is disposed to think that the Scripture system, be it what it may, is of a broader and more comprehensive character than some very exact and dogmatical theologians are inclined to allow: and that, as wheels in a complicated machine may move in opposite directions and yet subserve one common end, so may truths *apparently opposite* be perfectly reconcilable with each other, and equally subserve the purposes of God in the accomplishment of man's salvation.[1]

Simeon used to say that if he were asked whether he were a Calvinist he would reply that he was not. If he were asked whether he were an Arminian he would again reply that he was not. If he were then asked what in fact he was, he would answer, "A Bible Christian." That was the ultimate position of those whom God chose to employ in the work of Revival in the eighteenth century. Here lies the source of their unanimity and power. Hence they derived their essential message.

[1] C. Simeon, *Horae Homileticae*, Vol. I, p. xxiii.

CHAPTER XVI

THE INFLUENCE OF THE REVIVAL

THE FULL EFFECT OF REVIVAL IS ULTIMATELY INCALCU-
lable. No human yardstick can measure the overall impact
of a supernatural phenomenon of this order. The consequences of Pentecostal quickening defy computation. The impression is more than merely superficial. It penetrates below the
surface and exercises an uninterrupted influence long after the
outward manifestations have disappeared. It may well be concluded that revival represents an advance in depth and it is precisely these profundities which cannot be plumbed by normal
methods of investigation. Only the Spirit Himself can search the
deep things of God. This was the aspect of the eighteenth-century
Awakening which most struck John Wesley as he reviewed its
course in his now celebrated sermon at the foundation of City
Road Chapel, London. Preaching from Numbers 23 : 23, "What
hath God wrought?" he began by indicating the exceptional extent of the movement.

> This revival of religion has spread to such a degree as neither we
> nor our fathers had known. How *extensive* has it been! There is
> scarce a considerable town in the kingdom where some have not
> been made witnesses of it. It has spread to every age and sex, to most
> orders and degrees of men; and even to abundance of those who, in
> time past, were accounted monsters of wickedness.

Next the rapidity of this expansion engaged his attention.

> Consider the *swiftness* as well as extent of it. In what age has such
> a number of sinners been recovered from the error of their ways?
> When has true religion, I will not say since the Reformation, but
> since the time of Constantine the Great, made so large a progress in
> any nation, within so small a space? I believe hardly can either
> ancient or modern history afford a parallel instance.

But Wesley proceeded to dwell with great emphasis upon the enduring effects of the Revival.

> We may likewise observe the *depth* of the work so extensively and
> swiftly wrought. Multitudes have been thoroughly convinced of sin;

and, shortly after, so filled with joy and love, that whether they were in the body or out of the body, they could hardly tell; and in the power of this love they have trampled under foot whatever the world accounts either terrible or desirable, having evidenced, in their severest trials, an invariable and tender goodwill to mankind, and all the fruits of holiness. Now so deep a repentance, so strong a faith, so fervent love, and so unblemished holiness, wrought in so many persons in so short a time, the world has not seen for many ages.[1]

This must necessarily be regarded as the supreme consequence of the Awakening, for as Finney enquired, what is revival but multiplied conversions? At the head of our catalogue of influences this lasting transformation of innumerable lives must be set. And lest it might be suspected that Wesley's own judgment could scarcely be altogether unprejudiced, let us append the considered and impartial statement of Canon Overton:

If the faith which enabled a man to abandon the cherished habits of a lifetime and go forth ready to spend and be spent in his Master's service, which nerved him to overcome the natural fear of death, and, indeed to welcome the last enemy as his best friend who would introduce him to the better land he had long been living for; which made the selfish man self-denying, the discontented happy, the worldling spiritually-minded, the drunkard sober, the sensual chaste, the liar truthful, the thief honest, the proud humble, the godless godly, the thriftless thrifty—we can only judge by the fruits which it bore. That such fruits *were* borne is surely undeniable.[2]

It is inevitable that the direct impact of a religious revival should be felt within the Church. It is the very nature of revival to stir the people of God. Only indirectly, though none the less powerfully, does it bear upon secular society. Evan Roberts's prayer, "Lord, bend the Church and save the world!" suggests the pattern and procedure involved. So we are not surprised to learn that, in the language of W. J. Townsend, the Church of the eighteenth century "felt a Divine vibration" whilst the Spirit moved in the midst.[3] More balanced estimates of the Hanoverian Church do not remove the need for a spiritual influx nor render the resultant inspiration less remarkable. This was particularly evident within the Establishment. The Evangelical clergy, according to Lecky, "gradually changed the whole spirit of the English Church. They infused into it a new fire and passion of devotion, kindled a spirit of fervent philanthropy, raised the standard of clerical duty, and completely altered the whole tone and tendency

---

[1] Wesley, *Works*, Vol. VII, pp. 425-6.
[2] Overton, *op. cit.*, p. 13.
[3] *New History of Methodism*, Vol. I, p. 364.

of the preaching of its ministers."[1] Sir James Stephen rightly described the Evangelical fathers as "the second founders of the Church of England."[2]

The initial and determinative transformation took place amongst the clergy themselves. We have seen how almost all the great leaders of the Revival were converted in holy orders. Their experience of God's grace and love led them to a new conception of their pastoral duty and their tireless, devoted labours set a fresh and unprecedented standard of clerical fidelity and effectiveness. A truly apostolic ministry was reintroduced into the Church of England: holding the apostolic doctrines, fulfilling the apostolic mission, and displaying the apostolic spirit. This marked improvement in the discharge of clerical obligations and the accompanying rediscovery of ministerial vocation represents the major effect of the Revival upon the Church of England. "I have seen no change in my long life," wrote Thomas Grenville, "equal to the change in the habits and manners of the clergy."[3] The zeal and assiduity of the Evangelical incumbents stirred their associates to emulation. It was the exemplary devotion of John Newton which first impressed the careless Thomas Scott and led him towards evangelical conversion. On more than one occasion Newton had walked over from Olney to visit two of Scott's parishioners who were seriously ill and whom he himself had neglected. "Directly it occurred to me," he confessed, "that whatever contempt I might have for Mr. Newton's doctrines, I must acknowledge his practice to be more consistent with the ministerial character than my own. He must have more zeal and love for souls than I had or he would not have walked so far to visit and supply my lack of care to those who as far as I was concerned might have been left to perish in their sins."[4]

Church life as a whole was not unnaturally affected by this change of heart among the clergy. Congregations vastly increased; week-night services and classes were instituted; catechetical and Scriptural instruction became common. Holy Communion was administered with greater frequency and there is more than a touch of truth in G. W. E. Russell's assertion that the Evangelical Revival paved the way for the Oxford Movement in its renewed devotion to the sacrament.[5] The Evangelical contribution to

[1] Lecky, *op. cit.*, Vol. II, p. 627.
[2] J. Stephen, *Essays in Ecclesiastical Biography*, p. 445.
[3] Cf. Elliott-Binns, *Early Evangelicals*, p. 419.
[4] T. Scott, *op. cit.*, p. 24.
[5] Cf. *Theology*, Vol. LIII, p. 327.

hymnody can scarcely be overestimated and did much to raise the
level of worship. The replacement of what John Wesley justifiably
dubbed "the miserable, scandalous doggerel of Sternhold and
Hopkins"[1] by the uplifting hymns of Watts and Charles Wesley, of
Newton and Cowper, of Toplady and Olivers, of Cennick and
Montgomery, constituted a major revolution.

The impact of the Evangelical Revival was felt at least as much
upon Dissent as in the Church of England. Prior to the Awakening
Dissent was at a lamentably low ebb. Indeed, according to Isaac
Watts, "it was rapidly in the course to be found nowhere but in
books."[2] The inroads of Latitudinarianism had been perhaps even
more incisive than in the Establishment and political controversy
had drained the Nonconformists of their pristine spirituality. The
Revival supplied an overdue fillip to a decadent Dissent. So great
was the increase that it has been claimed that whereas at the opening of the century the proportion of Dissenters to Anglicans was
only one in twenty-two, by the end it was as much as one in eight,
and this did not include the Methodists. In the opinion of Piette,
it is unquestionable that the Awakening under Wesley "caused an
outburst of fervour in the Protestant world. Not only those disciples who have felt the direct influence of the master, but, in
addition, by emulation, Anglicans, Congregationalists, Baptists, in
short, all those for whom Christ was still a Divine Being, the
Arianized Presbyterians being the only exceptions—all experienced
a renewal of spiritual life."[3] It is a noticeable fact that such Inde-
pendents and Baptists as had been resuscitated by the Revival reported considerable increases whilst the Presbyterians who had
succumbed to Socinian views declined.

But the influence of the Revival was more than a matter of the
conversion of individuals and the rejuvenation of churches. It expressed itself most markedly in the establishment of a series of
agencies for the promotion of Christian work, of which the
missionary societies must be mentioned first. The astonishing
missionary advance at the close of the eighteenth century and the
onset of the nineteenth was a direct consequence of the Evangelical Awakening. The world church, which Archbishop Temple
hailed as "the great new fact of our era,"[4] was only made possible
by the outflow of missionary enthusiasm and endeavour which
stemmed from Great Britain after the Revival. The first English
missionary society had been founded as far back as 1649 for the

---

[1] Wesley, *Letters*, Vol. III, p. 227.   [2] Overton, *op. cit.*, p. 153.
[3] Piette, *op. cit.*, p. 651.   [4] W. Temple, *The Church Looks Forward*, p. 2.

purpose of propagating the Gospel in New England. In 1682 work was attempted in the East Indies and in 1691 the Christian Faith Society for the West Indies was inaugurated. These, however, were but local experiments. The formation of the Society for Promoting Christian Knowledge in 1698 and in 1701 its assistant organization, the Society of the Propagation of the Gospel, marked a new stage in missionary effort. Although the S.P.C.K. supported the work of Danish Lutheran evangelists in India its witness, like that of the S.P.G., was confined by charter to the British colonies. There was therefore abundant and pressing need for more explicit missionary enterprise. It was the Evangelical Revival which provided the stimulus and the pioneers.

In this the palm of priority must undoubtedly be awarded to the Moravians, although, as their missionary work was organized from their headquarters at Herrnhut, theirs cannot be regarded as a British society. But the repercussions of the enterprise begun as early as 1732 affected the entire evangelical movement and was instrumental in bringing about the missionary awakening at the close of the century. We cannot lightly discount this factor. "The vast missionary energy of the Church of the Brethren is a unique fact in the history of the whole Christian Church," wrote Warneck in his *History of Protestant Missions*, "and it is explained only by the fact that this Church, notwithstanding all the weaknesses attaching to it, is the manifestation of a fellowship grounded in the evangelical faith and rooted in the love of Christ. . . . In two decades the little Church of the Brethren called more missionaries into life than did the whole of Protestantism in two centuries."[1]

In his *History of the Church Missionary Society* Eugene Stock selected 1786 as the *annus mirabilis* of missionary development. He listed an impressive number of events each of which paved the way for the subsequent missionary recrudescence and each of which sprang from an Evangelical source. In that year William Wilberforce made his resolve "to live to God's glory and his fellow creatures' good."[2] In that year Thomas Clarkson published his famous essay against the slave trade and Granville Sharpe formulated his plan for settling liberated slaves in Sierra Leone. In that year the first ship-load of convicts sailed from England to Botany Bay and through the intervention of Wilberforce, Newton and Thornton, Richard Johnson was sent as chaplain. In that

[1] G. Warneck, *The History of Protestant Missions*, pp. 63-4. Towlson, *op. cit.*, p. 180, does not hesitate to call these Moravian efforts "the first modern missions".
[2] E. Stock, *The History of the Church Missionary Society*, p. 57.

year C. F. Schwartz, a Lutheran missionary of the S.P.C.K. in South India, visited Tinnevelley, David Brown, a former pupil of Joseph Milner, arrived in Calcutta as one of the chaplains of the East India Company and Charles Grant, the senior merchant, devised a scheme for a mission in Bengal. In that year Thomas Coke on his second American voyage headed for Nova Scotia, but repeated storms drove the ship off course to Antigua where he exercised a most fruitful ministry. In that year members of the Eclectic Society, composed of Evangelical clergy and laymen in London, discussed "the best method of planting and propagating the Gospel in Botany Bay" and elsewhere.[1] In that year William Carey first suggested at a meeting of Baptist ministers in Northampton that they should consider their responsibilities to the heathen. Prior to this in 1784 John Sutcliffe, a Baptist minister at Olney, who had been thrilled to read of the Great Awakening in America, had called the Northamptonshire Baptist churches to special intercession for an outpouring of the Spirit. As Dr. Payne observes, "it was probably these prayer meetings, as much as any other single influence, which prepared the little group of ministers to venture on the formation of a missionary society."[2]

It was when Carey was preaching the sermon at the Association gathering in Nottingham at Whitsuntide 1792 that he pleaded with his congregation to "expect great things from God and attempt great things for God." It seemed that his message had fallen on unresponsive ears and as the meeting was about to disperse Carey asked Andrew Fuller, "Is there nothing again going to be done, sir?" And so at the eleventh hour the resolution was carried to form a Baptist Society for propagating the Gospel among the heathen. On Tuesday, 2nd October, 1792, in Widow Wallis's back parlour in Kettering the project was launched and the sum of £13 2s. 6d. was placed in a snuff-box to start the work of world evangelization.

Before this, in 1790, the Methodist Conference had appointed a Committee of management to superintend the missionary witness in the West Indies begun by Coke, and Thomas Haweis, the Anglican Evangelical, had unsuccessfully attempted to send two of the Countess of Huntingdon's Trevecka students to the South Seas.[3] It was Haweis who was to prove instrumental in establish-

---

[1] Ibid., p. 58.   [2] E. A. Payne, *The Church Awakes*, p. 31.

[3] Allan Birtwhistle claims that the Methodist Missionary Society was really launched in 1786 when the Conference approved Coke's missionary design with the proviso that the Connexion itself should be responsible rather than a Society (*Proceedings of Wesley Historical Society*, Vol. XXX, pp. 25-9).

ing the next great missionary society in 1795. His review of Melville Horne's *Letters on Missions* in the *Evangelical Magazine* for November 1794 was followed by a specific proposal to form an interdenominational body. Along with John Eyre and David Bogue, Haweis may rightly be regarded as the co-founder of the London Missionary Society. The first missionary ship, the *Duff*, sailed in 1796 for Tahiti and thus Haweis's dream of taking the gospel to the South Sea islands was eventually fulfilled. The Church Missionary Society, constituted in 1799, was equally a child of the Evangelical Revival. Already the Eclectic Society had been concerned with missionary endeavour. In May 1795 at a meeting of an Evangelical Clerical Association at Rauceby in Lincolnshire it was announced that a bequest of £4,000 had been devised by Joseph Jane, the Evangelical Vicar of St. Mary Magdalene, Oxford, and later of Iron Acton, Gloucestershire, "to be laid out to the best advantage to the interest of true religion."[1] The matter was eventually referred to the Eclectic Society and Charles Simeon proposed the question, "With what propriety, and in what mode, can a mission be attempted to the heathen from the Established Church?" A discussion ensued and Basil Woodd, who was present, afterwards declared, "This conversation proved the foundation of the C.M.S."[2] In 1799 there was finally formed "A Society for Missions to Africa and the East" with Henry Venn as chairman, Thomas Scott as secretary and John Thornton as treasurer. In 1812 the name was altered to that of the Church Missionary Society.

But societies other than missionary owe their initiation to the Revival. In 1796 Thomas Bernard, William Wilberforce and the then Bishop of Durham, Shute Barrington, collaborated to form the Society for Bettering and Increasing the Comforts of the Poor. As far back as 1750 a Society for Diffusing Religious Knowledge amongst the Poor had been established, but the aim of this later body was to ensure that the health and safety regulations were duly observed in the rapidly expanding factories. In 1799 the Religious Tract Society came into being, mainly through the advocacy of George Burder, an Independent minister at Coventry who had been influenced by Whitefield and Romaine. Already Hannah More had circulated her Cheap Repository Tracts and John Wesley had been responsible for the distribution of similar pamphlets. The R.T.S., however, was intended to be more com-

[1] C. Hole, *The Early History of the Church Missionary Society*, p. 63.
[2] W. Carus, *Memoirs of the Life of Charles Simeon*, p. 229.

prehensive and, unlike the S.P.C.K., it was not confined to the Established Church. The work is now incorporated in the United Society for Christian Literature. The British and Foreign Bible Society, founded in 1804, had a predecessor in the Naval and Military Bible Society of 1780. The events which led to its formation date from as far back as 1787. It was in that year that an appeal was made from Wales, where the Revival had made such headway, for a further supply of Bibles. The S.P.C.K. had not issued a copy in Welsh for some considerable time and there was a distressing dearth. An edition of 10,000 in 1799 proved to be quite inadequate to meet the demand. The urgency of the situation was brought home to Thomas Charles of Bala when little Mary Jones tramped fifty miles over the Welsh hills with her six years' savings only to find that the last copy of the Scriptures in her native tongue had been sold. Charles thereupon dedicated himself to the task of securing Bibles for Wales and when the S.P.C.K. was unable to afford further help, he proposed to the committee of the R.T.S. the plan of forming a Bible Society of which the sole object should be "to encourage a wider diffusion of the Holy Scriptures."[1] The scheme was readily approved and one member enquired, "Surely a Society might be formed for the purpose, and if for Wales, why not for the Kingdom? and if for the Kingdom, why not for the world?" Thus was launched the British and Foreign Bible Society with the principal objective of disseminating copies of the Word of God "without note or comment" not only in Great Britain but throughout the world. It was interdenominational in character from the start and its constitution demanded equal representation as between Anglican and Nonconformist members of committee and joint secretaries. Its close association with the Evangelical Revival is sufficiently indicated by the first officers. Lord Teignmouth was chairman, with Wilberforce as vice-president. The secretaries were Josiah Pratt and Joseph Hughes whilst John Thornton was treasurer.

The Sunday School movement also had its roots in the Revival. Numerous attempts have been made to trace its exact origin. Of course, there had been experiments along similar lines before the eighteenth century, but they were not co-ordinated into a concerted policy. Hints may be discovered as far back as the time of Martin Luther, John Knox and Carlo Borromeo, who founded a Confraternity of Christian Doctrine for instructing children. Joseph Alleine, the Puritan author of *The Alarm to the Uncon-*

[1] Balleine, *op. cit.*, p. 133

verted, conducted a Sunday School in his meeting place in the latter part of the seventeenth century and Thomas Wilson, Bishop of Sodor and Man, introduced it in 1703. The Revival occasioned further efforts in this novel direction. John Wesley had formed Sabbath instruction classes for children in Georgia and advocated a similar practice in this country. The first Methodist Sunday School of which any record remains was started in 1769 at High Wycombe by Hannah Ball. Herself a convert of Wesley, she was led to employ this means of furthering the Christian education of the young. "The children meet twice a week, every Sunday and Monday," she told Wesley. "They are a wild little company, but seem willing to be instructed. I labour among them, earnestly desiring to promote the interest of the Church of Christ."[1] Hannah Ball persevered in this pioneer enterprise until her death in 1792, when her sister Anne took over. Other instances of such ventures also come to our occasional notice. These, however, were isolated and unrelated projects. It was only with the advent of Robert Raikes that the method became widespread.

Raikes himself was a wealthy Evangelical layman in the city of Gloucester. He was a friend of Whitefield and the Wesleys. His first philanthropic efforts were directed at prison reform but he soon realized that crime was often the result of ignorance and neglect. His attention was drawn to the need of the street urchins by Sophia Cooke, a Methodist, who afterwards married Samuel Bradburn, one of Wesley's preachers. It was she who pointed out to Raikes the crowd of young ragamuffins in St. Catherine's meadows and she marched with Raikes at the head of his tatterde-malion regiment when first they attended the Cathedral service. With the help of Thomas Stock, curate of St. John the Baptist's, Raikes opened his Sunday School from 10 a.m. until noon and from 1 p.m. until evensong. They returned to learn the catechism until 5.30 p.m. before being sent to their homes. When Raikes published an account of his experiment in the *Gloucester Journal* in 1783, three years after he had begun it, some of the London papers copied it and Wesley reprinted it in the *Arminian Magazine*. It attracted considerable attention and Evangelicals and Methodists alike implemented it in actual practice. Fletcher of Madeley started six schools in various parts of his parish and in the summer held open-air classes in the Shropshire woods. Thomas Wilson opened one at Slaithwaite. Cornelius Bayley at Manchester and Miles Atkinson at Leeds soon followed suit. Romaine reported that the

[1] Wesley, *Journal*, Vol. V., p. 104n.

plan had been "marvellously favoured" by God and Wesley said he found more springing up wherever he went.[1] "Perhaps God may have a deeper end therein than men are aware of," he added. "Who knows but that some of these schools may become nurseries for Christians."[2] In 1786 William Richardson, the Evangelical Vicar of St. Michael-le-Belfrey, York, founded a Church of England Sunday School Society, which began with ten schools and enrolled over five hundred children on the first Sunday. The interdenominational Sunday School Union dates from 1803. The Sunday School movement was fairly launched with its altogether incalculable consequences for good.

It must not be supposed, however, that the influence of the Revival upon education was confined to the work of Sunday Schools. The programme of day-school instruction was also affected. Indeed, John Richard Green went so far as to assert that the Evangelical Awakening "gave the first impulse to popular education."[3] But space does not permit us to elaborate.

We must close by examining in brief the social impact of the Revival. It is a fallacy to imagine that spiritual quickening bypasses the realm of communal relationships. Revival rouses the conscience of both Church and State and leads to the removal of injustices and the amelioration of living and working conditions. It affects society as a whole and its beneficial consequences extend to every man. It is not difficult to substantiate such claims so far as the eighteenth century is concerned. Perhaps the most obvious and impressive example lies in the abolition of slavery. Not only did the Evangelical Revival provide the protagonists but also the principles. "The two doctrines which contributed most to the abolition of slavery," declared Benjamin Kidd in his *Social Evolution*, "were the doctrine of salvation and the doctrine of the equality of all men before the Deity."[4] These were the very doctrines stressed by the Revival. They were to prove invincible even in the face of vested interest and ingrained prejudice. In the mid-eighteenth century the iniquitous slave trade was, in the language of Sir James Stephen, "converting one quarter of this fair earth into the nearest possible resemblance of what we conceive of hell."[5] More than two hundred English vessels were engaged in the monstrous traffic and yet such was the moral blindness of the age that many who even professed and called themselves Christians could see little wrong in it. It was in 1772 that the abolitionist

[1] Ibid., p. 104.   [2] Ibid.   [3] Green, *op. cit.*, p. 718.
[4] B. Kidd, *Social Evolution*, p. 168.   [5] J. Stephen, *op. cit.*, p. 538.

cause began to attract public attention when Granville Sharpe won the Somersett case. In 1785 Thomas Clarkson composed his Latin prize essay at Oxford on the subject of slavery and eventually persuaded Wilberforce to take up the issue in Parliament. In 1787 a Committee was formed and the twenty years' fight began. Amongst those who encouraged the abolitionist group was John Wesley who assured them of his deep interest in "their glorious concern."[1] In his *Thoughts on Slavery* published as early as 1774 Wesley had already expressed himself in unequivocal terms. Four days before his death he penned his famous letter to Wilberforce, urging him on in his crusade.

> Unless the divine power has raised you up to be as *Athanasius contra mundum*, I see not how you can go through your glorious enterprise, in opposing that execrable villainy, which is the scandal of religion, of England, and of human nature. Unless God has raised you up for this very thing, you will be worn out by the opposition of men and devils. But, if God be for you, who can be against you? Are all of them together stronger than God? O be not weary in well doing! Go on, in the name of God and in the power of His might, till even American slavery (the vilest that ever saw the sun) shall vanish away before it.[2]

The prayers of Wesley the aged were to be wonderfully answered and Wilberforce's strenuous agitation was to lead at length to the Act of 1807 which declared the slave trade illegal. Throughout the long years of protest the mainspring of support was the Clapham Sect, that small and much pilloried group of Evangelical laymen who consistently sought to translate the insights of the Revival into social action.

Slavery was by no means the only issue in which the influence of the Awakening was felt. "Both the onslaught of the slave trade and the other remarkable philanthropic efforts towards the last quarter of the last century," said Lord Morley, "arose in, and owed their importance to, the great Evangelical movement." Prison reform was a further result of revival. Long before John Howard published his book on *The State of the Prisons in England and Wales* in the year 1777, John Wesley had sought to arouse the national conscience on this matter. The Oxford Methodists had included prison visitation as one of their works of mercy and Wesley kept it up all his life. In 1761 he had written to the *London Chronicle* to describe the beginnings of reform at Newgate and to urge that the example might be followed. Wesley regarded Howard as "one of

---

[1] Wesley, *Letters*, Vol. VIII, pp. 6-7.   [2] Ibid., p. 265.

the greatest men in Europe."[1] and Howard was not slow to recognize his indebtedness to the father of Methodism. Writing of a meeting with Wesley at Dublin in 1787 he says: "I was encouraged by him to go on vigorously with my own designs. I saw in him how much a single man might achieve by zeal and perseverance; and I thought, why may I not do as much in my way as Mr. Wesley has done in his, if I am only as assiduous and persevering? and I determined that I would pursue my work with more alacrity than ever."[2] The relief of the poor, the care of the sick and aged, the feeding of the hungry were all undertaken as the expression of Christian concern. Labour homes were established, schemes of work devised for the unemployed, loan offices and banks opened for the poor and legal advice provided. The curse of the drink traffic was fearlessly attacked and the foundations of the modern temperance movement laid. Perhaps most surprising of all is the denunciation of war to be found in the writings of more than one of the Evangelical leaders and nowhere more trenchantly than in the works of Wesley. "There is a still more horrid reproach to the Christian name, yea to the name of man, to all reason and humanity," he declared in his treatise on original sin. "There is war in the world! war between men! war between Christians! I mean between those that bear the name of Christ, and profess to 'walk as He also walked.' Now, who can reconcile war, I will not say to religion, but to any degree of reason or common sense?"[3]

Such a passage as that, with its startlingly modern relevance, enables us to understand the ultimate significance of the Evangelical Revival. Its influence consists of something more than a series of immediate consequences, however practical and beneficial. It rests in what Fitchett called "the continuity of spiritual impulse."[4] The Revival itself may indeed have subsided. As we have seen, the years of actual visitation were comparatively few. But the impetus it provided carried the Church through the years of intensive evangelization which we have sought to survey, and led it out into all the challenge and adventure of a new century. And to this day we are debtors to the Revival. Its force is yet unspent. The Church is moving forward still along the channels that were cut when God warmed Wesley's heart. He only waits to bring His people now into the same experience of the Spirit's fullness in order to renew His former glories and add a fresh chapter of revival to the story of the Church.

[1] Wesley, *Journal*, Vol. VII, p. 295.   [2] Tyerman, *Wesley*, Vol. III, p. 495.
[3] Wesley, *Works*, Vol. IX, p. 221.   [4] Fitchett, *op. cit.*, p. 525.

SHORT GENERAL BIBLIOGRAPHY

(*The primary sources in the writings of the Revival leaders and in contemporary memoirs have been sufficiently indicated in the footnotes. More recent biographical studies have also been mentioned in passing. The present list consists chiefly of modern authorities found to be helpful in supplying a broader background and sharper perspective.*)

Abbey, Charles J., *The English Church and its Bishops, 1700–1800*, 2 vols., London, 1887.

Abbey, Charles J., and Overton, John H., *The English Church in the Eighteenth Century*, London, 1886.

Addison, William G., *The Renewed Church of the United Brethren, 1722–1930*, London, 1930.

Armstrong, Maurice W., *The Great Awakening in Nova Scotia*, Hartford, 1948.

Baker, Eric W., *A Herald of the Evangelical Revival: A Critical Inquiry into the Relation of William Law to John Wesley and the Beginnings of Methodism*, London, 1948.

Baker, Frank, *Charles Wesley as Revealed by his Letters*, London, 1948.

Balleine, G. R., *A History of the Evangelical Party in the Church of England*, London, 1951.

Bett, Henry, *The Spirit of Methodism*, London, 1937.

Bready, J. Wesley, *England: Before and After Wesley, The Evangelical Revival and Social Reform*, London, 1938.

Bretherton, Francis F., *The Countess of Huntingdon*, London, 1940.

Butler, Dugald, *John Wesley and George Whitefield in Scotland, or, The Influence of the Oxford Methodists on Scottish Religion*, Edinburgh, 1898.

Cannon, William Ragsdale, *The Theology of John Wesley, with Special Reference to the Doctrine of Justification*, New York, 1946.

Carpenter, S. C., *Eighteenth Century Church and People*, London, 1959.

Carter, C. Sydney, *The English Church in the Eighteenth Century*, London, 1948.

Carter, Henry, *The Methodist Heritage*, London, 1950.

Cell, George Croft, *The Rediscovery of John Wesley*, New York, 1935.

Chapell, F. L., *The Great Awakening of 1740*, Philadelphia, 1903.

Church, Leslie F., *The Early Methodist People*, London, 1948.

Church, Leslie F., *More about the Early Methodist People*, London, 1949.

Clarke, W. K. Lowther, *Eighteenth Century Piety*, London, 1944.

Colligan, J. Hay, *Eighteenth Century Nonconformity*, London, 1915.

Coomer, Duncan, *English Dissent under the Early Hanoverians*, London, 1946.

Curteis, George Herbert, *Dissent in its Relation to the Church of England*, London, 1873.

Dakin, A., *Calvinism*, London, 1940.

Davies, G. C. B., *The Early Cornish Evangelicals, 1735–1760*, London, 1951.

Dimond, Sydney G., *The Psychology of the Methodist Revival*, Oxford, 1926.

Doughty, W. Lamplough, *John Wesley: Preacher*, London, 1955.

Edwards, Maldwyn L., *John Wesley and the Eighteenth Century: A Study of his Social and Political Influence*, London, 1933.

Edwards, Maldwyn L., *Family Circle: A Study of the Epworth Household in Relation to John and Charles Wesley*, London, 1939.

Elliott-Binns, Leonard E., *The Evangelical Movement in the English Church*, London, 1928.

Elliott-Binns, Leonard E., *The Early Evangelicals: A Religious and Social Study*, London, 1953.

Figgis, J. B., *The Countess of Huntingdon and her Connexion*, London, 1892.

Fitchett, W. H., *Wesley and His Century: A Study in Spiritual Forces*, London, 1906.

Gaustad, Edwin Scott, *The Great Awakening in New England*, New York, 1957.

Gewehr, Wesley M., *The Great Awakening in Virginia, 1740–1790*, Durham, N.C., 1930.

Gregory, J. R., *A History of Methodism chiefly for the Use of Students*, 2 vols., London, 1907.

Green, J. Brazier, *John Wesley and William Law*, London, 1945.

Hamilton, J. Taylor, *A History of the Church known as the Moravian Church during the Eighteenth and Nineteenth Centuries*, Bethlehem, Pa., 1900.

Harrison, Archibald W., *The Beginnings of Arminianism to the Synod of Dort*, London, 1926.

Harrison, Archibald W., *Arminianism*, London, 1937.

Harrison, Archibald W., *The Evangelical Revival and Christian Reunion*, London, 1942.

Harrison, Archibald W., *The Separation of Methodism from the Church of England*, London, 1945.

Hassé, E. R., *The Moravians*, London, 1911.

Hennell, Michael, *John Venn and the Clapham Sect*, London, 1958.

Henry, Stuart C., *George Whitefield: Wayfaring Witness*, New York, 1957.

Hildebrandt, Franz, *From Luther to Wesley*, London, 1951.

Hildebrandt, Franz, *Christianity According to the Wesleys*, London, 1956.

Hutton, J. E., *A Short History of the Moravian Church*, London, 1895.

Hutton, J. E., "The Moravian Contribution to the Evangelical Revival in England 1742–1755", in *Historical Essays by Members of the Owens College, Manchester*, ed. T. F. Tout and J. Tait, Manchester, 1902, pp. 423–52.

Jones, Mary G., *The Charity School Movement: A Study of Eighteenth Century Puritanism in Action*, Cambridge, 1938.

Knox, Ronald A., *Enthusiasm: A Chapter in the History of Religion, with special reference to the XVII and XVII Centuries*, Oxford, 1950.

Lecky, W. E. H., *A History of England in the Eighteenth Century*, 7 vols., London, 1892.

Lee, Umphrey, *John Wesley and Modern Religion*, Nashville, 1936.

Legg, J. Wickham, *English Church Life from the Restoration to the Tractarian Movement*, London, 1914.

Lindström, Harald, *Wesley and Sanctification*, Stockholm, 1946.

Loane, Marcus L., *Oxford and the Evangelical Succession*, London, 1951

Loane, Marcus L., *Cambridge and the Evangelical Succession*, London, 1952.

McDonald, H. Dermot, *Ideas of Revelation: An Historical Study A.D. 1700 to A.D. 1860*, London, 1959.

MacInnes, John, *The Evangelical Movement in the Highlands of Scotland 1688 to 1800*, Aberdeen, 1951.

MacLean, Donald, *Aspects of Scottish Church History*, Edinburgh, 1927

McNeill, John T., *The History and Character of Calvinism*, London, 1954.

Maxson, C. H., *The Great Awakening in the Middle Colonies*, Chicago, 1920.

Middelton, John White, *An Ecclesiastical Memoir of the First Four Decades of the Reign of George III*, London, 1822.

Middleton, Erasmus, *Biographia Ecclesiastica*, Vol. IV, London, 1816.

Mossner, Ernest C. *Bishop Butler and the Age of Reason*, New York, 1936.

Nagler, Arthur W., *Pietism and Methodism*, Nashville, 1918.

Ollard, S. L., *The Six Students of St. Edmund Hall expelled from the University of Oxford in 1768*, London, 1911.

Orr, John, *English Deism: Its Roots and Its Fruits*, Grand Rapids, 1934.

Overton, John H., *The Evangelical Revival in the Eighteenth Century*, London, 1886.

Overton, John H., and Relton, Frederic, *The History of the English Church from the Accession of George I to the end of the Eighteenth Century, 1714–1800*, Vol. VII in *A History of the English Church*, ed. W. R. W. Stephens and William Hunt, London, 1906.

Perry, G. G., *A History of the English Church. Third Period. From the Accession of the House of Hanover to the Present Time*, London, 1890.

Piette, Maximin, *John Wesley in the Evolution of Protestantism*, London, 1938.

Plumb, J. H., *England in the Eighteenth Century*, London, 1950.

Plummer, Alfred, *The Church of England in the Eighteenth Century*, London, 1910.

Rattenbury, J. Ernest, *Wesley's Legacy to the World*, London, 1928.

Rattenbury, J. Ernest, *The Conversion of the Wesleys*, London, 1938.

Reynolds, John S., *The Evangelicals at Oxford 1735–1871*, Oxford, 1953

Rigg, John H., *The Churchmanship of John Wesley*, London, 1878.

Robertson, Sir Charles Grant, *England under the Hanoverians*, Vol. VI in *A History of England*, ed. Sir Charles Oman, London, 1947.

Rowden, A. W., *The Primates of the Four Georges*, London, 1916.

Russell, G. W. E., *A Short History of the Evangelical Movement*, London, 1915.

Ryle, John Charles, *The Christian Leaders of the Last Century*, London, 1869.

Shepherd, Thomas B., *Methodism and the Literature of the Eighteenth Century*, London, 1940.

Simon, John S., *The Revival of Religion in the Eighteenth Century*, n.d. (*c.* 1907).

Simon, John S., *John Wesley and the Religious Societies*, London, 1921.

Simon, John S., *John Wesley and the Methodist Societies*, London, 1923.

Simon, John S., *John Wesley and the Advance of Methodism*, London, 1925.

Simon, John S., *John Wesley, the Master Builder*, London, 1927.

Simon, John S., *John Wesley, the Last Phase*, London, 1934.

Smyth, Charles H., *Simeon and Church Order: A Study of the Origins of the Evangelical Revival in Cambridge in the Eighteenth Century*, Cambridge, 1940.

Snell, F. J., *Wesley and Methodism*, Edinburgh, 1900.

Sparrow-Simpson, W. J., *John Wesley and the Church of England*, London, 1934.

Stephen, Sir James, *Essays in Ecclesiastical Biography*, London, 1883.

Stephen, Leslie, *A History of English Thought in the Eighteenth Century*, 2 vols., London, 1881.

Stevens, Abel, *The History of the Religious Movement in the Eighteenth Century Called Methodism*, 3 vols., 1858–61.

Stoughton, John, *Religion in England Under Queen Anne and the Georges*, 2 vols., London, 1878.

Stromberg, Roland N., *Religious Liberalism in Eighteen Century England*, Oxford, 1954.

Sweet, William Warren, *Religion in Colonial America*, New York, 1942.

Sydney, William C., *England and the English in the Eighteenth Century*, 2 vols., London, 1881.

Sykes, Norman, *Church and State in England in the Eighteenth Century*, Cambridge, 1934.

Temperley, H. W. V., "The Evangelical Revival" in *The Cambridge Modern History*, Vol. VI, *The Eighteenth Century*, Cambridge, 1909.

Thompson, Edgar W., *Wesley: Apostolic Man; Some Reflections on Wesley's Consecration of Dr. Thomas Coke*, London, 1957.

Towlson, Clifford W., *Moravian and Methodist: Relationships and Influences in the Eighteenth Century*, London, 1957.

Townsend, W. J., Workman, H. B. and Eayrs, G. (ed.), *A New History of Methodism*, 2 vols., London, 1909.

Tracy, Joseph, *The Great Awakening*, Boston, 1842.

Turberville, A. S. (ed.), *Johnson's England. An Account of the Life and Manners of his Age*, 2 vols., Oxford, 1933.

Turnbull, Ralph G., *Jonathan Edwards the Preacher*, Grand Rapids, 1958.

Turner, George Allen, *The More Excellent Way: The Scriptural Basis of the Wesleyan Message*, Winona Lake, 1952.

Tyerman, Luke, *The Oxford Methodists*, London, 1873.

Walker, George L., *Some Aspects of the Religious Life of New England with Special Reference to Congregationalists*, New York, 1897.

Wauer, G. A., *The Beginning of the Brethren's Church in England*, New York, 1901.

Wearmouth, Robert F., *Methodism and the Common People of the Eighteenth Century,* London, 1945.

Whiteley, J. H., *Wesley's England: A Survey of XVIIIth Century Social and Cultural Conditions*, London, 1938.

Whiteley, J. H., *Wesley's Anglican Contemporaries: Their Trials and Triumphs*, London, 1939.

Willey, Basil, *The Eighteenth Century Background: Studies in the Idea of Nature in the Thought of the Period*, London, 1950.

Williams, Basil, *The Whig Supremacy, 1714–60*, Vol. XI in the Oxford History of England, ed. G. N. Clark, Oxford, 1939.

Williams, William, *Welsh Calvinistic Methodism. A Historical Sketch of the Presbyterian Church of Wales*, London, 1884.

Workman, Herbert B., *Methodism*, Cambridge, 1912.

INDEX OF NAMES AND SUBJECTS